How Rich
Is Too Rich?

How Rich Is Too Rich?

Income and Wealth in America

Herbert Inhaber and Sidney Carroll

PRAEGER

New York
Westport, Connecticut
London

Library of Congress Cataloging-in-Publication Data

Inhaber, Herbert.
   How rich is too rich? : income and wealth in America / Herbert Inhaber and
Sidney Carroll.
      p. cm.
   Includes bibliographical references and index.
   ISBN 0-275-93619-8 (alk. paper)
      1. Income distribution—United States.   2. Wealth—United States.
   3. United States—Economic conditions.   I. Carroll, Sidney L.
   II. Title.
   HC110.I5I54   1992
   339.2′2′0973—dc20   90-27541

British Library Cataloguing in Publication Data is available.

Library of Congress Catalog Card Number: 90-27541
ISBN: 0-275-93619-8

First published in 1992

Praeger Publishers, One Madison Avenue, New York, NY 10010
An imprint of Greenwood Publishing Group, Inc.

Printed in the United States of America

The paper used in this book complies with the
Permanent Paper Standard issued by the National
Information Standards Organization (Z39.48–1984).

10 9 8 7 6 5 4 3 2 1

Copyright Acknowledgments

The authors and publisher are grateful for permission to quote from the following:

A. B. Atkinson, *The Economics of Inequality* [Oxford: Clarendon Press, 1975].

From *Generating Inequality*, by Lester C. Thurow. Copyright © 1975 by Basic
Books, Inc. Reprinted by permission of Basic Books, Inc., Publishers, New York.

Reprinted with permission of Macmillan Publishing Company from *Macroeconomic
Theory* by Gardner Ackley. Copyright © 1961 by Gardner Ackley.

William S. Gilbert and Arthur S. Sullivan, *The Authentic Gilbert and Sullivan Songbook*,
James Spero, editor, Dover, 1978. Selection from ''The Gondoliers.'' Act II.

CONTENTS

TABLES AND FIGURES

TABLES

FIGURES

PREFACE

With the advent of the Presidential primaries and caucuses in early 1992, questions about income distribution and wealth again echo throughout the land. True, it's mostly the Democrats who are making noises about unfairness. Senator Al Gore Jr. of Tennessee proposed an increase in tax rates for the most affluent in May 1991, in order to reduce the overwhelming budget deficit. In September, House Majority Leader Richard Gephardt accused Ronald Reagan and George Bush of carrying on a "class war against middle-class families to benefit the wealthiest people in our society."

But Republicans have paid attention to the issue as well. Teddy Roosevelt, an idol of George Bush, advocated a vast redistribution of income and wealth that most Democrats today would shy away from. Newt Gingrich, one of the more unconventional Congressional Republicans, has suggested publicly that conservatives should do some serious thinking about economic redistribution.

Missing from most of the political accusations and counter-claims is some understanding of just how rich is too rich. Quite often, the decision as to what level of income or wealth is "excessive" is based on some multiple of ten, which in turn is based on the number of fingers we have on our two hands.

For example, Citizens for Tax Justice, a lobbying group, has said that tax cuts in the 1980s for the richest million Americans added $1 trillion to the national debt. Kevin Phillips, in his book *The Politics of Rich and Poor*, spends considerable space charting the rise of the top 1%—one out of 100—of the income and wealth pyramid. Paul Posner of the General Accounting Office defines high incomes as those exceeding $100,000 annually.

Other measures of a dividing line are about as arbitrary. The annual Forbes 400, one of the major headline-makers on large wealth accumulations, has the number in its title based on the size of a party given in 19th-century New York. Lawrence Hilibrand, a 31-year-old stockbroker at the disgraced investment firm of Salomon Brothers, made $23 million in 1990 and thus his name made the news. Would he have remained obscure if he had earned $10 million or $2.3 million?

Truth is, all these measures—who gets written about, who gets on what list, who gets accused by politicians of being filthy rich—are semi-arbitrary at best, and often completely arbitrary. If we're going to get away from the demagoguery that often passes for political and social discussion on income and wealth distribution, we have to be a little more rational. This book lights the path to that goal.

We began in an unusual way. One of us, a physicist, came across some strange graphs on income distribution buried in a statistics book. Not knowing much about economics at the time, he was unsure whether serendipity had struck, or whether he was reading something that all economists took in with their mother's milk.

Enter the economist of our team. He had long been concerned about income distribution or maldistribution, but had abandoned its pursuit. The physicist and economist met. We debated whether the peculiar charts and graphs meant anything, whether a general conclusion based on them could be developed, and whether economists already knew everything worth knowing about income distribution.

We decided they didn't. What's more, we realized we could formulate some new and basic understanding of the age-old question: How rich is too rich?

There are no absolutely new ideas, only combinations of old ones. Yet the concepts we put together suggest practical solutions to the problem of excessive wealth.

When Carlyle called economics the dismal science in 1850, he coined a powerful but ultimately wrong phrase. We are awash in a sea of economic thoughts and actions, even on a day when a dollar bill doesn't cross our palm. And economics is perhaps most fascinating when we consider the very wealthy. The actions—or lack of actions—that we take about this small group strongly influence the nation's economic fate.

Writing on economics has an often-deserved reputation for being as dry as driftwood. Because our message deserves to be heard outside dusty academic meeting rooms, we have attempted to write for a broader audience.

If we decide how rich is too rich, what next? There are many measures we could take. Some of them may hurt our economic health, that is, provide less goods and services for those who aren't rich. Some actions may actually *increase* our economic well-being. We've outlined a way to deal with the question of how rich is too rich, yet at the same time making our economy healthier than ever. It still allows the rich a reasonable number of Rolls-Royces, trips on the Concorde, and castles in Spain.

At the conclusion of this lengthy task, we would like to thank Betty Carroll, who worked on computer input for the drafts, developed graphs, and helped organize the bibliography. Reba Inhaber made many helpful editorial suggestions. Both tolerated the many hours we put in, and the seemingly endless discussions. We are deeply appreciative of their support.

__1__

A GRAND PARADE

Alexis de Tocqueville, that perceptive observer of American life, once said, "The love of wealth is therefore to be traced, as either a principal or accessory motive, at the bottom of all that the Americans do."[1] The wise Frenchman usually made more cogent observations about the United States in a page than most historians do in a book, but in this case he may have gone too far. To ascribe all—or even most—American actions to "love of wealth" is a bit exaggerated.

Still, there is no denying our fascination with money, wealth, and their inevitable handmaiden, disparities. Pick up the paper and you will see it in black and white: "Congress Moving to Limit Tax Breaks on Luxury Vehicles for Business"; "Taxes Held Less Progressive than Law Implies"; "The Return of Inequality"; " 'Fairness' and Income Equalization"; "America's Income Gap: The Closer You Look, the Worse It Gets."

What do these claims of fairness or unfairness mean? The headlines are random ripples in a vast sea of thoughts on income and wealth. Unless we focus our reasoning, much as a wave-energy device takes water motion and transforms it into power, we will be tossed back and forth intellectually.

If everyone in this nation had exactly the same income and wealth, this book would end prematurely at this point. However, if everyone had the same degree of intelligence, there would be no such word as "smart." So a key to understanding income or wealth is knowledge of how it is —or could be—distributed. In other words, who has what.

When it comes to money, we frequently assume much more understanding than we possess. We can be liberals, trying to fiddle with the divine economic rules that Moses forgot to bring down from Mount Sinai. Or conservatives, who prefer to leave the well-off enough alone. But if there are laws governing income and wealth, they should transcend our personal political beliefs.

Although true "natural" laws in economics sometimes seem rare, there is one in income distribution: The lower 97% or so of the population is governed by one system; we will define it shortly. About the upper 3%—the "filthy rich" or "builders of society," depending on your philosophy—is ruled by another. We can use these two interlocking rules to decide *how rich the rich should be*. To make these rather abstract percentages more specific and vivid, once you get past the approximately $110,000 income level (in 1987 dollars), you move into the second and upper distribution. The place where the two distributions part company is the "kink," or the backwards bend. That is because when we depict the two rules graphically, there appears to be a kink in the lines.[2]

We are not satisfied with merely describing what happens to income. Later, we will propose the ADS, or Alternative Distribution System.[3] We believe that our proposal will *add* to the total fairness of our society, hence the acronym. ADS is based on the fact that much of the income of the well-off is due to wealth. It is thus an inheritance plan that will bring the distribution of the lower 97% and upper 3% closer together. There will still be the good and the not-so-good life, but the extremes will not be as great as they now are.

This book is *not* a reworking of the familiar "rich get richer and the poor get poorer" theme, a common motif in many volumes touching on economics. The natural laws of income distribution are more profound than the commonplace observation that there are rich and poor, or that most of the latter would like to join the former. With slight variations, the law we will describe holds in most democratic countries. There is an international pattern in the way that societies reward their members. Knowing these laws, we can better understand why so many of the never-ending rules and regulations designed to redistribute income and wealth have failed.

A few words on what this book is *not* about: poverty and corporations. We do not generally talk about destitution, although the subject may arise from time to time. President Johnson's War on Poverty may have ended in a crushing defeat—for whom, we cannot yet tell—but its chronicles, and the mopping-up operations for the last two decades, are not part of our story. The division between the superwealthy and the rest of us *is*.

THE ROBIN HOOD DREAM

If society decides that the rich are a little too much so, in principle we could expropriate some of their wealth. This, according to some, would eliminate poverty in the United States, if not all over the world. Then the words of Saint Luke would finally come true: "He hath filled the hungry with good things, and the rich he hath sent away." On that day of gnashing of teeth and shouts of joy, depending on the size of one's bank account, "excess" wealth would be confiscated. Mercedes would revert to being only a girl's name.

It is only a beautiful dream. If all the money that could be taken from the rich were given to relieve poverty, much penury would still exist. It was once said that the French Revolution made the rich poor, but did not make the poor rich. Even in a wealthy country like the United States, there are far more needs of poor people than there are dollars we could take away from the rich. And even that assumes that the rich would allow their wealth to be taken away without a struggle.

We will use a partly hypothetical example to prove that point. Consider Gordon Getty, at one point, according to *Forbes* magazine, the richest man in the nation. (A more recent issue of *Forbes* has John Kluge, the Virginia media magnate, at the head of the list, but the results of the calculations change only slightly.) We do not have access to Mr. Getty's army of accountants, so we have no idea whether his reported accumulation, $4.1 billion, is accurate. In a later chapter we will discuss whether or not the rich play hide-and-seek with the tax collector and financial magazines.

Exactly how many poor there are in this country is a matter of debate, a debate that can never have a real conclusion. Politicians talking about poverty will invariably quote numbers to their advantage. Democrats will point to the shabbiness of many of our center cities. Republicans will note that our Gross National Product (GNP) continues to reach new highs.

Leaving the rhetoric aside, if we take the so-called official poverty level, itself subject to much argument among economists, we might find about 30 million people in poverty. This in turn would be about one in eight citizens. The proportion will vary depending on whether we are going into or coming out of a recession, the size of the family in question, whether they live in a city or on a farm, and a host of other factors.

Now suppose that just before Mr. Getty is hustled off to a rest farm by his concerned relatives and business associates, he decides to divide his entire fortune among all the nation's poor. A little division would show that each poor person would get a weekly check of about $2.70. And this would be for only one year. At the end of that time, Mr. Getty, having exhausted his fortune, would have nothing left to donate to the poor.

No doubt Mr. Kluge, the Hunt brothers, Sam Walton of Arkansas, and other wealthy men would have been impressed by this selfless act of Mr. Getty's, and also emptied their wallets upon the poor. But similar calculations show that stripping the wealthy to their skins, while it may be morally satisfying to some, will not, by itself, solve the problem of poverty. There are just too many poor, and not enough wealthy.

Because of this, we cannot follow the advice given by Gilbert and Sullivan:

He wished all men as rich as he
(And he was rich as rich could be)
So to the top of every tree
He promoted everybody.[4]

So why bother? Why not let the rich have what is theirs, the poor eat spaghetti, and the rest of us avoid rocking an already unsteady economic boat? A question like this links morality to income distribution or redistribution. The greatest philosophers have tried to decide how rich the rich could be without at the same time being immoral. They never came to any conclusions, other than there had to be some unspecified bank balance that was too high.

While relating who gets what of society's fruits to questions of morality has made lots of work for printers, very little has ever been proved or universally accepted. One man's justice is another's expropriation. If one message emerges from plowing the endless fields of philosophical discourse on wealth, it is that wise men often disagree.

In other words: *there is no way to prove that one income distribution is fairer than any other*. If everyone agreed on what was fair in terms of income and what was not, we might be able to decide who should get what. But conflicts abound.

We are taking a different tack here. The two of us each have our own private ideas on how rich is rich enough, based on our personal experience, readings in economics and other factors. Just like the philosophers, we are not quite in agreement on the basis of these individual influences. Yet we believe that the laws of income and wealth distribution, as opposed to what we may feel in our gut, set the level of excessive wealth and income themselves.

CORPORATIONS AND PEOPLE

A second area that we will *not* touch on, except indirectly, is corporate wealth and income. There have been no end of stories on how much profit an individual oil company or General Motors have been piling up in recent years. In the five years from 1984 to 1989, profits of U.S. automakers alone totalled some $53 billion.[5] But this money eventually ends up in human hands, not stashed between the pages of the account books of some abstract corporation. As a result, we have concentrated on wealth going into wallets and pocketbooks, not cash registers. People establish or invest in corporations in the hopes of making themselves wealthy, not the company.

In summary, long before the first socialist trod the earth, many were concerned that the fruits of man's labor were somehow maldistributed. But how could this maldistribution be measured, let alone corrected? The first part of this question could not be answered until governments started to collect financial data, usually from income and death tax forms. Accountants and economists then analyzed it. Only then could the second part of the question be considered, let alone answered.

This book resolves the question that stumped ancient thinkers: How rich is too rich? The Bible, in Acts 4, said that distribution was made unto every man according as he had need. (This is echoed in Marx). However, its author had no way of specifying exactly how that distribution was to be made in terms of goods and services. This book does.

INCOME AND WEALTH

We will be talking about both income and wealth. There is a distinction between the two. They are not the same, although both are based on money. The confusion between wealth and income is brought about partly by the English language, in which someone who is wealthy is generally regarded as having a high income. This is not always true. Other languages are better at distinguishing between the two concepts.

In separating the two ideas, we can use the analogy of rivers and dams. The flow of water in a river is similar, in a sense, to income. The flow can be great in some rivers; our highest-paid financiers, entertainers, and athletes like the three Michaels—Milken, Jackson, and Jordan—can be regarded as the Mississippi of incomes. Invalids, those on the lower end of Social Security with nothing else coming in, and the unemployed are the creeks and back streams of income. They have little flow in the best of times and none in the worst.

Wealth can be likened to the dams, both for hydroelectricity production and irrigation, that block the flow of many rivers. Behind each dam is a substantial volume of water, storing at least some of the flow. If he wants to, the dam operator could shut off the flow completely. This would be analogous to a wealthy man having no income at all. This has probably happened from time to time. Occasionally we read about someone who starves to death, and is found to have thousands of dollars stuffed under mattresses or in cupboards.

Yet we do not read in the *New York Times* around Christmas of the "100 Neediest Wealthy Cases." That is because some of that wealth can be converted to income at any time. A rare painting can be sold, a piece of land auctioned off—these and other steps are available to the wealthy. Not to many of the rest of us, though; the flow in our own rivers is usually not something we can change all by ourselves.

So to be wealthy implies at least the potential for high income. On the other hand, having a high income does not always imply wealth. Joe Louis had some of the world's biggest paydays from the 1930s to the 1950s. Decades later he was fighting the Internal Revenue Service, not boxers, to stay out of jail for failing to pay taxes. We wonder how many of today's top entertainers and sports figures will find in coming years that they have had enormous incomes, but accumulated little wealth.

THE RELATIONSHIP BETWEEN INCOME AND WEALTH

The relation between income and wealth has three parts. The first is something that for simplicity we will call *earned income*. This is compensation paid to individuals for personal services rendered. Earned income could be the wages paid to the construction worker, the royalties of the inventor, or the fees of the surgeon. All involve specific functions performed by an individual.

Two things can happen to earned income. It can be consumed or saved. If it is saved, as in the dam analogy, we can see the creation of wealth. So it takes earned income to generate the beginnings of wealth.

The second concept relates income and wealth. Savings as capital earns income. When capital, from whatever source, is allowed to earn income that is reinvested, wealth can increase dramatically. Remember that we cannot tell the difference, in a given bank account, between wealth that derives from earned or unearned income.

Look at the sugar in your sugar bowl. Some of it may have come from beets, vastly different from cane. Yet the grains in the bowl from the two sources are indistinguishable.

While the ability to earn wealth-producing income is not easily transferable (Michael Jordan's children will probably not play in the National Basketball Association), wealth itself is. Someone who amasses wealth through his or her own effort can pass on these assets capriciously—or even wisely—to progeny or others. This transmission process continues generation after generation. Those in the second, third, or later generations have done nothing personally to earn or deserve wealth, other than being born to the right parents.

This transmission from one generation to the next is our third aspect of the relationship between income and wealth.

In addition, wealth—whether earned or unearned—can grow through its own unearned income, increasingly in a never-ending spiral. Once accumulated, it is relatively easy to husband. This yields the gigantic and seemingly perpetual fortunes which we will address in more detail later.

To recapitulate, there is earned income, unearned income, and the pure wealth resulting from the two. It is these last two—coupled with the transmission possibility—that lead to long-run maldistribution of wealth in society.

Because of the crucial link between earned income, unearned income, wealth generation, and preservation, we can now clearly see why analyzing income distribution is the first vital step in understanding wealth.

Changing wealth distribution will shift income distribution, resulting in a more logical income pattern, a less peculiar sharing of the riches of society, and a more productive population. What we later propose—the Alternative Distribution System (ADS)—is the vehicle for these happy results.

A GRAPHIC EXAMPLE OF INCOME DISTRIBUTION— THE PARADE OF JAN PEN

What do we know about the actual, as opposed to the guesses about, distribution of income and wealth? Statistics on income abound. Each of us is required, under penalty of law, to tell the government most pertinent facts about our annual income. On the other hand, numbers on wealth are systematically gathered only on death. Even then, they are usually calculated only for those in the very top income and wealth brackets. Nonetheless, in the last few years information on wealth covering the entire nation has become a little more common. In previous decades it was almost nonexistent.

What data we do have will be used to buttress our contention that income and wealth follow what statisticians call a lognormal (or Gibrat, after a French economist) distribution. At very high incomes, the lognormal is replaced by another distribution called Pareto (after the Italian economist). Things are very different beyond the kink between the two distributions.

On hearing the words "income distribution," you may have visions of bloodless tables of numbers, your eyes blurring as you try to bring the masses of digits into focus. Income distribution can be thought of in this way, but Jan Pen, the Dutch economist, has brought the admittedly dull figures to life. While the columns themselves may be sleep-inducing, they represent millions of real Americans trying to make a living, doing the best they can for their families. We should not forget this when we are confronted by the inevitable numbers. The following is a condensed adaptation of Pen's work.[6]

Suppose we know the income of everyone in the nation. In reality, this is not possible. For example, the poorest—hoboes, the homeless, street people, and the like—may live from hand to mouth, not trying to add up their few quarters and dollars. Members of the Mafia may leave the bookkeeping to their accountants, with careful instructions to keep most of their ill-gotten gains out of the tabulations. In spite of these and other exceptions, it is fair to say that the bulk of the population, at least by April 15, knows approximately what they made the previous year. For our purposes, "approximate" is close enough; we do not have to have it down to the last dollar.

The next question is, How can we handle this vast array of numbers representing people? In a recent year, there were a total of about 107 million tax returns (of which about 20 million were nontaxable).[7] So the sheer volume of data is intimidating.

There are, in principle, an infinite number of ways to answer this question. One extreme would be to fling an enormous computer printout at the reader, at least figuratively. In effect, we would be doing nothing with the numbers. Another way would be to visualize groups of taxpayers, with so many thousands in the no income to $1,000 bracket, another number for the $1,000 to $2,000 bracket, and so on up the line. While we will have some tables later, there are sometimes better ways to present the information.

Professor Pen proposes a grand parade, at least in our minds, in which everyone with an income marches by. We could, in our imagination, give everyone a big sign to hold up, stating his or her earnings. It is far more interesting if we did the opposite of Procrustes. That early specialist in alterations shrank or stretched his victims to make them all the same size. What we will do is shrink or stretch everyone, to make their size *proportional* to their income. Since there is a wide array of incomes in a given year, there will be a correspondingly wide array of heights.

Pen's parade is previewed in Figure 1.1. The average income of each group is measured by the height of the curve. As the horizontal axis shows, the parade lasts one hour, by our self-imposed rule.

The parade is organized by income, so that those with the smallest incomes are on the left. The height of the curve at each point represents the average income of the individuals at that level. This works quite well until the last minute of the parade. The incomes at this level are so large that it would require an additional *nine pages* to represent accurately their incomes. This is a major element of the argument that will be made in this book.

So in this grand and fanciful parade, stretching for miles, the tallest people will have the highest incomes. The midgets will have the lowest. And to avoid complicating matters further, we will not bring in questions of wealth as opposed to income. As we will see later, if we had a parade of *wealth*, the results would be even stranger than the ones we are about to see.

A few more words as we hear the band in the distance. To keep the show from getting tedious, everyone will march by in exactly one hour. We know that it is impossible to get 250 million people to move past the reviewing stand in that short a time, but it is no more impossible than getting the group to assemble in the first place. So we pretend that we are latter-day versions of Cecil B. DeMille, with superhuman powers, and can get everyone across the line within the appointed time.

We are going to ignore people in the parade with no direct income, but who share in it. Mrs. Getty may not have gotten any oil royalty checks addressed to her, but she was certainly not destitute as a result of that

Figure 1.1
Professor Pen Captures the Income Distribution in 1987 in an Imaginary One-Hour Parade

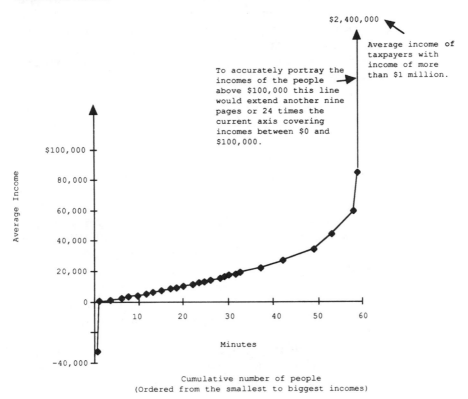

Cumulative number of people
(Ordered from the smallest to biggest incomes)

omission. You can live well without any income by being married or related to the right people. This applies to men as well as women. The husband of Chris Evert, one of the highest-paid women in sports, shares in her enormous income. However, our parade cannot take account of situations like this.

THE PARADE BEGINS

Now the parade begins, with the smallest in front. But even before we see the tiniest of people, we notice something even more unusual: people with negative height. These are the people who lost money in the course of the year. In the United States in recent times, there were between 800,000 to 900,000 of them.

If it is difficult to visualize the extremely small and gigantic people we will see later in the parade, it is even harder to imagine negative height.

But if we can organize a marchby of everyone in the country in less than half the time of a football game, anything can be accomplished.

For people of negative height, we see their feet on the ground, and their heads somehow burrowing under the earth, like human moles. Through unknown means, they move forward. The greater their losses, the deeper their heads are in the ground.

Who are these strange creatures? They are mostly businessmen who have suffered capital losses during the year. Our tax laws encourage people to take tax losses every few years, so there are far more people in this group than we would expect in prosperous times. The tax reform law of 1986 reduced this incentive somewhat, so we may see a smaller negative height group in the parade in coming years.

Those who suffer losses in one year generally do not in the next. If incomes were averaged over five or ten years, there would probably be very few with negative incomes over that period. Yet in any one year we will find hundreds of thousands.

Most of the people with negative incomes do not seem miserable in spite of their large losses. These losses averaged $32,000 for the entire group in the year 1987, more than the average national *positive* income. And isn't the man who leads the parade, with his head perhaps sixty yards beneath the surface, the same one whose picture was featured a few years ago in the *Forbes* list of the wealthiest people in the country? How can he be heading the march, when he should by all rights be at the end?

Have no fear. The gentleman in question is not likely to be found in the nearest breadline. If we held the parade again next year, he would likely be in his rightful place in the back, towering over most of the other marchers.

After the big losers, we find smaller ones, whose negative income is probably not a result of the tax lawyers' manipulations. They are a varied group, but they may include people whose homes have burned down without insurance, and business people whose enterprises folded. About a third of all new firms fail within a year or two.

By way of proof of these results, consider the 1987 tax returns. Of those with negative or zero income, about 3% had tax-exempt interest. These generally derive from municipal and state bonds. Rather than the pittance you might expect from this negative income group, their average income from these bonds was about $21,000. If the average return on a tax-free bond that year was about 6% (lower than corporate or federal bond rates because of the tax-free aspect), this implies an average wealth from this source alone of about $350,000 for this group. Not bad for people with negative incomes.

We can investigate this subterranean group further. About half of them received taxable interest from banks and the like. Their average income from these sources was about $4,700. If we assume an average interest rate of about 8%, this in turn implies about $58,000 in the bank. This is less than the $350,000 in municipal and state bonds we mentioned above, but still more than most Americans have in a savings account.

The marchers with heads in the ground are numerous, but they go by in about half a minute. The rest of the parade is above ground, which makes it a little easier to see.

THE TINIEST PEOPLE

Before we see the miniature people heading up the above-ground parade, we should mention the rule we are using to proportion income to height. We are assuming that the average real height of all people, male and female, is about 5ft. 7in., or 67 inches, give or take an inch. In 1987, the average reportable taxable income in the United States was about $26,000. We obtained this value by dividing all adjusted gross income (less deficits) by the 107 million taxpayers in that year.

We will take this income as corresponding to the average height. Thus if someone has an income of $52,000, or twice the average, he or she would be assigned an imaginary height, for purposes of the parade, of twice 67 inches, or 134 inches. This in turn is slightly more than 11 feet tall. Similarly, someone with an income of $13,000, or half the average, would be assigned a height of half 67 inches, or 34 inches. This is less than a yard.

Now back to the reviewing stand. We have been promised that the real parade would begin after the first half-minute of the economic moles buried in the earth, but where are the people? As time goes by, almost no activity is seen except some dust rising from the ground. In exasperation we seize a handy telescope, and there they are—tiny people, marching side by side, the size of a match stick or key. No wonder they were not visible from a distance. As we squint at them, and try to make out their minuscule bodies, we realize that this is truly when the faint go marching in.

Who are these people? They are truly a mixed group. Some are people who may have worked for just a short time, because of illness, lack of employment skills, or other reasons. Because they have held a job for such short times, they are not eligible for unemployment insurance benefits, which help out people in more prosperous classes.

We may personally recognize some of these economic midgets. Some are the teenagers bagging or checking groceries at your local grocery store for spending money. The cash earned would be the only income attributed to the teens in the parade. Allowances from parents or money from neighbors or family for mowing lawns or baby-sitting would not be represented, since they generally do not show up on tax returns. The appearance of the teenagers at this stage then does not necessarily mean they are poor.

But there are also many people in this group that we do not recognize, unless we have seen some television documentaries on poverty. There are a goodly number of dirt farmers, some from Appalachia. These people are not as badly off as their puny size might indicate, because of the food crops they raise for themselves. Remember, this is a parade of money, not goods or food. The height of the group of stunted gnomes varies, but all of them are ten inches or shorter. It is no wonder we had some difficulty in seeing them from the reviewing stand.

The procession of the smallest midgets has taken longer than we would have guessed—about four minutes in all. Recall that the parade is an hour in length, and that about four and half minutes have gone by. There are clearly more low-income people around than we had imagined.

UP TO THE WAIST

Now the marchers are getting bigger—10, 12, 20 inches and on up to knee height. There are also a lot more of them. This array is composed of some old-age pensioners with small Social Security checks, some divorced women without alimony, people on welfare, and yet others who have been jobless a substantial part of the year. A few of these unemployed, such as artists and actors, may be in that condition voluntarily. They may describe themselves as being "between engagements" or "between sales" of a canvas. Next year, they may hit it lucky, with a choice part or a big sale. In next year's parade, we may find them grown dramatically, and near the rear of the marchers. But this year, they are close to the front, and reach just above our kneecaps.

This group, between 10 inches and 2 feet in height, has taken about ten minutes to go by. You will note that this group is much larger in number than the two previous ones. About a quarter hour has gone by. Yet we are still seeing people no taller than preschool children. When will the normal people get here?

Not quite yet. For first must come those who have regular or almost regular employment, but who are the lowest paid of steady workers. If you go into an office building late at night, some of them—the cleaning crews and the guards—will be there. A few of this group are at your local fast food restaurant, and you may recognize familiar faces. Not the managers, of course—they will be seen later in the parade—but the order takers and hamburger flippers. Now clerks, unskilled manual laborers, and grocery workers, slightly above the minimum wage, file by. And since this parade is American, we see hundreds of thousands of minorities—blacks, Hispanics and others—coming by now. In fact, the proportion of minorities seems quite high. We would try to make a quick estimate of the proportion, but the people are moving by so fast that we can not.

How tall are these people? They go up to about three to four-and-a-half feet high. But we can make a somewhat more exact estimate for those who are paid exactly the minimum wage. In 1987, the federal minimum was $3.35 an hour, although some states had higher values. If someone worked forty hours a week at that rate, their equivalent height would be a foot and a half. Because of this, many in the latest group now filing by who are paid the minimum wage work considerably longer than forty hours a week.

HALF THE PARADE HAS GONE BY

By this time, we may have stolen a nervous glance at our watch. About twenty-five minutes of the parade have passed, and yet the marchers hardly reach to our chests. Where are the regular people, those who are supposedly the backbones of our communities and nation?

They still have not arrived. As Professor Pen puts it, we still keep seeing dwarfs. The marchers are gradually getting bigger, but painfully slowly. Now we begin to see the masses of so-called ordinary workers, who start to reach up to our armpits. Then on to skilled industrial workers, generally those who are not employed at the very largest corporations like General Motors. We also see office and computer employees. This latest group reach up to our shoulders. This height is referred to in the women's department of clothing stores as "petite," but the marchers in this group are mostly men.

Time goes on. Another seven minutes have flown by, bringing the elapsed time to about thirty-two minutes. We might expect that at the half-way point people would be at the exact average, but this is not so. Looking straight ahead brings no eye contact yet. Only after about thirty-six minutes, with twenty-four minutes left in the parade, do people with average income march by.

Who are these average types? They are middle management civil servants, for example. However, these civil servants are federal, not state or local. The latter two groups have already passed us by, on the whole.

Others at this point in the parade are experienced teachers and some principals, some junior officers and senior noncommissioned officers in the military, junior industrial managers, and some low-ranking executives just a few years out of college. A few retired couples with substantial Social Security checks and perhaps income from a company pension are also represented.

Now only about twenty minutes remain. Heights are starting to rise more rapidly now, much faster than in the first half hour. During that first period, the rate of change seemed excruciatingly slow. By the forty-five-minute mark, with only fifteen minutes left to go, people are about as big as the tall man in the circus or the biggest player in the National Basketball Association, at about seven-and-a-half feet tall. We see a few university professors, mostly at the associate professor rank and at medium to smaller colleges. Full professors at Harvard, Cal Tech, and Yale will come by later. We also see a few people just a year or two out of college who have chosen a lucrative profession, such as chemical or petroleum engineering.

Now the smaller ranks of giants wheel onto the field. After apparently endless minutes of almost imperceptible height changes, we see visible alterations with each new glance. Over the next ten minutes, up to the fifty-five-minute mark, successful businessmen and women, advertising agency mangers, and some prosperous midwestern farmers march by. They are accompanied by the top scientists. A few Harvard and Yale professors are found in this group, but the top ones are yet to come. The height of this group is ever-increasing. They grow past the ten-foot barrier up to around twelve feet, much taller than any real human being has ever grown. It is around this point we decide to measure these giants in yards, not feet.

THE LAST FIVE MINUTES OF THE PARADE

The last five minutes of the parade are the most startling and memorable of all, even more astounding than the armies of matchstick people we saw almost an hour ago. By this point, the swarms of midgets have almost faded from our memory.

In the next minute or two, a few doctors loom into view. They are not the most successful surgeons, who appear just before the end of the march, but younger physicians, some of whom may work for the government in such agencies as the National Institutes of Health: five yards high. Successful engineers, top federal civil servants, and other high executives are all about the same height. The top professors, whose books appear in the *New York Review of Books* and who have consulting and royalty income in addition to their professional salary, are also here. Three- and four-star generals and admirals, with swagger sticks about six feet long, start to appear.

Now there is only one minute to go. While we have seen many of the major groups in our society, there are still a large number of movers and shakers of the money tree to go. Here come members of Congress, at about seven and a half yards. However, some of the more affluent Senators, with private income in addition to their salaries, will appear later at a height of ten to fifteen yards.

A little farther down the line comes the president. In calculating his height, we take account only of his direct salary. His fleet of aircraft, ability to live for free in one of the largest and most historic mansions in the nation, and an army of servants, do not play any part in our estimate of his height. In fact, we have done the same underestimation for many of the top executives that appear in this section of the parade. Their perks do not appear in their paycheck or capital gains. However, we will see that these executives are already so tall that it does not make all that much difference if their perks would have boosted their height by half.

Finally the president strides by. He is about twenty yards high. His security guards, being only about three yards tall, have passed by many minutes ago. Obviously, at that height they would have been of little use in protecting the president, even if they could accompany the Chief Executive in this part of the parade. Even standing on each other's shoulders, they could not keep the president out of harm's way. After all, they come up only halfway to his shin bone.

Now the top surgeons, for heart, lung, eye, and all the other interesting organs, file by. Their height is sometimes greater than the president's: ten, twenty, up to thirty yards high. It is a good thing that the parade will end quickly, because we would get a stiff neck from peering up at these gigantic figures. In fact, since the heads of the marchers are becoming difficult to see without binoculars, we tend to focus on their feet, which are much easier to see. The feet of the last surgeon we saw were about five yards long, about the size of a compact car.

In the last few seconds of the parade are many of the people we read about in the news. Their names often appear in newspapers like the *Wall Street Journal* and magazines like *Fortune*, *Forbes*, and *Business Week*, although entire articles in these publications are not yet devoted to them. They tend to be the subject only of paragraphs in these national stories. However, these executives are often the theme of lengthy articles in their hometown newspaper business pages. Here we see the businessmen who run large—but not the largest—firms: twenty or thirty yards tall. No, we are not being discriminatory here. Almost all the Brobdingnagians on the field are male.

Here come the basketball, baseball, and football stars, representatives of a different kind of business. Their heights vary tremendously, just as there was a grand variation in the heights of business executives. We saw the heights of these executives range from that of the manager of a McDonald's fast-food establishment, many minutes ago, to that of the gargantuan executives we are seeing—rather, partly seeing because of their size—now.

The smallest of the basketball players came by a few minutes ago, at around twelve yards tall. These are players who were drafted in late rounds by their teams, or who are just starting their careers. Most of those with some experience are about five or six times as high. One towering and well-muscled figure from the sports world strides by at around 100 to 150 yards high. His thighs are so large that we can not make out his face, so we can not tell which sport he plays. Since we have almost given up on estimating heights, we concentrate on the length of his feet. They are fifteen to twenty yards long, about the size of a railway car.

By now, we are almost overwhelmed. The president was about the size of a ten-story building. This athlete is about thirty-five to forty-five stories high, bigger than the tallest buildings in all except a handful of American cities.

The parade continues. The mix changes rapidly, with fewer entertainers and sports figures. More people appear who seem to have thatches of white hair, and who occasionally carry canes. True, Johnny Carson is there, about a quarter mile high. Bob Hope might also be that height. By now, people are approaching the height of the Sears Tower.

THE LAST GROUP IN THE PARADE

Who are the last group in the parade? They are people with accumulated wealth, mostly. Their income from that wealth can be, in some cases, astronomical.

In general, we do not recognize most of the faces. Some of them have appeared in annual compilations in magazines like *Forbes* or *Fortune*. However, even the excellent journalists attached to those publications have missed a large number in this last section. The journalists would say, in defense, that theirs is a compilation of wealth. The parade is one of income. They would be right.

Some of the giants striding by, such as Daniel Ludwig and John Kluge, make a point of staying out of the press, occasionally paying well for the privilege. In any case, almost everyone who appears in this last section is not known by face or voice to the average reporter. They have long passed the point where they got a thrill out of seeing their name in the newspaper or on television.

With only a second or two to go in the parade, we could not tell whose heads those enormous legs belong to, even if we could recognize the faces. The shoulders are literally in the clouds. If we had enough time, we might estimate the heights from the size of the gigantic shoes pounding by, but it all happens too fast.

One of the people in the reviewing stand says that he has made a rough calculation. Using surveyor's instruments, he has estimated that the length of the shoes of one of the last men in the parade—for they are almost exclusively men now—was about sixty football fields. From that, he invites us to calculate the height. But we are so astounded by what we have seen that we decline the invitation.

There is some dispute over the identity of the last man who strides by, the earth quaking under his footsteps. Is it a Getty heir, or one of the owners of the DuPont billions? Or is it Michael Milken, the junk-bond king, who in a court case was reported to have earned about $550 million in 1987? Nobody knows for sure. Even if we questioned one of these gentlemen, we might not get an accurate answer, assuming the respondent was perfectly honest. The fortunes and complicated stock and land transactions are too great and abstruse for all except the most ingenious accountants to decipher.

Still, the impression made by the last marcher is overwhelming. The average sole of a man's shoe is about one-quarter inch thick. If that was indeed Mr. Milken at the end of the parade, the soles of his shoes are about *620 feet* tall. His soles alone are higher than all the marchers who appeared in the first fifty-nine minutes of the parade.

THE PROCESSION ENDS

Suddenly, it is all over. The procession of millions has finished, and the field now rings with an unbearable silence. The ground gradually stops shaking.

What have we learned? At least two major facts: First, we reach the average height much after half the time has elapsed. Most of the parade consisted of small men and women, as well as the dwarfs, midgets, and matchstick figures. The reason? The average is boosted considerably by the large figures in the last ten or so minutes. Each of the towering figures bringing up the rear changes the average by himself only slightly, however.

Second, the end of the hour is stunning. Rather than seeing an increase of an inch or two every few minutes, as we did at the beginning, the heights rise by leaps and bounds. By the end, the increase is a yard per second or more. The size of the very last behemoths is so immense that we have difficulty in measuring it. We abandon the binoculars we used before and bring out a telescope. The last minute starts with marchers seventy yards high and then extends up into the stratosphere.

The parade is a lot like the familiar analogy about the age of the earth. If that age could be represented by an average-sized book, all the time that humans have existed would be shown by a page or two at most. Everything since Columbus would be fit into a paragraph or so. Finally, the changes since the first atomic bomb would be the last few words, or even the very last one. This condensation of recent history, the years we are usually most interested in, is similar to the last minute or so of the grand parade.

One thing we have not learned from the procession is how rich the rich *should* be. The heights seem to rise gradually, so that there is no obvious break in the ascent to the heavens. As a result, there is no clear way to say how tall is too tall. Yet it can be done. We will have to use graph paper to do it.

For most of us, the amount we receive or earn in comparison to others is more important than any analogy about the age of the earth. Even before the imaginary march, we knew that some people made far more than the average, but what else is new? The vast line of marchers went by so quickly that it was difficult to draw any quantitative conclusions, other than the two listed above.

Yet by analyzing the data in a more leisurely way than one hurried hour, it is possible to find "natural" laws about the distribution of both income and wealth. The rest of this book will be devoted to determining how we can find those laws—by ourselves, not relying on the words of economists—and how we can use them to build a better society.

__ 2 _____

A HISTORY OF
WEALTH AND
INCOME DISTRIBUTION

Anyone who tries to summarize what is known about a given subject should do so with trepidation. Lord Acton's saying rings in our ears: ''Advice to those about to write history—don't.''[1] Since he disregarded his own counsel, we feel we can, too.

In this chapter, we will briefly trace the history of wealth and income distribution. There is no attempt to cover all that has been said on the subject. Anyone trying to do this should go into the encyclopedia business.

Trying to find the first mention of the fact that some people had more wealth and income than others is like trying to decide conclusively who invented the first automobile. Little bits and pieces of the puzzle, just like the modern car, were brought into being at various times and places. Some of us can remember sketches of a steam car that supposedly ran in France in the seventeenth or eighteenth century. Otto, appropriately named, invented the forerunner of the modern internal combustion engine in the late nineteenth century. The list of inventors or popularizers could be extended indefinitely. At some point, we realize that there was no single inventor of the auto.

In the same way, there is no single first document drawing attention to the fact that income and wealth are not spread evenly. We suppose that somewhere on a Sumerian clay tablet, the first writing that survives to this day, there is a complaint that someone was making more money, or hoarding more wealth, than somebody else. Regardless of what came first, there is no doubt that inequality has formed the basis for many ancient writings and aphorisms.

A Confucian statement is apparently one of the first on the subject: ''Where wealth is centralized, the people are dispersed. Where wealth is distributed, the people are brought together."[2] This thought, or varia-tions on it, has been the goal of most economic reformers in the three millenia since. However, exactly what is meant by centralization, disper-sion, and bringing together is not known. As with almost all the philosophical statements in this chapter, truth or falsity hangs on the precise definition of the terms, and these meanings are never given.

Plato said that wealth was the parent of luxury and indolence, poverty of meanness, and both of discontent.[3] For the first time we see the idea that excess wealth has some relation to poverty, if the former does not actually create the latter. Others said that the more overall wealth, the less overall poverty. Twenty-five centuries later, the battle still rages be-tween supply-siders and more conventional economists.

The Book of Good Counsels, written in Sanskrit around 300 B.C., notes that wealth is held (or taken) for wisdom, and that it should be so is a shame. Here is an initial instance where the personal characteristics of the wealthy are denounced. In spite of the fact that many, if not most, ancient works of literature were written with the patronage of the rich, they usually do not get many words of praise. Of the major statements on wealth and income, probably not more than a tenth are even neutral, let alone favorable.

The specific patron who funded the work may get hosannas, but the wealthy as a group, from which the specific patron comes, get mostly brickbats.

A later Greek, Aristotle, noted the relationship between political systems and wealth distribution. Before we go further, we should note that almost everything the ancients wrote on the subject dealt with wealth rather than income. It was clearly assumed that high income implied great wealth, and vice versa. In the ancient world, this was probably close to the truth.

Aristotle said, "Democracy arose from men's thinking that if they are equal in any respect, they are equal absolutely . . . the real difference be-tween democracy and oligarchy is poverty and wealth." Was Aristotle right? There have been democratic countries with highly skewed wealth distributions. England, from which we derived many of our concepts of democracy and freedom, is one such example.

In backward Albania, people may earn about the same amount. Yet democracy is as alien to that country as bananas are to Alaska. Most of us think we would be better off if wealth were not so maldistributed, but we would only be fooling ourselves if we blamed all the ills of society on this maldistribution.

By the time of the Romans, Cicero, himself a wealthy man by ancient and modern standards, had little good to say about his class: "Beware of ambition for wealth, for there is nothing so characteristic of narrowness and littleness of soul as the love of riches; and there is nothing more honorable than indifference to money."[4] Again and again, we come across similar statements. The well-to-do, in the words of the old Al Jolson song, warble, 'I didn't want to do it.'' Whether or not this was true, or just a psychological defense before psychology itself was invented, is unclear. Certainly most of those who made statements of this type did not quite manage to dispose of all their wealth before they died, in spite of the alleged burden of all that money.

Lucretius, who lived in the first century B.C., echoed Plato's thought: ''The greatest wealth is to live content with little.''[5] This may be so, but at that period the Romans were creating the largest class of wealthy men the world had ever seen.

WHAT THE BIBLE SAYS

If the devil can quote Scripture, so can the economists. The Bible is an almost unending source of observations on poverty, wealth, possessions, and money. While neither of us can claim to be Biblical scholars, we have been unable to find any Biblical rule suggesting what the upper limits on wealth or income should be.

Is this because the Bible deals only in moral generalities? Not quite. It contains many numerical references to the size of animal herds, numbers of soldiers in an army or in battle, ages (remember Methuselah), and the like. Whatever the authors of the Bible were, they were not innumerate. Yet there is no numerical guide to how much one can have and still be acceptable to God.

The Old Testament is of two minds on wealth. On one side, a wealthy man is legitimate in certain contexts, as long as he regards the money as coming from the Lord.[6] If good fortune brought wealth, it was not to be avoided or escaped. The event was somehow part of God's mysterious plan. However, the recipient had to ensure that the wealth did not dominate him. (We use the masculine pronoun because there are few Biblical instances of wealthy women).

One proverb put the ideal simply: ''Neither poverty nor riches.''[7] This implies indirectly that there could be those with too much wealth, but this statement is so brief that its implications are vague.

There are precursors in the Old Testament to the later anti-wealth preachings of Jesus. About ten psalms equate ''rich'' with ''wicked'', and ''poor'' with ''righteousness'' and ''godly.'' The Book of Job denounces the idea that living justly will bring wealth.

Yet wealthy men like Abraham are regarded as blessed by the Lord. The patriarch's riches were in flocks of animals, one of the greatest sources of wealth in those early agricultural days. Solomon, also praised lavishly, had his riches in gold, jewels, and other precious items. It is fair to say that the Old Testament was split on the question of how rich is too rich.

JUBILEE!

The Jubilee year in the Old Testament is one of the few systematic redistributions of wealth we have been able to identify in ancient times.[8] Of course, there had been redistributions even in prerecorded history. A king or prince would be overthrown, and his town or palace pillaged by marauding soldiers. However, this was far from systematic, and had no basis other than naked greed.

The word "Jubilee" is derived from the Hebrew *jobel*, a ram's horn or trumpet. It was announced this way on the Jewish Day of Atonement. Jubilee has come to mean any day of great celebration, but in Biblical times it was a statement of God's word about wealth distribution.

The key Jubilee rule as far as we are concerned was the provision that all slaves were to be set free every fiftieth year. While the number of slaves in Palestine at that time is not known exactly, slavery was one of the main sources of wealth in the ancient world. To require that they all be freed, even though the wait was half a century, could have been a drastic form of wealth redistribution.

Was the Jubilee really carried out? Again, we do not know for sure, but one authority says, "The elaborate system . . . though logical and finally legal, exerted no widespread influence on common culture either in old testament or new testament times."[9]

In spite of the apparent lack of enforcement, it remains an intriguing concept. The ancients apparently realized that at some point, wealth had built up excessively in certain hands. One way of passing it around was to let it literally walk away.

Concentrating on slaves avoided problems of dividing land, another major source of wealth in those—and present—days. If a rule had been made about the land that had to be given away every Jubilee, there would have been endless arguments over who retained the choicest portions, and who should get the rest. It would also have required numerical calculations about the size of land, leading to complicated legal tangles. Setting the slaves free was a simple and bold stroke.

But not every year—every fifty, instead. If slaves had been freed every few years, there would have been little incentive to accumulate the wealth that the slaves represented. We then see that the Biblical authors were balancing the need for society to build up wealth with the requirement to spread some of it around to the less fortunate.

From the viewpoint of the slaves, Jubilee did not help much. Many lived and died without seeing that blessed year. But at least there was the possibility of freedom down the road.

THE NEW TESTAMENT

The New Testament, while sometimes as inconsistent as the Old in the area of wealth and income, generally comes down strongly against excess wealth. One of Jesus' most quoted sayings, "How hard it will be for those who have riches to enter the Kingdom of God!"[10] makes the point clearly.

The question of whether riches are a deserved blessing from God for a virtuous life is rarely discussed in the New Testament. Jesus generally did not believe that a man could be mentally separated from his possessions. As described by Luke, a rich fool is a fool precisely because his whole life is wrapped up in his wealth.[11]

In one of the most telling commentaries on the wealthy, a rich young man who hopes for eternal life goes away sorrowful when Jesus tells him, "Go, sell what you have, and give to the poor, and you will have treasure in heaven, and come, follow me."[12]

The New Testament bubbles over with passages of this nature. It is apparent that Jesus' followers were usually below what we would now call the poverty line. It would have been remarkable if He had spent much time praising the wealthy. While condemning riches—not merely "excess" wealth—Jesus did not avoid all well-to-do men. He did dine with the wealthy. At least one rich Jew, Joseph of Arimathaea, honored Him.[13]

In spite of the many references condemning wealth and riches in the New Testament, there is no formula stating where excess wealth begins. Because of that, Jesus' followers, at least in the first century of Christianity, had difficulty interpreting exactly what He meant them to do about money.

On one side, the disciples apparently carried a common purse,[14] indicating perfect financial equality. The Epistle of James denounces ring wearing and elaborately attired worshippers, who presumably could afford expensive attire. First Timothy also warns against the pitfalls of wealth.

Yet as the early Church grew in complexity and power, Christians were torn between what seemed to be the clear teachings of Jesus and their own growing store of worldly possessions. The conflict is still not resolved. In recent years, Catholic bishops in the United States denounced financial inequality in scathing terms.[15] At the same time, some of their parishioners were among the wealthiest in the nation. But even the bishops, with far more access to financial and statistical data than the often unlearned authors of the Bible, were unable to specify how rich is too rich.

THE EARLY CHURCH

The early Church fathers of the fourth and fifth centuries continued the tradition of the New, not the Old, Testament. Saint Chrysostom said, "The rich man is a thief. . . . Riches are not forbidden, but the pride of them is."[16] Saint Jerome: "The rich man is unjust, or the heir to an unjust one."[17] Saint Ambrose: "The earth was made for all, rich and poor in common. Why do you rich claim it as your exclusive right?"[18] Saint Augustine: "The superfluities of the rich are the necessaries of the poor. They who possess superfluities, possess the goods of others."[19]

Some of these thoughts bounce around in time-warped echo chambers, being recapitulations of what has been said before and the precursors of modern versions. The notion that wealth is theft rings down through the ages. A small part of wealth or high income is indeed garnered illegally—rum running during liquor prohibition, cocaine smuggling in the present day, the numbers game before the state muscled in, and so on. The IRS estimates that $9 billion in taxes alone in 1981 were evaded through these and other illegal sources.[20] But $9 billion is still small potatoes compared to all of the legal sources of wealth in our society. Buy a piece of land that just happens to contain black liquid underneath, and you can be wealthy in short order.

Is this theft? It is, if you believe that the proceeds should be shared among everyone, not just the fortunate owners of a specific piece of property. Chrysostom clearly thought that.

Saint Jerome's statement is a softening of Chrysostom's: the rich man may not be a thief in every instance, but he is at least unjust. The key to Jerome's aphorism is that even if a particular man of wealth is upright by some fluke of personality, he is descended from an unjust father or grandfather. In that sense, wealth is analogous to that spot in *Macbeth*: try as one might to wash it out, it never quite disappears. It curses generation upon generation until the wealth disappears through wars, revolutions, charity, or other causes. While our conclusion in this book is that there is more income and wealth disparity than is necessary according to the economic law we will describe, Saint Jerome's curse seems to be going a bit far.

St. Augustine's comment is a restatement of the "constant pie" theory of economics. There is only so much to go around. So if some are wealthier than others, it must be at the expense of the poor. In St. Augustine's day, before the Industrial Revolution with its explosion of total wealth, this was probably a reasonable statement. If the pie was expanding at all in fourth-century North Africa, the time and place of his life, it happened so slowly that nobody noticed it. For all practical purposes, it was constant.

THE MUSLIM WORLD

There seems to be little written in the Muslim tradition on wealth and who may have too much. Part of the reason for this may be the fact that the religious leaders were often wealthy themselves, and saw no reason to denounce their own class. One of the few Muslim personages to mention both wealth and its implications was Abd-el-Raham, Caliph of Cordoba in the tenth century:

> I have now reigned above fifty years in victory and peace, beloved by my subjects, dreaded by my enemies, and respected by my allies. Riches and honors, power and pleasure, have waited on my call, nor does any earthly blessing appear to be wanting for my felicity. In this situation, I have diligently numbered the days of pure and genuine happiness which have fallen to my lot: they amount to fourteen. O man, place not thy confidence in this present world![21]

The Caliph says that troubles of the rich do not disappear as their bank accounts increase. Job was an Old Testament forerunner of this. We tend to forget that this sorely afflicted man was originally wealthy, with herds of oxen, sheep, camels, and other property. If he had started out with nothing, God would have had more of a challenge in besetting him with disaster.

TOWARD THE MIDDLE AGES

The Dark and Middle Ages saw no cessation of the stream of discussion about and invective heaped upon the heads of the wealthy. But as before, there was no indication given of how we would differentiate a wealthy man from a middle-class one, or what, if anything was to be done. Dante wrote: "And what else, day by day, imperils and slays cities, countries and single persons, so much as the new amassing of wealth by anyone?"[22]

After the fall of the Roman Empire, most sources of wealth in Western Europe had disappeared, with the exception of nondestructible land. It was only in the early shoots of the Renaissance in Italy that wealth was again being produced on a large scale. Dante, always alert, noticed this. But he seems overly negative. Wealth and its acquisition produced many harmful effects in Renaissance Italy as it did in previous ages, but "slaying of entire countries" surely is hyperbole.

John Wycliffe, the fourteenth-century English reformer, said, "Lords devour poor men's goods in gluttony and waste and pride . . . and so in a manner they eat and drink poor men's flesh and blood."[23] Again, this is a restatement—in a highly dramatic manner—of the "constant pie" theory. If you have a big slice, it is because somewhere, someone has a smaller one. This was still probably close to the truth at the time Wycliffe wrote, although by the fourteenth century improvements in agriculture and trade were making England richer than in past eras.

As far as we can tell, Erasmus, the great Dutch jurist and philosopher of the early sixteenth century, was one of the first men of the Renaissance to advocate doing something specific about inequality. Before this time, the difference between rich and poor had often been noticed and frequently decried. Yet with the exception of the Jubilee year we mentioned above, it was as if God, instead of merely giving Adam the breath of life with his outpointed finger depicted on the ceiling of the Sistine Chapel, had with His other hand conferred inequality on the race of man. Erasmus wrote, in distinction to that assumption: "The prince should try to prevent too great an inequality of wealth. I should not want to see anyone deprived of his goods, but the prince should employ certain measures to prevent the wealth of the multitude being hoarded by a few."[24]

Noble sentiments, and radically different from those being told to another prince by Machiavelli around this time. But how great is "too great" an inequality? This, Erasmus leaves for others to decide.

And what are these measures that will produce greater equality? Presumably they are some sort of taxes. Since there was very little slavery in Europe at the time that Erasmus wrote, the Jubilee solution of distributing wealth would have accomplished little or nothing. If taxes are the vehicle for redistribution, there are more varieties and types of taxes than there are excuses for being late to dinner. Which one or ones Erasmus and his prince would have chosen are not disclosed.

A last point on this quotation: Erasmus was not quite sure if he still followed the "constant pie" theory, almost a law in world economic thinking to that date. He implies that reducing inequality might involve taking goods or money from those well off, and he hesitates at that point. By the sixteenth century, enough new wealth was being created to inspire the hope that inequality could be reduced without merely taking from Peter to feed Paul.

In spite of Erasmus' baby steps towards wealth or income redistribution, the other side was still powerful. Martin Luther, a contemporary, said: "An earthly kingdom cannot exist without inequality of persons."[25] The fiery religious leader may have been referring to social status, intelligence or other human attributes, yet it is likely that most of its intent dealt with wealth. Luther says, in effect, "Let it be. Why tamper with something that God Himself may have planned?"

Three centuries later, the lexicographer Noah Webster, in a letter to the statesman Daniel Webster, put it another way: "The distinction of rich and poor does exist, and must always exist; no human power or device can prevent it."[26] Again, if it has always been that way, why not continue it? Using that reasoning, of course, you would be reading this in a dim grotto with your fellow cavemen.

At the start of the seventeenth century, Francis Bacon, the English philosopher, wrote: "Of great riches there is no real use, except in the distribution; the rest is but conceit."[27] A nice argument here. Bacon says that the whole idea of riches is pointless, without defining at what stage accumulation crosses the boundary between being worthwhile and being useless. Our society's intermittent searches for wealth via lotteries and other games of chance shows that many of us do not accept his philosophy.

Cervantes, a contemporary of Bacon, simplified the question of inequality: "There are two families in the world: The Haves and the Have-Nots."[28] It is an exaggeration for the sake of effect, although some similar arguments have formed the basis for twentieth-century socialist literature. It is obvious to anyone consulting income or wealth data that there is a gradation from the richest to the poorest. It was almost certainly that way even in the Spain of the late Middle Ages, although Cervantes did not view it that way.

This gradation makes the question of how rich is too rich much more difficult than if there were indeed only two classes, each member of which had exactly the same wealth or income. If Cervantes were right, "too rich" would be anything or anyone above the presumably large class of "Have-Nots."

Thomas More, in constructing his *Utopia* in 1516, did not neglect the question of wealth distribution: "an unjust and unkynde publyque weal, which giveth great fees and rewards to gentlemen, as they call them . . . and of the contrary parte maketh no gentle provision for poor plowmen, coliars, laborers . . . without whom no common wealth can continewe."[29] Yet in this blessed land of More's mind, there is still no indication of how wealth or income is to be distributed. More felt that the distribution of his day was "unjust," but that is only the first step on the road to justice. The omission is all the more glaring since More was explicitly constructing a Utopia, in which all rules of society could be restarted from the beginning.

THE INDUSTRIAL REVOLUTION CREATES ENORMOUS NEW WEALTH

With the dawn of the Industrial Revolution in the eighteenth century, philosophers wrote ever more on inequality and wealth. In part, this was because more wealth was being visibly created with the passage of each decade, in contrast to ancient times. Whether or not the wealthy became more arrogant in the process is unknown. However, by 1778 Samuel Johnson was noting, in accordance with the views of many previous writers: "The insolence of wealth will creep out."[30]

Jefferson and Carlyle, on the two sides of the Atlantic, echoed the same thought: "There is a natural aristocracy among men. The grounds of this are virtue and talent. . . . There is also an artificial aristocracy founded on wealth and birth."[31] So Jefferson. Now Carlyle: "Aristocracy of Feudal Parchment has passed away with a mighty rushing; and now, by a natural course, we arrive at Aristocracy of Moneybag".[32] Both thinkers decried the old aristocracy of position and the new one of gold, but failed to realize that the latter is transformed into the former if you wait long enough. In this country, the Rockefellers are regarded as an elite of birth—Laurence Rockfeller had a special gold medal given to him by Congress. The Perots, Gettys, and Waltons are thought of as an elite of money alone. Yet it was not that long ago that John D. Rockefeller (the first) was looked upon by most as an upstart in comparison with the old wealth of the Vanderbilts. And in turn, Commodore Vanderbilt, who had once operated a ferryboat, was viewed down the noses of the Astors. The chain extends a long way back into history.

Neither Jefferson nor Carlyle advocated specific measures to eliminate the looming aristocracy of dollars and pounds. In fact, if we look at the early history of the United States, it was only under the administration of that social conservative, the second U.S. president, John Adams, that a modest wealth tax was imposed by Congress. Jefferson railed at the maldistribution of wealth, or at least its maldistribution with respect to those with virtue and talent. However, he did little or nothing, beyond writing, to correct it. As has often been the case in history, those who complain most about a problem are not necessarily those who do something about it.

We will show later that some of the effects that Jefferson grumbled about were probably less severe at the birth of the new republic than in most other times and places. There was indeed inequality in those times. Yet when wealth is plotted on the probability graph paper we will use to illustrate our points about the super-rich, the United States during Jefferson's time exhibits a much smaller "kink" than most other periods and nations. Based on our calculations, the era of the Founding Fathers saw few super-rich even by standards of the time. This can be shown objectively. So Jefferson, one of the most perceptive philosophers in history, was off the mark on this point.

ADAM SMITH SPEAKS

It was in the time of Washington and Jefferson that Adam Smith wrote. In fact, one of the editions of *Wealth of Nations* was dated 1776. Clothed in figurative robes of ermine by such latter-day admirers as George Gilder, Smith supposedly laid the theoretical and moral basis of modern capitalism. Yet in his writings, we can find throwbacks to the old constant pie theory.

In that way of thinking, there was only so much to go around, no matter what economic theory one followed or how the government manipulated matters. Our ignorance of Smith's viewpoint may be due to the fact that, as John Kenneth Galbraith has pointed out, the Bible, Smith's *Wealth of Nations*, and Marx's *Capital* are the three books that everyone quotes but nobody reads. In any case, Smith said: "Wherever there is great property there is great inequality . . . for every one rich man, there must be at least five hundred poor."[33] Not, mind you, "follow my theories of the invisible hand of capitalism and all will be rich, or at least there won't be more than 200 poor for every wealthy person." Rather, Smith seems to hold this ratio of 500:1 as an iron law of economic nature. Since he is only re-stating in his usually clear and direct way what previous writers had suggested, we will not analyze his seemingly immutable ratio.

James Madison, the author of our constitution, echoed Plato's thoughts about the conflict between inequality and democracy: "The most common and durable source of faction has been the various and unequal distribution of property."[34] Showing more specific concern, he said, "Our Republic will be an impossibility because wealth will be in the hands of a few". How few are a few? How concentrated is concentrated? And if definitions could be supplied, what should be done to save the republic for which Madison had so valiantly struggled? *The Federalist* papers addressed many topics, but never answered these questions.

NINETEENTH-CENTURY AMERICA

Andrew Jackson's time was heralded as the age of the common man, because of such vivid images as the near riot at his inauguration, with muddy boots tramping through the White House. But observers of the scene, such as de Tocqueville, were noting less equality than at the founding of the republic. This decrease can be precisely measured by our probability graph paper, where the tell-tale kink of the upper few percent shows up clearly for the first time in American history.

President Jackson found it opportune to inveigh against the wealthy, even while a member of that class himself. In an 1832 veto of a Bank Renewal bill, he said: "Many of our rich men have not been content with equal protection and equal benefits, but have besought to make them richer by Act of Congress."[35] The way Jackson tells it, he had discovered a phenomenon new to history. Nothing could be further from the truth. As long as there have been governments, the wealthy have sought its protection, and used it wherever possible to enrich themselves. The battle for democracy over the centuries can be viewed in one light as the measure of how much was granted by governments to the nonwealthy.

Peter Cooper, the philanthropist and one of the wealthiest men of his time, also noted the looming problem as the United States turned away from its revolutionary origins: "There is fast forming in this country an aristocracy of wealth, the worst form of aristocracy that can curse the prosperity of a nation."[36] At first glance, this statement appears similar to Jefferson's of a generation or two before. The analysis which we supply in this book allow the distinction to be made. Jefferson was wrong: Cooper was right. The next section shows why.

AN EXAMPLE FROM 1798

Although the concept of income tax forms and their numbers being fed into calculators and computers is a relatively new one, economic historians have found evidence that the kink in income distribution we later describe in more detail existed hundreds of years ago. This gives credence to our assertion that the change in slope at around 2% or 3% of the income pyramid is almost a law of economic nature.

By way of proof, we present some data gathered by Lee Soltow, for the year 1798, just after the U.S. was established.[37] The graph in Figure 2.1 represents only wealth, because income data from long ago is not easy to find. As well, there are qualifications to Soltow's data, in spite of the fact that he is probably the leading expert on revolutionary-era income and wealth.

The information is shown on an unusual type of graph paper, known as logarithmic probability. The reason for this will be explained in the next chapter. The key lesson to be drawn from the graph is that the points do not all fall on a straight line. They lie on two. What this means will also be discussed in the next chapter.

Briefly, the wealth coordinate is the vertical axis, and ranges from less than $1,000 to over $100,000. The horizontal axis is the cumulative population up to that point in terms of wealth. For example in 1798 about 99% of the population had a total wealth of less than about $10,000. About 60% had a total wealth of less than about $1,000, and so on.

What does the graph mean? For our purposes, the main feature is what we call the "kink", or break in the line as it moves to the right-hand side of the graph. In the figure, the kink is rather small. The curve is almost a straight line throughout. This means that the distribution of wealth in revolutionary America followed what we will call a "natural" path. Wealth and income distributions of later eras have a much more noticeable kink. We will describe the implications of this kink later in this book.

THE LATER NINETEENTH CENTURY

As the nineteenth century progressed and disparities became ever more evident, the verbal onslaught against excessive wealth became ever more strident. Matthew Arnold, the English writer, laid almost every wrong

Figure 2.1
Wealth Distribution in the America of 1798

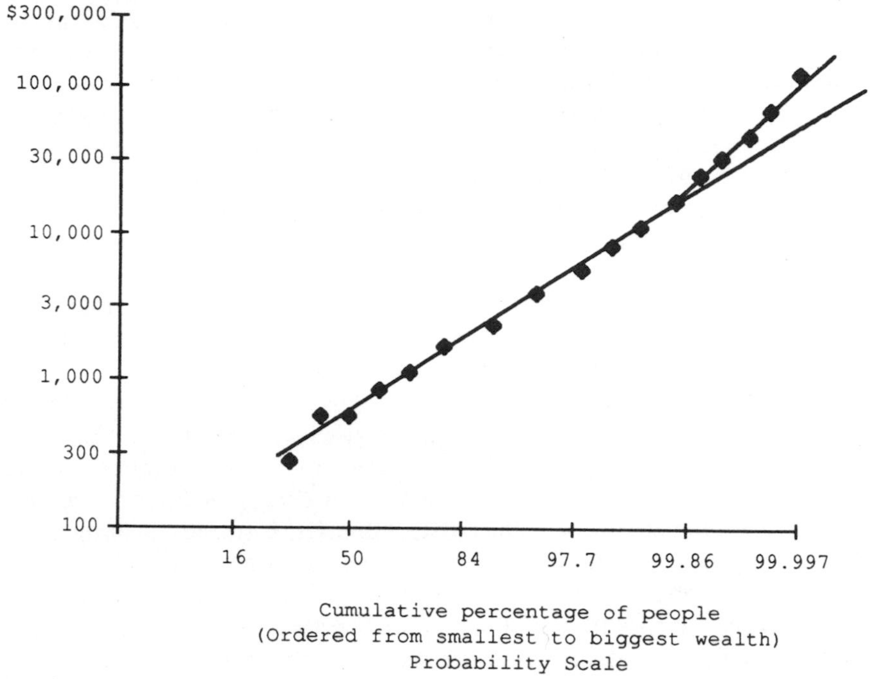
$300,000
100,000
30,000
10,000
3,000
1,000
300
100
16
50
84
97.7
99.86
99.997
Cumulative percentage of people
(Ordered from smallest to biggest wealth)
Probability Scale

in society at the doorstep of these disparities: "Our inequality materializes our upper class, vulgarizes our middle class, brutalizes our lower class."[38] Charming words if you do not like inequality, but held under the microscope they reveal only mist. No doubt there are materialistic members of the upper class, members of the middle class who do not raise their pinkies while drinking, and members of the lower class who engage in mud wrestling. All of the adjectives that Arnold used could also be applied to members of the other two classes, however. Even if the three adjectives were directed solely at the class for which they were intended, there is no way of showing that inequality caused it all. There was brutality in the lower class long before great concentrations of wealth came on the scene. Similar statements could be made about the other two classes.

In the Gilded Age that marked much of the second half of the nineteenth century in the United States, there was a curious dichotomy among the wealthy. On one hand, there were those such as George Baer, railroad industrialist of Pennsylvania at the turn of the century, who regarded their wealth as semidivinely given, or at a minimum due to their clearly superior brains.[39]

On the other hand, there was a small minority who felt some discomfort with the wealth they had either grabbed or had fallen into their hands. For example, J. P. Morgan, often regarded by the public as one of the great white sharks among financiers, said: "Of all forms of tyranny, the least attractive and the most vulgar is the tyranny of mere wealth."[40] Certainly Morgan resisted—with great success—the attempts of governments of the day to tax away large parts of his wealth or income, so exactly what he meant by that almost revolutionary statement is not clear. The financier may have thought of himself as more cultured, having acquired a vast treasure house of art, than the crude parvenus with whom he had to associate.

And the effect of this wealth on its possessors? Benjamin Franklin once said of an acquaintance: "He does not possess wealth: it possesses him."[41] That is true in some cases, false in others. The Rockefellers and Kennedys are certainly exceptions to this alleged rule. Three Rockefellers have served as governors of states as diverse as New York, West Virginia, and Arkansas, a record probably unmatched by any other family. Three Kennedys have served as president and/or senators. The financial reports of the U. S. Senate shows many with inherited fortunes, leaving them free to channel their ambition to political rather than financial pursuits.

Around the time that Morgan was speaking, Congress debated the question of inherited wealth, and what should be done about it. This was one of the few times that Congress has looked at the question in depth. In 1912, a great contest took place on the question of estate versus inheritance taxes. Estate rather than inheritance taxation won the day.

Returning to the robber barons, Andrew Carnegie was unique in that he attempted to give it all away, with almost complete success. Joseph Patterson, the publisher of the New York *Daily News*, spoke about his class as if he were almost on the other side of the barricades. He had been a radical socialist while attending Yale, and apparently some of his youthful ideas clung to him in later life: "While [the working people] support me in splendid style, what do I do for them? Let the candid upholder of the present order answer, for I am not aware of doing anything for them."[42]

One might think that with a statement like this, the *Daily News* would be printed on pink paper, with a silhouette of Karl Marx atop the editorial page. Readers of that newspaper know that its editorial stance is generally just the opposite.

Was Patterson just a wealthy man with a momentary twinge of guilt, or does his statement say something about inequality? To respond, we would have to set sail on the stormy seas of psychology. But we are not equipped for the voyage. There is little question that the wealthy sometimes wish they were not that way. In the case of the Caliph of Cordoba, quoted above, some of the well-to-do find that wealth has not brought them as much happiness as they had expected. Conversely, the poor, represented only tangentially in this collection of thoughts on wealth, sometimes aspire to higher financial states. On other occasions, they are satisfied with their meager lot in life.

In this book, we are trying to go beyond these transitory thoughts about wealth to the fundamental facts of what is *excessive* income or wealth, and what could or should be done about it. Only after this is accomplished can we decide if these or other aphorisms, guilt twinges, and all the rest really mean something.

THE TWENTIETH-CENTURY UNLIMITED WEALTH

Our present century has brought so many observations about wealth, income, and inequality that merely listing the names of those who have spoken or written on the subject might take up as much space as the total statements of the past. This does not prove, of course, that wealth or income inequality in this century is any worse—or better—than in previous ones. It may only show that more is being written on everything under the sun and beyond. As well, being that strange breed of people called "contemporaries," we are naturally more familiar with that which is written recently.

Unfortunately for those who think that the turning of a calendar page automatically heralds the dawn of a new age, we can find no new thoughts on inequality which are not, to some degree, a rephrasing of what has gone before. Gandhi said: "All amassing of wealth or hoarding of wealth above and beyond one's legitimate needs is theft. There would be no occasion for theft and no thieves if there was wise regulation of wealth and social justice."[43] This idea has clearly echoed across history.

There is indeed a grain of truth in what Gandhi says. But robbery? To test the Mahatma's assertion, we would have to know the "wise regulations" to which he referred, put them into practice, and then see if the sale of burglar alarms fell off.

Knowing the writings of the saintly Indian, we suspect he would have said, if pressed, that all should have equal shares of wealth and income. If this state could be achieved—and we would definitely *not* advocate it—it is by no means certain that thievery, in the broad sense, would disappear.

We can cite at least two reasons for this. First, in poor neighborhoods, where almost everyone has the same income (and no wealth), theft still takes place. The poor can and do rob the poor. Second, if there is one thing clear in many of the thoughts cited above, it is that the wealthy are ascribed unpleasant characteristics of greed and lust after money. Would these attributes vanish overnight if the wealthy were reduced to the same level as everyone else? You could make a case that their greed, if they do have it, would become even greater than before, as they tried to get back into their old position of superiority. Gandhi might have been in for a surprise if his policies had ever been carried out.

TWO BRITONS ON WEALTH

Perhaps the most famous twentieth-century statement on inequality is that of George Orwell: "All animals are created equal, but some are more equal than others."[44] In twelve words, he cut through most of the hypocrisy that surrounds the question of wealth and income inequality.

In 1984, the year in which his most famous novel was set, Orwell was celebrated like no other socialist in the last few decades. His widely quoted aphorism explained that the appearance of equality is insufficient; it must be matched by deeds. This then is applicable to what we are saying here. As we note elsewhere, governments have passed progressive income tax laws, estate tax laws, and a host of others designed to reduce, to some degree, inequality. Most of these taxes and laws have looked intimidating on the statute books, but have had less effect than planned. The gap between legislative intent and what happens after the tax forms are filled out remains as great as ever. In spite of Orwell's wisdom, how we could reach the semblance of equality, let alone the reality was unexplained. If some animals are indeed more equal than others, how do we bring them down to the same level of equality?

George Bernard Shaw took another tack. Many of the previous thoughts have implicitly asked the wealthy to share with the poor in some way. Shaw said: "Instead of sympathizing with the poor and abolishing the rich, we must ruthlessly abolish the poor by raising their standard of life."[45] This sounds reasonable, but are the standards of the poor to be raised by taking away from the rich, or by tapping some other source of wealth? This Shaw leaves unsaid.

One of the first problems assigned in elementary physics courses is estimating what fraction of an iceberg is above water level. You take the density of saltwater and ice, plug them into a formula, and find that most of the iceberg is below sea level. So it is with the thoughts of philosophers, writers, poets, and politicians on wealth and income disparities. We have presented only the iceberg's tip on the subject.

SOME CONCLUSIONS

What have we learned from all this? Much has been said against the rich over the millennia, but most of the effect has been lost because there have been no adequate definitions. Almost anyone with any degree of reasoning ability can tell that the most well-off man or family in a city or state is indeed wealthy. But what about the second wealthiest, or the ten-thousandth? Should the sometimes drastic measures advocated against the wealthy apply to those down the list as well? Silence reigns on the part of almost all writers on the subject.

Let us be fair. Few of those whom we have quoted knew much about economics or statistics. As a result, their analysis is inevitably diffuse. Still, the implication often is that the identification of the wealthy is as clear and simple as labelling biological specimens. An animal either is a horse or it is not. A wealthy man may be just that to you, but not to an even wealthier man living down the block. It is precisely because there is so much confusion on this topic that the remedies for correcting inequalities have often been ineffective.

Another thread running through most thought on the subject is the confusion between income and wealth. Let us amend that; income is only mentioned rarely, if at all. Yet the two concepts are different. To put it succinctly, income is the flow of wealth and wealth is the accumulation of income. There have undoubtedly been vast numbers throughout history who have had large incomes during their lives, and for one reason or another were unable to turn it into wealth and pass it along to the next generation. Merchants were probably the most numerous in this group, but in recent times entertainers and sports figures have often fallen into this class. The philosophers generally lump the wealthy with the high-income earners. For our purposes, they are not always the same.

The constant pie theory, or the immutability of total wealth or income, is another chord frequently struck. In ancient days, with its infinitesimal economic progress, this was a reasonably accurate description of society. Yet we hear echoes of this down to the nineteenth century, and occasionally even today. What we will advocate as our solution to the problem of maldistribution, our Alternative Distribution System, is based on precisely the opposite view. By spreading the wealth and income somewhat more evenly than now—but *not* perfectly evenly—we expect that the economic pie will grow faster than it normally would. More people will have a chance to put their ideas and inventions into effect, with money backing them up and incentive to make the try successful.

What are the Rich Really Like?

Much that has been written on wealth deals with the personal characteristics of the wealthy. Are they avaricious, or in reality generous to those less fortunate? Do they suffer terribly from the burden of wealth, or do they live a happy and carefree life, as those who followed the television series *Lifestyles of the Rich and Famous* imagine they do? It is true that the subject is fascinating to many. *People* magazine would be mostly blank space if it did not cover the wealthy. While we include some discussion of this topic, this is not our primary focus. In our opinion, analysis of how rich the rich should be and what should be done about it has often foundered on the reefs of the personalities of the rich. Here we concentrate on what their fortunes represent. We realize that there is a person or family behind every large bank account or oil well, but we cannot decide public policy on whether the rich are charming or mean. We suspect, as Hemingway is reputed to have said to F. Scott Fitzgerald, that the rich are like you or me, except they have more money.

Democracy and Inequality

Another constant theme is the threat to democracy posed by vast accumulations of wealth. While we would like to sound the tocsin to reinforce our case, we cannot, in good conscience. There is no question that if there is enough concentration, democracy suffers or disappears. The case of Nicaragua, where the late dictator Somoza was alleged to have owned half the real wealth of the entire nation, is a case in point. Yet that benighted land has had dictatorships, or at least semi-dictatorships, before and after the portly despot, with varying degrees of income inequality. The relationship is weak, at best.

Closer to home, in the United States the greatest degree of income equality was in revolutionary and pre-revolutionary times. We know this from a variety of sources. The revolutionary era is often held up in history texts as the epitome of direct democracy, with almost everyone gathered in town halls to debate the vital issues of the day. Yet, to take a few examples at random, there never was a direct vote to declare war on Britain, the franchise was restricted mostly to property owners, and women did not vote. Neither did slaves, who made up almost one-fifth of the population. None of this suggests that Washington, Jefferson, and the other Founding Fathers were undemocratic. Rather, it points out that the relation between the level of democracy and the extent of wealth and income inequality is far from certain.

One subtle distinction which is often missed in philosophical musings is the difference between greed and income distribution. The desire for gold and other valuables has existed at least since the dawn of recorded history. This desire is sometimes equated with the fact that there are wealthy and poor people, but it should not be. Greed probably exists in equal measure in all classes. The wealthy merely have more opportunity to indulge in it.

If there is one area where the great thinkers of history are found wanting, it is in recommending measures to correct or alleviate disparities. We could find few, if any, statements indicating how the problem they illustrated so vividly was to be overcome, or what the chances were that a proposed measure would actually work.

Gandhi, surely one of the most perceptive figures in world history, could only suggest "wise regulations" to correct the injustices he saw. How is a government to apply this? Or, if one relies on market forces to solve most economic problems, how is the market to be adjusted to bring about greater equality? We do not know what Gandhi would have replied, but other writers have said that this is a problem for government agencies or economists to solve.

That is the difficulty in a nutshell. There are incessant cries for economic justice ringing down the corridors of time. We also have legislatures and government departments who, from time to time, are seized with the idea of "doing something right" economically. The gap yawns between the concept and the action. With our Alternative Distribution System, we have constructed at least a rope bridge over the gap, if not the Golden Gate.

A LAW OF INCOME
DISTRIBUTION

Figure 3.1 summarizes the 1987 income tax data in an unusual way. First
we will examine this graph, then briefly the economic theory behind the
graph, and then the necessary mathematical tools to analyze it. This
presentation is common to our arguments for both wealth and income.
It provides us with a powerful and objective instrument for comparing
distributions across time and place.

The graph paper we are using is probability paper, and it allows us
a view of the income depicted in Pen's parade in a new way. Remember
that the last few percent of people had incomes nine pages above the
rest of us, according to the very first figure in this book. This type of graph
paper allows us to examine those few in great detail, while still viewing
the other 97% or 95%. It is as if we could look at all ten pages of that
original graph at the same time.

The graph is simple, once we understand how it works. We will ac-
complish that by illustrating the distribution of 1987 U.S. income, as
reflected by tax returns.[1] Then we will explore briefly the economic
theory and develop the mathematics necessary to understand it.

THE DISTRIBUTION OF INCOME

First, tax returns are sorted by the adjusted gross income (AGI). Then
a table is drawn up, showing how many people had incomes in various
brackets, for example between $10,000 and $11,000. The final step is
determining the total income of all the people who reported incomes
in this range. For the example we have chosen, the total income in
this bracket will be close to $10,500 times the number of people in this
range.

Figure 3.1
U.S. Income Distribution in 1987

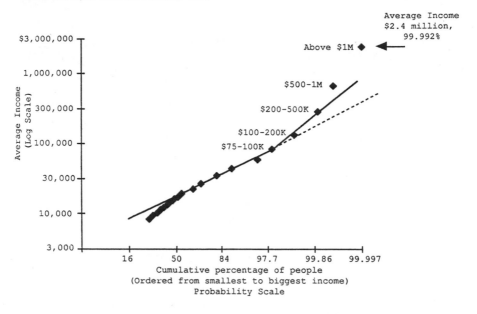

Source: Hostetter and Bates, Individual Tax Returns, p. 19

These calculations result in Table 3.1. As we progress down the table, we tabulate for each group how many taxpayers were at or above them in the table. This is shown in the third column, entitled "Cumulative Percentage of Returns with Positive AGI", which starts at 2.67 %. This means that 2.67% of the returns with positive AGI had an income of between $1 and $1,000. At the bottom of the table, we have counted 100% of the people. For each group, there is an associated average income—the total adjusted gross income of the group divided by the number in that group.

Note that between $17,000 and $18,000 we reach the halfway point of incomes. Fifty percent of the people report incomes below this amount; 50 % are above. The average income, the total amount of money reported on all returns divided by the total number of people who filed returns, is significantly larger—about $26,000. The difference between these two numbers ($18,000 and $26,000) is important. In Pen's parade, each individual's income is tallied in order of size. Fifty percent means the place where half the people are below and half above. Average incomes include the very richest. This makes it appear that this income is enjoyed by 50 % of the people—something that does not happen.

Table 3.1
U.S. Income Distribution in 1987[1]

	Number of Returns (thousands)	Adjusted Income Less Deficit (AGI) (billions)	Cumulative Percentage of Returns with Positive AGI	Average Income of Group
No adjusted gross income	891	-28.8		-$32,400
$1 to $1000	2,833	1.7	2.67%	$610
$1000 to $2000	3,696	5.5	6.15%	$1,500
$2000 to $3000	3,728	9.3	9.66%	$2,500
$3000 to $4000	3,352	11.7	12.82%	$3,500
$4000 to $5000	3,327	15.0	15.95%	$4,490
$5000 to $6000	3,304	18.2	19.06%	$5,500
$6000 to $7000	3,109	20.2	21.99%	$6,490
$7000 to $8000	3,217	24.1	25.02%	$7,500
$8000 to $9000	3,093	26.3	27.93%	$8,510
$9000 to $10,000	2,984	28.3	30.74%	$9,480
$10,000 to $11,000	2,973	31.2	33.54%	$10,490
$11,000 to $12,000	2,821	32.4	36.20%	$11,500
$12,000 to $13,000	2,766	34.6	38.80%	$12,500
$13,000 to $14,000	2,736	36.9	41.38%	$13,490
$14,000 to $15,000	2,567	37.2	43.80%	$14,500
$15,000 to $16,000	2,504	38.8	46.16%	$15,490
$16,000 to $17,000	2,285	37.7	48.31%	$16,500
$17,000 to $18,000	2,292	40.1	50.47%	$17,490
$18,000 to $19,000	2,195	40.6	52.53%	$18,490
$19,000 to $20,000	2,119	41.3	54.53%	$19,500
$20,000 to $25,000	9,062	203.3	63.06%	$22,430
$25,000 to $30,000	7,494	205.5	70.12%	$27,430
$30,000 to $40,000	11,605	402.5	81.05%	$34,700
$40,000 to $50,000	7,866	350.5	88.46%	$44,600
$50,000 to $75,000	8,144	485.7	96.13%	$59,600
$75,000 to $100,000	2,043	173.8	98.06%	$85,000
$100,000 to $200,000	1,520	201.2	99.49%	$132,400
$200,000 to $500,000	432	124.0	99.89%	$287,100
$500,000 to $1 million	77	51.9	99.97%	$673,000
Over $1 million	36	87.2	100.00%	$2,402,000
Taxable returns, total	86,750	2,706.6		
Nontaxable returns, total	20,320	81.4		
Total	107,070	2,788.0		

Average of all returns with positive AGI	$26,529
Median of all returns with positive AGI (to nearest thousand)	$17,000

Two numbers—the cumulative percentage of returns (column 3) and average income (column 4)—are used to plot the graph in Figure 3.1. The horizontal axis represents the cumulative percentage of people, and the vertical axis represents incomes at each level on a logarithmic scale. We will explain this scale, and why we are using it, later.

Now return to the graph. Its vertical axis shows the average annual adjusted gross income (AGI) for most of the 31 brackets used by the Internal Revenue Service. The logarithmic scale depicts incomes from about $5,000 to over $1 million. The horizontal scale shows the *cumulative* percentage below a given income level. For example, if we trace the 50% line vertically, we hit the sloping line at the median income of about $17,000.

The line falls fairly close to the actual data points until around the top 3% of the population (corresponding to about 97% on the horizontal scale), when it takes a sudden leap upwards. A dotted line continues the original line to the right. This break in the two lines is the key to our analysis.

The graph makes an almost straight line from about 36% to 95% of the income distribution. The lower 36% had incomes below $12,000 in a year in which the average poverty level for a family of four was $11,611. Incomes below that level are usually supplemented by a number of government programs, the incomes from which are not reflected in tax returns.

Beginning around the $50,000 to $75,000 income levels, a sharp and ever-increasing change occurs. Incomes begin to rise very strongly relative to the lower part of the curve. This fits quite well with the results of Pen's parade and economic theory. You will recall that the last few minutes of the parade saw some grotesque effects.

The crucial point that we make here is that there are *two separate lines*, not one. If there had been only one, we could have said that technically, everyone is described by only one distribution. There would have been no obvious break or cut-off point between the two groups, and this book would not have been written.

The case we will present below argues that *it is the group above the dotted line that could be called "too rich."*

In 1897, Vilfredo Pareto noted that the distribution of income in various countries, when plotted as a cumulative frequency function—that is the technical name for what we have been doing in Figure 3.1—had a characteristic shape. Professor Pen describes the relationship this way:

> In words, Pareto's Law amounts to saying that the number of income recipients earning at least a given income decreases by a fixed percentage, if we let them increase by 1%. This percentage is A. Suppose that we have established that in a given country A = 2, then we can state the law as follows: Imagine a certain income—the Selected Income Level—and count how many people earn this or a higher income; now perform the same operation with an income 1% higher, and the number of income recipients will have become 2% smaller. Whichever Selected Income Level we start with, the same percentage always emerges. The A is therefore a member of the large class of elasticities. The law can also be formulated this way: The elasticity of the number of persons above each Selected Income Level is constant, and therefore independent of the choice of this Selected Income Level.[2]

For example, there are about 36,000 tax returns at the $1 million level or above. How many are at $1.1 million or above? This is a 10% increase. If A = 2, there should be 20% less, for a total of about 29,000. Similar calculations can be performed for other income levels.

Subsequent work by the French economist, Gibrat, determined that much of the rest of the distribution was better described by a lognormal curve (explained below).[3]

To restate what we have learned: Starting from low income, the distribution is lognormal up to a rather high income, at which it follows the Pareto law or curve.

All that we have to know now is that a lognormal distribution is a *straight line* on probability paper, and anything that curves upward from this straight line indicates massive increases from one part of the population to the next. Figure 3.1 shows that the U.S. income distribution follows the laws of Gibrat and Pareto. The "kink," or the place where the two curves meet, is around the 97% level (i.e., the top 3% of incomes).

SOME MATHEMATICAL POINTS

Now that the main point about the kink between the two lines has been made, we have to do a little mathematical tidying up. First, we have to admit that all the dots in the graph do not fall exactly on the straight lines. Anytime you do see an economic graph with every dot precisely on a line, it is possible that the artist drew the line first and then added the dots. What we see in Figure 3.1 is about as close to a law as we can get in economics. Because we are trying to include everyone who files a tax return, there is inevitably some uncertainty and variability in the data.

Second, as we implied above, the 3% point is not set in concrete. The graph shows that the cut-off point or kink is a bit fuzzy. It might be 2.5% or 3.5%, depending on how we drew the straight lines. The exact point is not of great consequence in any case. The important idea is that the slope of the lower line definitely changes as it melds into the upper line.

The cut-off point has been around 3% in the United States for years—sometimes a little higher, in other years a little lower. In other countries, with different social systems, salary structures, and other economic factors, the kink will be at a different point.

Third, the upper 3% of the income distribution occupies more than 3% of the graph paper's width. This is in contrast to ordinary or regular graph paper, where the top 3% would fill exactly that proportion of the paper. The strange result is because of the peculiarities of probability paper. It stretches out the last few percent so they can be studied in detail, and compresses the region around the midpoint. If we had been studying the bottom of the income pyramid, rather than the top, we would also have been able to concentrate on the lowest few percent.

The lines of the graph do not appear radically different at first glance. In part, this is an optical illusion due to the vertical scale of the graph, which is logarithmic. The distance from $10,000 to $20,000 is exactly the same as from $100,000 to $200,000, a hallmark of the logarithmic scale. This type of measure compresses differences of slope.

As an example of the differences in the two slopes when dollar amounts are evaluated—in contrast to physical distances on the graph paper—consider travelling from the 95th to the 97th percentile of income. We rise from about $89,000 to about $112,000, a difference of about $23,000. Now we reach the elite on the right. If we travel another 2%, exactly the same as in the previous example, from 97% to 99%, we rise from $112,000 to about $240,000, a difference of about $130,000. The ratio of the two differences is about $130,000/$23,000, or about 5.7. This indicates that there really is a substantial change between the slopes when we transfer from the cryptic notation of the graph to dollar amounts.

WHY THE POOREST ARE NOT ON THE STRAIGHT LINE

The straight lines we talked of above are not quite arrow-like. This is especially evident on the left-hand side of the graph, where the data points go below the line as we approach the poorest part of the population.

This means that there are really more poor people than we would expect on the basis of our simple model. For example, at around the $7,000 income level, we would expect about 14.5% of the population to be below it, on the basis of the straight line we have drawn. In truth, about 20% of the population is below. Given that there were about 107 million returns in 1987, this means that 5.5%, or about 5.9 million, of the returns are not accounted for in our model at this income level. Is this due to teenagers working a few hours at a fast food stand, mothers employed while their children are in school, and other part-time workers?

This book is not about poverty, so we will say comparatively little about the lower part of the income distribution. This is not because the poor are unimportant; how society treats its less fortunate is truly a measure of its civilization.

Rather, the subject is so vast that it deserves a treatment of its own. When 40% of the entire population, according to *USA Today*, would have trouble paying off an unexpected bill of $1,000, poverty or near poverty is more common than we might imagine.[4]

Tens of millions of people past retirement age have little beyond their Social Security checks. Average annual payments for retired workers was about $5,300 in 1984; that for disabled workers was about $200 more. This huge mass of retirees with comparatively little income would account for part of the bulge at the lower end of the scale. In turn, this bulge shows up on our graph as points below the straight line at lower percentages.

Part-time employment is another cause. In 1982, about 16 million people worked part time out of a labor force of about 110 million. We do not know exactly how much they earned, but there is a good chance that it was substantially less than the values for full-time employment. For example, about four million teenagers, traditionally the lowest-paid workers other than migrant workers and illegal aliens, are employed part time. They must file with the IRS, even though they may be covered by their parents' returns.

Another reason why some of the dots at the bottom of Figure 3.1 are below the straight line is that many in this group receive what the economists call non-cash benefits. When someone gets Medicare or Medicaid benefits, it is not counted in their income. The money is sent directly to doctors or hospitals without appearing on W-2s, the record of earned income.

For example, one study of so-called "in-kind" benefits in 1970 showed that for one of the lowest-income brackets ($1,000 to $2,000 annually) in-kind transfers were about 50% of cash income.[5] The ratio gradually dropped as cash income rose, reaching a proportion of 22% in the $4,000 to $5,000 bracket. If these and similar benefits were indeed counted as income, as in a sense they are, some of the dots falling below the left-hand side of the lower line in Figure 3.1 would rise considerably.

THOSE WHO DROP OFF THE GRAPH

There were about 890,000 taxpayers in 1987 reporting no gross income or a loss. This is almost 1% of the total of 107 million returns. There is no way we can show this group on the vertical axis of Figure 3.1, since it does not go down to zero or to negative values. This omission is a fundamental property of a logarithmic axis.

Because this class with a net loss is a small fraction of all taxpayers, we might be tempted to dismiss them as changing the results very little, especially when we cannot even portray them on the graph. This would be a mistake, for at least two reasons. First, while 1% is indeed a small proportion, it is greater than the fraction of all returns with an adjusted gross income of about $150,000 in 1987. Second, the average loss by this group sheds considerable light on how some taxpayers shield their income from the IRS. This hidden income generally does not show up on our graphs or in our calculations.

This is the mysterious group that appeared at the head of the grand parade in Chapter 1, buried in the earth. Their average loss was about $32,000.

Almost everyone suffers a good-sized financial loss in the course of a lifetime. Some property gets stolen, a business fails, a partner absconds with funds, or an uninsured building burns down. In most cases, income during the year of the loss outweighs the financial damage, so that total net income is still positive.

For example, the average loss from all residential fires was about $5,000 in 1982. If the average family income was about $20,000 in 1982 (in 1982 dollars), it seems unlikely that many citizens would suffer a net loss—total income minus the loss—due to fires. Besides, most homeowners have at least some fire insurance, cutting down on the total number of net losers even more.

The group of those with net losses clearly includes many who have arranged their otherwise prosperous business affairs to have a paper loss in a given year. Many in this group cannot be the ghetto downtrodden, who have all their possessions stolen. The poor do not own $30,000 of goods in the first place. In the second place, they do not often report losses to the police or insurance companies. Rather, by judicious manipulation of profits and losses, the often well-to-do people in this "losers" group can create a negative balance for the year. The people who have losses this year, and are not even on the graph at all, may show up next year on the extreme right-hand side, in the top 3%.

By way of example, we noted in Chapter 1 that those in this group who hold tax-free municipal and state bonds have an average income from these sources of about $21,000. This suggests that their average holding was about $350,000. More than half of this loss group had taxable interest from banks, averaging about $4,680. This in turn implies an average bank account of about $58,000. About a quarter of this group received dividends worth about $3,300. It is difficult to translate this into stock holdings, but they would be substantial.

Nobody can exist for long on average losses of $32,000 a year. Average liquid assets, such as cash in the bank, of American families is much less than this amount. In 1982, 49% of the population had less than $5,000 in savings and investment assets.[4] If these losses occurred to the average household, they would have one and only one chance to get off the loser's list. The group of the purported victims must then be made up mostly of wealthier citizens. We suspect that few of them go hungry.

Why have this discussion of people not even on the graph? While 890,000 tax returns is only a few drops of water in the bucket of all form 1040s, they illustrate why the slope of the line for the top 3% in the graph (the upper right-hand side) may be even steeper than we show. If some of the wealthy can appear to the tax man to have losses in some years, a true reckoning would produce an even sharper slope on the right-hand side of Figure 3.1.

PSYCHOLOGY AND THE LOGNORMAL DISTRIBUTION

Taking logarithms may seem unnecessarily abstruse for something as straightforward as tax returns, but the mathematics corresponds to some of our psychological feelings about money. Since this book is ultimately about cash, it is important to know what relationship logarithms have to both the flow and quantity of money.

Consider someone who earns $10,000 a year. The economy booms, and he is rewarded with a raise to $12,000. Now look at his boss, the chief executive officer of this firm. The CEO may earn $100,000 annually. Because of his hard work, he gets a bonus of $20,000, for a total of $120,000.

How does this pair feel about their new-found gain? Feelings cannot be measured accurately. Still, a reasonable case is that their joy is about the same, even though the monetary amounts involved are vastly different. The 20% increase they have both received should provoke each to sweet dreams—one of Nikes, the other of Mercedes.

Logarithms enter into psychology because they are a measure of the *ratio* between two numbers, not their differences. In this instance, the ratio of the dollars after to the dollars before the windfall in both cases is 1.2 ($12,000 divided by $10,000; $120,000 divided by $100,000). The logarithm of 1.2 in both cases is obviously equal. The difference in dollars is clearly not. So if we say that the two recipients of extra money are even approximately equal in their joy, we are in effect saying that humans react *logarithmically*.

Further evidence comes from a *USA Today* survey of 2,400 households.[4] The less well-off people considered an income of $100,000 "rich." Among those with high incomes, it took a million to reach that category.

Logarithms allow a mathematical formulation of an ancient maxim: The more you get, the more you want. Give a battered jalopy to a teenager who does not have wheels, and you will be greeted with jumps or squeals of joy depending on the gender of the recipient. Want to try this with Donald Trump or Leona Helmsley? The advantage of logarithms is that it allows us to be quantitative about vague thoughts and emotions.

INFLATION EFFECTS

According to Frederick Leith, inflation is like sin: Every government denounces it, and every government practices it. Does inflation change our conclusions?

Not really. If we had said that $110,000 was the point where the income distribution line changes slopes or kinks (it is, for 1987), always had been and always would be, we would be wrong. Inflation has been around almost as long as systems of economic exchange. Nobody expects it ever to disappear.

What does inflation do to our results? Our conclusions—that there are two income groups dwelling in the bosom of one nation—changes little if at all. In a given year, the kink may wander from 2% up to 4%, depending on inflation, the way people report their income to the IRS or hide it, and a host of other factors. Yet the two slopes persist on each yearly graph.

What *does* change is the vertical scale, or the amount of money earned per household or tax return. From 1960 to the mid-1980s the consumer price index rose by a factor of about three. An income of $30,000 in the latter period would correspond to about $10,000 at the time of John Kennedy's election, if incomes kept in exact lock step with prices. This means that if the kink for 1987 in Figure 3.1 was about $110,000, it was probably $30,000 to $35,000 in 1960.

So the point where the slopes change has altered in dollar value over the years. But it is still there. If it appeared in some years and not in others, like a lighthouse blinking on and off, our contention would be weakened beyond repair. The fact that the kink or elbow remains, through thick and thin, shows that it expresses a fundamental rule about how American society is organized.

WHAT DOES A FAIRER INCOME DISTRIBUTION MEAN?

We have described the two types of income distribution, one for the lower 97% and the other for the upper 3%. A fairer distribution for the nation would comprise *one* distribution, not two.

How would this work in practice? For those adept at interpreting complicated graphs, the answer to that question leaps out immediately from Figure 3.1. The rest of us may need a little help.

From that figure, we can see the dotted line continuing the distribution of the lower 97% up to the right. It diverges from the *actual* income distribution of the upper 3%. But what does this mean in terms of actual dollar amounts and numbers of people?

Figure 3.2 answers this question. It still is not on simple linear graph paper. The numbers of people involved and dollars in question change too drastically for so-called "normal" graph paper to handle all the information. For example, on the left-hand side of Figure 3.2 we are considering about five million households, and on the right-hand side about 10,000.

The horizontal axis, scaled in units of 10,000 people or tax returns, runs backwards. It travels from five million people on the left-hand side to the top 10,000 earners on the right. Incomes, on the vertical axis, run in the correct (upward) direction. Scaled in units of $100,000, they range from $100,000 at the bottom to over $2 million at the top. The upper black dots represent *actual* income levels in 1987, derived from the right-hand side of Figure 3.1. The lower blank dots are an extension of the lower 97% curve in Figure 3.1. It is shown as dashed in that figure. The left-hand bottom corner of this graph is the "cut-off" point of Figure 3.1, so the two curves shown here come together. They diverge as income rises.

Consider a few examples from Figure 3.2: At the bottom left-hand corner, about three million households had an adjusted gross income in 1987 of about $110,000 or more. At this point, the theoretical and actual lines meet. The three million households correspond to about 3% of the 107 million tax returns in 1987.

The rest of Figure 3.2 is concerned with households earning more than $110,000. It then corresponds to the right-hand side of Figure 3.1, where the two lines diverge. In effect, we have expanded the right-hand side of Figure 3.1 by scrutinizing it more closely.

Figure 3.2
A More Rational Income Distribution above the 3% Cutoff Point

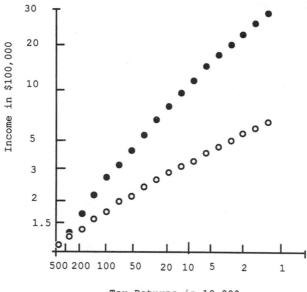

Tax Returns in 10,000

If we move somewhat to the right in the figure, we come to the top two million households, or the highest 2% of tax returns. We start to see a divergence between the two curves. The *actual* income is about $170,000, but the "fairer" distribution is about $135,000. The difference is about $35,000, and amounts to about 20% of the total income at this level.

At one million households, or the top 1% of income, the divergence is greater. The actual level is about $280,000, but the more rational distribution corresponds to about $180,000. That is a difference of about $100,000, or about 36% of the actual income. While a drop from $280,000 to $180,000 may seem substantial, the remaining amount is still about seven times the *average* household income in 1987.

Now proceed a little to the right, to the top 500,000 households. The top one-half percent of the population had an *actual* income of at least $430,000. We propose a more rational income of about $200,000. This is a drop of about 50%, but the remaining amount is still *eight and one-half times* the average national income. There would still be far more than enough for European trips and Yale tuition.

The highest 50,000 earners correspond to the top one-twentieth of one percent, or one in 2,000. In a town of 50,000 people whose income distribution was similar to that of the entire nation, there would be 25 people in this group. Their *actual* income was at least $1.5 million. From the way that incomes are rising as the groups get smaller and smaller, we are approaching an almost vertical cliff.

From this group, we propose an income, based on the lower curve, of about $430,000, a drop of about 70%. This, we admit, is a substantial proportion. However, this elite group, even with the reduced income, would still rank in the top 500,000 as of 1987. They would still have an income level 16 times the average.

As we mentioned above, *we are setting no fixed limits on income*. This implies that the lower curve of the figure would keep rising indefinitely as the number of tax returns being considered became smaller and smaller.

The major difference between what actually happened in 1987 and our proposed curve is that the *slopes* are radically different. The actual upper income curve kept rising. Ours tends to slow down after a while.

Figure 3.2 shows clearly how our more rational distribution system differs from what really took place in 1987. Under what we propose, the rich would still be rich by usual standards. They would just be a little less so.

WHAT DOES IT MEAN TO SAY A DISTRIBUTION IS LOGNORMAL?

Before we can build a house, we have to assemble all the tools and materials. Since our analysis of income and wealth distribution depends upon logarithmic and lognormal distributions, we have to deal, to some extent, with mathematics.

Many distributions, of birds, trees, or money, exhibit a pattern that we can describe by an equation. In fact, such a large proportion are similar mathematically that they are called "normal". We can illustrate a normal distribution by something everyone is familiar with: human height. We all have a vertical dimension. There are obvious differences in height. Do they fit some type of mathematical description?

Suppose we went out in the street and wrote down, on slips of paper, the heights of the first thousand men we met. We could do the same for women, and find a similar normal distribution, centered on a shorter average. For simplicity, we will not do this.

Tossing the thousand slips into a hat, we then select the height with the largest number of slips. It probably would be around 5 ft. 9 in., about the average height for men in this country. Now we go three inches in either direction, to 5 ft. 6 in., and an even 6 feet. We would probably find close to equal numbers of slips of paper, corresponding to numbers of men in each category. This is the key point in determining if a distribution—the thousand men—is a normal distribution. If we go an equal distance in either direction from the maximum, the values should be about equal in a normal distribution.

Because we have already said that the height of 5 ft. 9 in. has the most men, there would be fewer at 5 ft. 6 in. and at 6 feet. The exact decrease in numbers is not important for this analysis. We would probably also find equal numbers for any pair of heights equally distant from the maximum: 5 ft. 4 in. and 6 ft. 2 in, 5 ft. and 6 ft. 6 in., and so on.

Now we plot our findings on ordinary (linear) graph paper, as shown in Figure 3.3, Panel A. We use the word "ordinary" to preface the phrase "graph paper," because later in this figure we will use some unusual graph paper. In Figure 3.3, Panel A, the average height is the maximum, and the curve gradually slopes down on both sides. There are many fewer men at 6 ft. 5 in. and 5 ft. 1 in. than the maximum.

Mathematicians call this curve a normal distribution, because it describes many—though not all—of the phenomena of the universe. Most common measures, from the diameter of peas to the lengths of index fingers, tend to assume this shape when plotted on graph paper. The distribution is sometimes called bell-shaped, for obvious reasons. The bell can be flat or tall, depending on the quantity we are considering or the scale of the graph.

For example, if in Panel A of Figure 3.3 we had used a horizontal scale of six inches instead of two inches, the resulting curve would not have looked much like the Liberty Bell. It would have been tall and narrow. Real bells do not deviate much from a standard shape. Since we are in the realm of theory, we can stretch or squash our bell-shaped curve like Play-Doh.

The normal distribution is *statistical* in nature. Suppose you took the heights of 20 men and plotted them on a graph like Panel A of Figure 3.3. Chances are you would get a lumpy curve, looking roughly like a bell that had seen battle. There would be gaps—your group might not include anyone from 6 ft. 1 in. to 6 ft. 3 in., for example—and excesses. There might be a cluster around 5 ft. 8 in. The smaller the group, the more irregular the bell-shaped curve.

On the other hand, fan out across the city, making thousands of measurements, and the curve that you draw at the completion of your labors will almost certainly be nearly smooth. This is basically what we mean when we say that the normal curve is statistical. Enough measurements even it out.

So *most* things we can measure, from the number of hairs on our heads to the times it rains in July, will show up as a bell-shaped curve on graph paper. The key word in the previous sentence is "most." For a variety of reasons, not all distributions are normal.

It is tempting to call everything that is not a normal distribution abnormal, but nature makes no such distinction. It chooses its distributions in ways that are still somewhat mysterious. Putting these distributions on graph paper and giving them a name are human artifacts, not those of nature.

Figure 3.3
Graphing Techniques Used in This Book

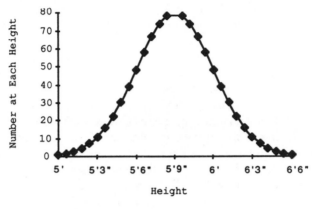

Panel A

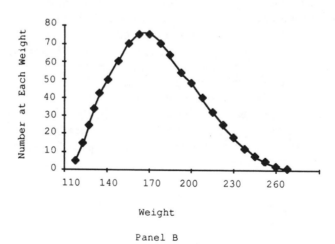

Panel B

Figure 3.3 (Continued)

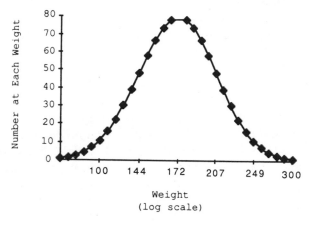

Weight
(log scale)

Panel C

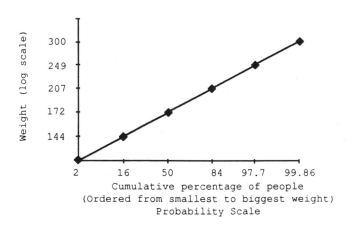

Cumulative percentage of people
(Ordered from smallest to biggest weight)
Probability Scale

THE LOGNORMAL DISTRIBUTION

The spreads of wealth and income *do not* follow simple bell curves. It turns out that money matters tend to be best described as a lognormal distribution, a cousin of the normal or bell-shaped curve. Then why bother talking about normal distributions in the first place?

The normal curve was exemplified by something we all know about, height. So will the lognormal. The first syllable of lognormal is a contraction for logarithm. The dictionary defines logarithm as the index of the power to which a fixed number (i.e., the base) must be raised to produce another given number. For example, the logarithm of 100 is 2. This means that if we raise 10 to the second power or square it (i.e., 10×10) the result is 100. Logarithms can also be a decimal number like 2.78. In this case, we have to turn to a hand calculator to determine 10 raised to the power 2.78. Most calculators have a key marked "log," so doing the computation is much less of a challenge than it once was.

What is an example of a lognormal distribution? Consider something we all know about, some of us all too well: weight. Human weight is close to a lognormal distribution, as opposed to the normal distribution of height. We can recognize a normal distribution by its shape on graph paper. How can we identify a lognormal distribution? The statisticians say that a lognormal distribution is *skewed*, or not symmetrical. It will tend to look like Panel B in Figure 3.3, with a long tail on the right.

Suppose we go back to the thousand men whose heights we measured, and this time put them on the scales. After the beam has been tipped for the last time, suppose we find that more men are around 170 pounds than any other weight. This is actually close to the national average. In Figure 3.3, Panel B, we can see that the maximum is close to that value.

Now we can do as we did with heights; proceed in both directions from the maximum. Let us move 30 pounds, to 140 and 200 pounds. We will probably find more men at 200 than at 140, although we might first ascribe this to ordinary variation in the numbers. This is our first indication that the weights are nonsymmetrical.

Now let us proceed 70 pounds from the midpoint, to 100 and 240. There are very few men of the former tiny size, but we see many of the second group every autumn Sunday afternoon on our TV screens. The number of 240-pound men is far higher than the 100-pound variety, as we can deduce from the left-hand side of Panel B. In fact, the graph suggests few if any 100-pound men. The nonsymmetrical nature of the graph is becoming evident.

Even if we had never seen a game of professional football, we could prove the skewness of the weight curve. Every so often we read of someone who, beset by glandular problems, dies at a weight of 400 or more pounds. This is obviously more than 170 pounds from the midpoint of

170 we assumed above. To produce symmetry in the weight curve, someone would have to have a negative weight (i.e., more than 170 subtracted from 170) to correspond to that unfortunate person.

Peter Pan was supposed to have the ability to fly, implying some sort of weightlessness. He remains confined to the realm of imagination. Nobody else has zero or negative weight. As a result, the curve of human weight is unbalanced or skewed.

Not every skewed distribution is lognormal. There are types of distribution other than the two we have discussed, some of which are nonsymmetrical. One, the Pareto distribution describing the very top of the income pyramid, is a vital part of our argument.

RECOGNIZING A LOGNORMAL DISTRIBUTION

How would we know a lognormal distribution if we were given a series of numbers? The simplest way is to take the logarithms of each of the quantities involved. If we plot the *logarithms*—as opposed to the original numbers—and get a bell-shaped curve, the original distribution was lognormal. If we do not get a bell-shaped curve, then the original distribution *was not* lognormal.

Let us go back to the weight example we used before. The most common weight for men that we showed in Panel B was 170 pounds. Suppose that there were 78 men at that weight. The logarithm of 170 is 2.23, according to our hand calculator. Instead of plotting a value of 78 on the graph paper above the mark for 170 pounds, we proceed horizontally 2.23 units, and then mark a value of 78. At 200 pounds, there may be 55 men. The logarithm of 200 is 2.30. We mark a vertical point of 55, and a horizontal value of 2.30. We continue on in this way, until all the original weights have had their logarithms calculated and plotted.

If, after performing these mathematical operations, we find a bell-shaped curve forming on graph paper, we know that the original distribution was lognormal. We see this shown as Panel C, which is a transformation of Panel B according to the above rules. If we still do not get a bell-shaped curve, then there is no telling what the original distribution was.

Panel D of Figure 3.3 is a replay of Panel C—same data, different presentation. This time we are using probability paper, which allows us to spread out the last few percent of a curve and examine its characteristics more carefully. On probability paper, a normal curve (i.e., bell-shaped on regular graph paper) becomes a straight line. The units may correspond to everyday numbers—heights, for example—or they may be logarithms of numbers. Both will produce a straight line if the scale corresponds properly to the underlying distribution.

In Figure 3.1, we used this paper with income shown vertically on a logarithmic scale. If a number is above the straight line on a probability graph, it means that it is *much* above the corresponding number on the original normal or lognormal graph. The line in Figure 3.1 starting from the bottom left-hand corner is the Gibrat curve, which is strictly lognormal. Pareto's distribution appears whenever a point is above the line.

All the incomes in Figure 3.1 are expressed on a logarithmic scale. That is, to get from one rung of the ladder to the next, you multiply, rather than add. The Richter scale for measuring earthquakes works the same way. The quake of 7 on the Richter scale did massive damage in San Francisco; at 8, the energy unleashed would have been ten times greater. In other words, going from 7 to 8 on the Richter scale does not mean devastation only one-seventh greater.

Thus a number above the projection of the Gibrat line (the lower left-hand curve) ascends into Pareto's realm. It is massively bigger than it would have been if it had remained on the Gibrat line. In terms of Pen's grand parade, to go from one rung of the ladder to the next would require a lift in a helicopter.

THE LORENZ CURVE

Economists are sometimes accused of not coming up with new ideas. The invisible hand that Adam Smith wrote about in the eighteenth century may have been the one that wrote "Mene, mene, tekel," on the wall before Belshazzar's downfall.

This also applies to theories of equality and inequality. If you took Economics 101, you may have been told that experts in the field had shown that nothing could be done about income distribution. A Lorenz curve may have been offered up as proof.

This diagram, invented decades ago, is a rough measure of inequality. A sample is shown in Figure 3.4. We start off in the bottom left-hand corner with no population and no income. We end up in the upper right-hand corner with 100% of the population and 100% of the income.

To get from the starting to the final point, we plot the *cumulative* income distribution on the thin solid line. For example, Mortimer Zuckerman, editor-in-chief of *U.S. News & World Report* (himself one of the wealthiest men in America) noted that in 1988 the lowest tenth of the population had about 1.2% of total national income, the next tenth had about 2.6%, and so on.[6] In terms of plotting this on a Lorenz graph, the first point is 10% population and 1.2% income. The next point is 20% population and 3.8% (= 1.2% + 2.6%) income. We can continue the process until all the tax returns are included. The curved solid line in Figure 3.4 is then a typical curve for an industrialized country.

If the robber barons of the 1890s had continued on their merry way, accumulating most of the income and wealth of the country, the Lorenz curve would have been much different. It would have looked like a slightly

Figure 3.4
Lorenz Curves of Income

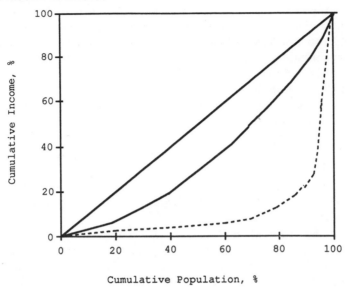

Cumulative Population, %

bent reverse "L," rising very slowly until it jumped to the top in the last few percent. We show this as a series of dashes in the figure. If a group of us lesser mortals happened to get on an elevator with John Kluge, the Sultan of Brunei, or Sam Walton, a Lorenz curve plotted for all of us would look like that reverse "L."

If, on the other hand, everyone in the elevator or the nation earned exactly the same amount, the Lorenz curve would be the straight solid line in Figure 3.4. It extends like an arrow from zero income, zero people to 100% income, 100% people. In this scheme, the lowest 20% of the population would have 20% of the income; the lowest 40%, 40% of the income; and so on up to the top. We would have the perfect egalitarianism suggested by Rawls's philosophical theories of income distribution.

PERFECT LORENZ EQUALITY

Could we ever approach that solid line of perfect equality? Although the United States has more reform movements per square mile than perhaps any other nation, there have been few interested in reducing income inequality as a primary goal. This inequality has been sometimes lessened as an indirect result of other political goals, such as public welfare and Social Security, but this was not the main aim of the movements that inspired these government programs.

One of the few campaigns in recent decades to try to reduce income inequality explicitly was Senator Huey Long of Louisiana's "Share the Wealth" scheme of the 1930s. The Kingfish was unquestionably a demagogue on some of his other political issues, and observers had wondered about his sincerity on this one. Since it was never put into practice before Senator Long was assassinated, we do not know how far "Share the Wealth" would have moved the curved solid line in Figure 3.4 toward the straight line of perfect equality.

How far is the straight line from the curved solid one? That will depend on whether we are considering 10% of the population, 90%, or some fraction in between. A Lorenz curve cannot be described mathematically except by drawing it. To solve this problem, the economist Gini measured the area between the straight line of perfect equality and any Lorenz curve. It is a measure of how far the total curve, not just one point, is from the straight line. The Gini coefficient is proportional to the area between the two curves.

If the robber barons came back to life, the area between the dotted and solid lines would be large, as would be the Gini coefficient. If Senator Long had become dictator of the United States during the Great Depression, as many feared, the area between the diagonal line and the resulting Lorenz curve would have been small. So would the Gini coefficient.

What do Gini and Lorenz have to do with our lognormal distribution? The two Lorenz curves in Figure 3.4 are smooth, so there is no obvious cut-off point or break in the distribution. In the language of mathematics, they are *integrals* of the income. We therefore cannot use these curves to estimate how rich is too rich. The Lorenz curve can tell us, along with its computational friend, the Gini coefficient, how unequal society is as a whole. But that is as far as it goes. The Lorenz curves can show whether some people are getting bigger slices of the pie than others, but not if some slices are too big.

PARETO'S THOUGHTS REVISITED

Finally, Pareto again. Recall that this Italian economist was the first to note that the top of the income curve could be described by a special distribution, forming a straight line on the type of probability graph paper we have been using.

Pareto's pathfinding work was recognized by Montroll and Schlesinger,[7] whose work was the partial inspiration for this book. Before quoting them, we note that in the following passage they use a 99% cut-off, rather than the 97% we use here. Their work was done in the 1980s, but for some unknown reason they used data from 1935 to 1936 rather than more recent income information. It is possible that the cut-off point was somewhat different in previous generations, but our object here is not to discuss all historical trends. Montroll and Schlesinger write:

> [The analysis] gives us no insight of the Pareto inverse power tail beyond the 99 percentile. No one would dispute the fact that the wealthy differ from the lower 99% in the manner that they accumulate income. While most people are paid by the hour, the wealthy frequently accumulate their extra wealth by some amplification process; that process varying from case to case. At the height of the Beatles' popularity, any new recording by them was purchased by millions of fans. The leverage people in the investment business have their own style of amplification. During certain periods of prosperity easy money becomes available for investment, sometimes in stock, sometimes in real estate, or perhaps in silver or Rembrandts. A common characteristic of such times is that the daring may exploit the easy money to acquire some speculative commodity through a small margin payment, say 10 percent, with a promise to pay the remainder later. If the commodity doubles in price, a 10 percent margin payment is amplified into a 9-fold profit.
>
> J. P. Morgan was given his first million by his father. He reinvested a considerable fraction of that in the manner described above, reinvesting the profit, etc., to become much richer than he would have had he accepted the offer of a privatdozentship [a type of professorship] in mathematics at Göttingen University offered to him by Felix Klein [a famous mathematician].

We will later discuss in more detail how wealth can be leveraged in this way. We will show that the power of compound interest provides a cushion to the already wealthy that is almost impossible to deflate.

Pareto's Calculations

Using difficult-to-find data around the turn of the century, Pareto found that the arithmetic means of incomes in many countries were below the centers of the income distributions. He saw no symmetric bell curves. Rather, the curves were skewed. As has been noted, the curve on the high side of a mean was radically different from that on the low side, because there was no limit to possible income, but everyone below a bottom limit died of starvation, reducing the curve to a straight line at that point.

Changing Pareto's Iron Rule

Because Pareto found his law to be almost universal, the question then arises: Is it possible to change it? Some economists have said that the Paretian conclusion shows that income distribution is as fixed as the laws of supply and demand. Those latter laws are occasionally altered by governments, but always seem to break through, like a car driving over thin ice, the regulations designed to restrain them. Is it the same for Pareto's law?

Pareto himself didn't think so, at least for the lower end of the income scale (i.e., the bottom 97% or so). He noted, for example, that fewer people starved to death in late nineteenth-century Europe than in previous centuries, in contradiction to the predictions of Marx. This meant that somehow, either through private charity or government intervention, the poor were getting more income than they had in the past. In turn, this implied that their portion of the income curve had risen. Pareto's law was flexible, at least on the lower side.

We share one strong interest with Pareto: The *top* of the income curve. But we part company with the venerable economist. He believed that progress in what used to be called the "lower orders" depended on not disturbing the upper orders.

Pareto thought that efforts at redistribution from the top to any lower ranks were doomed to failure. However, he supplied little or no justification. It apparently was a matter of personal philosophy. His charts could not be used to prove or disprove his contention.

So one reason Pareto is remembered in economics is for his discovery of the mathematical formula that accurately predicts the income distribution for the top few percent of incomes. It is enormously tilted to the very richest. Later, economists discovered that when logarithms of income are plotted against the cumulative number of people in each class, the result is a straight line—*except* for the top 2 or 3 percent. It is the intersection of these two distributions which concerns us.

THE 3% SOLUTION

The laws of physics and chemistry are usually thought of as being immutable. For some members of the public, the social sciences, such as economics, are still regarded as having weak, if not unenforceable, laws and rules. Our 3% solution is a widely applicable rule that can be put into practice to determine just how rich is too rich.

4

WEALTH AND INHERITANCE

The focus of this chapter will be wealth in its many aspects: What qualifies as wealth, how it is distributed in the United States, how that distribution has changed over time, and the power inherent in great wealth. The intellectual allure of the properties of wealth has attracted economists over the ages to questions such as these. They have traced the origins of wealth, its transmission from one generation to the next, and the impact and scope of taxation systems devised by governments on the wealth of citizens both dead and alive.

The facet of wealth that distinguishes it from all other elements of life is that it can be passed to others through inheritance. Even from the grave, assets can be controlled. Only a person's directions for control of assets can outlast his last breath.

We earlier defined wealth to be the current value in money of all assets held by an individual or family at a point in time. This wealth can be created through past earnings, interest, dividends on savings or stocks, through gifts, inheritances, lotteries, oil strikes, or any other source. Since our concern is strictly financial, we ignore human capital—earning ability, talent, or health—in the tabulation of wealth. Federal Reserve Board studies offer authoritative data about wealth:

1. It is highly concentrated. In 1986, the bottom 50% of the population held only 4% of the wealth. The top 5% held over half.[1] Wealth can be divided into rough thirds: the bottom 90% of the population held 33.4%, the 90% to 99% group held 35.1%, and the top 1% held 31.5%. A further breakdown of the top 1% reveals the extraordinary disparities even at this rarefied level. The lower half of this 1% held 7.2% of all net worth, while the top 0.5% held 24.3%, or $2.6 trillion.[2]

2. The distribution is quite stable over time. Between 1963 and 1983, the relative distributions were remarkably constant.[3] The shares for the lower 90%, the 90 to 99 percentiles and the top 1% for 1963 were 36.1%, 30.0%, and 31.8%, respectively. In 1983, the respective shares were 33.4%, 35.1%, and 31.5%, as we noted above. From Kennedy to Reagan, tremendous changes occurred in both the U.S. and the world economy. Yet the distribution of American wealth changed only very slowly. Pareto, in the nineteenth century, would not have been surprised at this result.

Particular individuals, as opposed to a group, can gain or lose wealth. Movement on or off the *Forbes 400* list is to be expected. William Bunker and Herbert Hunt left the list after their failed speculation in silver. Yet some of H. L. Hunt's children have retained their share of that fortune.[4] A few drop off the list of the wealthiest deliberately. Andrew Carnegie, believing that "The man who dies rich . . . dies disgraced" gave away 99.5% of his nearly $400 million fortune before he died.[5] Some put their assets into private foundations. Some of these foundations in turn give the donors of their *largesse* the use of mansions, private aircraft, and other luxuries, so that wealth is transferred without too much being given up to the taxman.

For a graphical description of wealth distribution, we can again use the Gibrat-Pareto system, shown on probability graph paper. Figure 4.1 presents the wealth distribution reported in 1984 by the Census Bureau in its survey of household net worth.[6] From about 50% to around 99%, the distribution forms an almost straight line. For the last 1% or so, the soaring line reflects the almost one-third of our national wealth they own. The Census Bureau's last category is denoted only as "above $500,000", so we can not gauge the very top wealth. Still we see the Pareto distribution of the top 1% (as contrasted to the top 3% in the *income* distribution) shooting skyward.

The key point here is that the "kink" reappears in wealth distributions. It's at a different place, with a different slope from its income manifestation. But it has returned, like Dr. Seuss's cat who came back.

In the summer of 1990, much of the above information was updated.[7] The richest 1% of U.S. adults had total holdings of $4.3 trillion in 1986. This was greater than the gross national product of that year of $4.1 trillion. There were 941,000 adults in 1986 with a net worth of $1 million or more, in contrast to the 180,000 who had that wealth in 1976, a decade earlier. Previous studies had shown the wealthy as having the biggest portion of their investments in real estate, but now corporate stock was the number one investment. This was based on the sharp rise in overall stock prices from 1982 to 1986.

Figure 4.1
Wealth Distribution in the United States in 1984

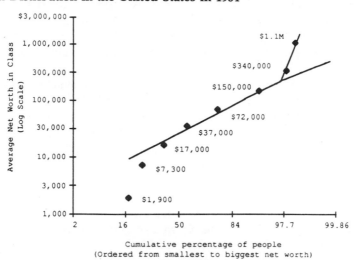

Cumulative percentage of people
(Ordered from smallest to biggest net worth)
Probability Scale

PROOF FROM BEYOND THE GRAVE

In spite of the previous paragraph, comprehensive wealth statistics in the United States have always been notoriously scarce. No systematic assessment by a government agency, even the Census Bureau studies noted above, documents wealth in the same rigorous way that income is tallied. We do not recommend such an agency.

The one time that wealth is reported to the government is when wills are probated and assets passed to new generations. The disposition of these wills in county courthouses across the country makes direct evidence of wealth concentration undocumentable. It is also difficult to trace the path of assets from one generation to the next, given the mobility of Americans. Even if such data were collectible, it would not tabulate large assets which pass directly to other generations in the form of trusts. These legal instruments do not require documentation at death in federal or local records.

In 1977, estate taxation began at $60,000. Today, the level is $600,000. As a result, the number of estate tax returns filed has fallen from 200,000 in 1977 to 40,000 in 1987.[8] This represents a significant information loss about assets for most Americans, but still generates a stream of data for those who die owning more than $600,000. The statisticians assume that the wealthy die as randomly as the rest of us. They then make statistical inferences about the wealthy still alive.

GAINING WEALTH

Schemes to become rich abound, but how does it actually happen? An individual can gain vast wealth in basically two ways. Entrepreneurs, entertainers, or lottery winners typically experience an explosion of affluence. The sensation is yeasty, entirely unprecedented, and quite pleasant.

For children and subsequent generations, there is usually no such fortune shock. They accept wealth as a birthright. It can be husbanded by careful stewards at a bank, brokerage firm, or law office. The fortune becomes a fixture. Under such circumstances, compound interest ensures that this wealth is preserved and grows without effort by the owner.

Darwin and Wealth

It was not long ago that the newly wealthy were regarded as a product of some mysterious Darwinian force. William Sumner, an economist at the turn of the century, wrote:

> The millionaires are a product of natural selection . . . it is because they are thus selected that wealth—both their own and that entrusted to them— aggregates under their hands . . . They may be fairly regarded as the naturally selected agents of society for certain work. They get high wages and live in luxury, but the bargain is a good one for society.[9]

This passage suffers from the same tautology as do some aspects of Darwinian selection theory. If someone becomes wealthy, it proves, according to Sumner, that he (rarely she) was naturally selected for entrepreneurship, intelligence, and other desirable skills. If someone tries to become rich and fails, the theory still holds: The individual did not have the right genes. This *ex post facto* reasoning is, by now, all but discarded among reputable economists. It is not surprising, however, to hear it espoused by second- or third-generation inheritors.

How is this instant wealth created? Chester gives an illustration:

> Suppose an entrepreneur figures he can build and equip a plant to build widgets at a cost of $10 million and that he will be able to sell them at the price of $3 million a year, or a 30% rate of return. If other forms of capital investment are yielding returns that average 10%, the widget manufacturer is in an above-average disequilibrium situation. Since at the average 10% rate of return it would take a capital investment of $30 million to yield the $3 million return, it becomes possible to sell shares in ownership of the widget plant for $30 million, even though it cost only $10 million to build. The entrepreneur has suddenly added $20 million to his wealth.[10]

Professor A. B. Atkinson has spent his life in the study of wealth. He has identified five important routes to vast wealth:

> The first is the invention or development of a new technique or product. The wealth of such men as Steven Jobs of Apple or Ray Kroc of McDonald's represents the monopoly rent that can be extracted by inventors or innovators. Invention by itself is not enough, there being many instances where the originator was not the person who obtained the monopoly rent, and the commercial exploitation of the idea is clearly of great importance. Commercial success depends to a large degree on an ability to forecast consumer needs, and indeed this responsiveness to market trends is itself a second major source of self-made fortunes. The success of many entrepreneurs derives not so much as from inventing a new product or mode of production, as from being in a rapidly growing industry.
>   A third, rather different, element is the ownership of natural resources. The discovery of oil or other minerals has led to many self-made fortunes, often unrelated to any active entrepreneurial effort. The substantial increase in the value of building land has, on a smaller scale, had a rather similar effect. The ability to exploit natural resources depends in some cases on decisions of government bodies, particularly planning and routing. This introduces a forth element, the impact of government restriction and the gains that can be made by those able to circumvent the restrictions. This has been apparent in the case of property development . . . The fifth and final element is that of pure luck, of being in the right place at the right time, or of a gamble coming off. In this context it must be remembered that the generation of self-made fortunes very often involves a substantial element of risk taking. Whether it arises from uncertainty concerning the outcome of an invention or of exploration for natural resources, whether it arises from uncertainty concerning the decisions of competitors or the government, there is an ever-present risk of loss or failure. The successful entrepreneurs discussed here are only a small fraction of those who set out to make money that way.[11]

In the above passage, we have taken the liberty to substitute some recent prominent names from the *Forbes 400* list. Atkinson goes on to prescribe how to transform an idea into a fortune:

> to enter a business at or near the ground floor, to hold a major interest and to resist selling during the hard times. Not only is the return to the successful likely to be much higher than from armchair investment, but the process of accumulation is favoured by the tax system. A businessmen can set the costs of expansion against taxable profits, and when he floats his company on the stock exchange, the resulting capital gains are taxed at a lower rate than investment income. [This was the case in the U.S. until the tax bill of 1986]. It is the result of this . . . that one can see really successful new business owners become millionaires or even multi-millionaires

in 10 or 20 years, even in very highly taxed countries where top salaried men are very tightly pinched.[11]

A difference between the fortune-generating power of Steven Jobs and Michael Jackson, both of the same generation, illustrates our point about the two types of instant fortunes. Jobs possesses capital, a different form of wealth than does Jackson. He owns—or owned—shares in an industrial company, which has and will typically grow in value over time. These shares also confer legal ownership over part of the company's material assets, and offer the potential to produce dividends. Moreover his shares are marketable.[12]

Jackson must make another record or do another tour to keep the mega-dollars coming in. His earning ability cannot be transferred to someone else. While Jackson has the option of starting his own record company, thus receiving unearned income, his proven money-earning talent is limited to himself, and possibly only to a short time span.

Jackson may become one of the few entertainers whose popularity—and high income—lasts over decades, such as Frank Sinatra. Then again, he may not. The number of former hit record stars who a year or two later were washing dishes for a living is legion. To put it simply, Jobs' fortune is based on capital. Jackson's is dependent solely on himself and the all-too-fickle public.

THE SITUATION IN 1987

The bare income tax returns of 1987 do not tell us who invested in what, or how long they held onto stocks, bonds, property, or art. They report only on the income from wealth, not wealth itself. However, by using the tables carefully, we can deduce some facts about the 36,299 households who reported incomes of more than $1 million in 1987.[13] Their number has risen in six years from 5,286, an increase of 585%.

We noted previously that, based on the taxable and tax-exempt interest that most in this group reported, we could deduce wealth of about $4.5 million for those who reported both sources. Over 90% in this richest group reported receiving dividends, at an average value of about $160,000. It is difficult to estimate the wealth behind this number. Some growth stocks pay no dividends at all, whereas stocks that have fallen in value may have a high dividend-to-price ratio. If one assumes an average dividend rate of 4%, this implies a wealth in stocks of about $4 million.

We have said that the wealthy hold more than stocks and bonds. They have Rembrandts, real estate, and jewelry. Neither we nor the wealthy know exactly how much these nonfinancial investments are worth until they are sold. Then they show up as a capital gain (rarely as a loss). The

IRS lumps capital gains in with capital losses in its classification, so we do not know how any losses would affect the results.

In any case, the IRS finds that about 94% of those in this richest class reported capital gains (less losses) in 1987. The average was $1.06 million, or about 44% of the total average income of $2.4 million they stated. Knowing the value of $1.06 million unfortunately does not tell us what was sold, or the wealth that still remains. In any given year, some in the very richest bracket may sell very little; others may make profits of tens if not hundreds of millions.

By way of contrast, the approximate average income in the United States, as described before, was about $27,000 in 1987. In the $25,000 to $30,000 bracket, the average capital gain (less loss) was about $2,200 for the one in eight in this group who had any capital gains at all. Putting it another way, capital gains constituted 1.1% of total income for the ''average'' group; it was 41% for the richest group.

While wealth is not always equivalent to high income, the values we have shown indicate that they are strongly associated.

FORTUNES AT THE TOP

Writing in *Esquire,* Donald Katz estimates the *increase* in accrued capital to the *Forbes 400* between 1985 and 1986 as $22 billion.[14] Katz notes that since the passage of the Tax Reform Act of 1986, some of the wealthiest are paying somewhat higher federal levies. He says that between 1985 and 1986, the extra taxes on this tiny group for one year should be about $2 billion. This would pay for an aircraft carrier of the *Nimitz* class, or the current budget of the Securities and Exchange Commission for the next 15 years.

In 1987, the total estimated net worth of the *Forbes 400* was $220 billion. In comparison: retail sales of alcoholic beverages in the U.S. during 1983-86 were $220 billion; U.S. military expenditures in 1986, $278 billion; U.S. budget deficit in 1986, $205 billion; value of mergers and acquisitions in the U.S., $173 billion; foreign investment in the U.S., $209 billion; U.S. investment abroad, $206 billion.[15] To be blunt, these 400 individuals are wealthy beyond normal imagination. And they all could fit into one section of a football stadium, or into a small theatre.

What do we know about the composition of these fortunes? As we noted above, in a 1990 report dealing with 1986 data the IRS reports that for estates over $1 million, corporate stock was the most important asset. For those with estates above $10 million, it formed about two-thirds of their net worth at death.[16]

For most of us, our home is our most important asset. As we move up—assuming we are that fortunate—real estate starts to diminish in comparison to stocks, even though the former source of wealth is still the largest one among the top quarter- to half-million wealth holders.

But curiously enough, for the very top wealth holders (i.e., those listed in *Fortune, Forbes, Money,* and other popular magazines) real estate makes a comeback. Of course, the real estate of these lofty wealth-holders is not simply their own residences, luxurious as they may be. It is the *business,* as opposed to the personal possession, of real estate.

In 1988, 59 of those listed in the *Forbes 400* made real estate their primary business, and another 32 on the list had real estate as a major sideline. Real-estate magnates on the list included Harry Helmsley (husband of the unfortunate Leona), valued at $1 billion or more; Donald Trump (since fallen on hard times), at about $700 million; Trammell Crow, at $600 million; and Daniel and John Galbreath, at more than $400 million.[17]

The annual compilations by *Forbes* and *Fortune* are a snapshot of those at the top. The listings tell how much they have, how they got there, and what family they have. We also get a feel for how fast the turnover is at that level—who left or joined the group since the last tally.

A departure from or fall down the *Forbes* list may be due to a number of factors. For example, someone may suffer a business reverse and have to sell off some holdings. Sam Walton, the Arkansas drug magnate, was reported in 1989 to have divided some of his extensive stock holdings among relatives. He then personally dropped down the list.

Perhaps the greatest source of change has been the increase in the minimum level needed to get into the group of 400 notables. While a fortune of $100 million may have been impressive a decade ago, your name would not get into *Forbes* in its latest compilation if your fortune had not bested that level substantially in the interval.

How Accurate is *Forbes*?

The *Forbes* list—or any other listing of this type—has enormous uncertainties. The main one is that the list of assets of the supposed wealthiest people is not made public to reporters. Even if it were, the financial affairs of the wealthiest are often so complicated and convoluted that reporters would have to have advanced degrees in finance or accounting to interpret them adequately. Few do.

For example, in the summer of 1990, Donald Trump, the New York real estate financier, ran into some monetary difficulties. Some reports said he was on the brink of personal bankruptcy; others said that he still had a net worth of hundreds of millions.

As well, the time that would have to be spent analyzing the financial reports of the wealthy, even if they were made available, would outstrip the resources of even relatively affluent magazines like *Forbes* and *Fortune.* For example, suppose that a mere four hours was spent on each of the favored 400. This would mean a total of 1600 hours of reporters' time. If ten reporters were assigned to the task, they would each have to spend about a month on this single story. We suspect that if reporters showed up at our house and had free access to all our financial records without any hindrance, they would probably have to spend much more than four hours determining our level of assets. It must be much more difficult to do this on people who have no interest in cooperating and possess vastly more elaborate financial dealings and records.

So the listings have to be taken as estimates. If they were better than that, the listings from one magazine to the next would be about the same. They are not.

CURIOSITIES OF THE RICH AND SOMETIMES FAMOUS

While reading publications of the IRS may sometimes be prescribed for those with insomnia, the listings for the very wealthiest—those with adjusted gross incomes of more than $1 million—make fascinating reading. A *Wall Street Journal* article for the 1986 crop turned up some curiosities.[18]

Of the 35,785 in the group, 7,585, or about 21%, claimed the deduction for working couples. Social Security income appeared on 5,928 returns, or about 17%. From time to time, some members of Congress propose putting in a means test on Social Security income, excluding those with substantial income from other sources. This presumably would exclude those in this $1 million-plus group.

The very wealthiest are not immune to the marital troubles that beset most of the rest of us. While it is impossible to determine whether this select group is happier in their married or unmarried state than others, we do note 68 in this group reported receiving alimony. Their alimony payments were naturally at a higher level than any other income group, averaging $126,000 annually.

While some read the Bible to mean that all should tithe, the very wealthiest do not quite come up to that holy mark, in spite of their substantial income. Of the $82.3 billion received by the group in total, about $7 billion was donated to charities. This comes to about 8.5% of their total income.

Perhaps the strangest statistic of the lot is the fact that 65 of the returns, or about one in every 550, reported unemployment compensation. Exactly how this comes about is unclear. The *Journal* says, "only one spouse on a joint return may have been jobless, of course, perhaps before marrying in 1986." It still seems peculiar to us.

ART AND CARS

The wealthy invest in belongings that are inaccessible to the rest of us due to their high cost. Picassos and Chippendale furniture are prominent examples. Most of us would find it difficult to price an oil painting or antique furniture. It would be even more of a challenge to determine if its price, or the price of an entire class of paintings or furniture, were rising or falling. As a result, most readers would not find it easy to evaluate our claim that the value of such goods tends to rise faster than many other investments.

Now some evidence is at hand. It is supplied by Sotheby's, the famous international auction house, and other agencies.[19] It is summarized in Table 4.1. The first column shows what a certificate of deposit invested at 8% would have yielded from 1980 to 1989. It would have reached about 200 in the latter year, taking 1980 as equal to 100.

The Dow Jones industrial stock index did much better, even allowing for the sharp fall in 1987. By 1989, it had about tripled in value compared to 1980. This was better than the performance of bank accounts, assuming the rate of interest noted above, by about 50%. We stated earlier in this chapter that the wealthy hold a disproportionate share of common stocks and other business investments. As a result, they would have profited more than smaller investors who placed their savings in banks.

Very few of us can afford an original Old Master or Impressionist painting. The table shows that, over the long run, these are apparently better investments than bank deposits, and perhaps superior to the stock market. The sole exception in the period considered was 1981-82 for Old Masters, where their value dropped below their original price. However, they had recovered by the following year. By 1989 they were outpacing even the Dow Jones industrials, compared to 1980.

Impressionist paintings were an even better group of art investments, perhaps due to their great popularity in Japan. By 1989, they had reached an index of about 1,000, or ten times their value in 1980. No bank certificate of deposit in 1980 could make that claim. By November 1989, a Manet

Table 4.1
A Comparison of Investments from 1980 to 1989

Year	Certificate of Deposit*	Dow Jones Industrials	Old Masters Paintings	Impressionist Paintings	Ferrari 250 GTO
1980	100	100	100	100	100
1981	108	106	78	118	118
1982	117	100	82	136	140
1983	126	136	100	184	165
1984	136	136	136	211	195
1985	147	152	156	242	211
1986	159	206	160	279	420
1987	171	262	184	468	495
1988	185	242	211	737	528
1989	200	300	327	1,000	2,000

* At 8%.

street scene, "La rue Mosnier aux drapeaux," was expected to sell for between $30 and $40 million. While most Impressionist paintings sold for much less than this range, there is little question that their overall prices rose dramatically in the 1980s.

Want to Buy a Used Car?

Once we get into even more exotic objects, the possibility for gain may be even higher. The last column of Table 4.1 shows the prices of Ferrari 250 GTOs. Their price rose by about a factor of 20 in the 1980s. In late 1989, a fund to invest in classic and historic cars was established, and paid about $5 million for a 1938 Alfa Romeo Spyder. Until that time, most of the increase in value from classic cars was collected by the already wealthy.

Some might think that the art business is small scale, with only a few well-publicized pictures, like "Irises" by Van Gogh, changing hands. At one time, this may have been true. Now it is not. Sotheby's Holdings 1989 auction sales of $2.93 billion represented a 61% increase over its 1988 business. Christie's International was not far behind, with $2.08 billion in 1989 sales, a 40% increase over 1988.[20] These values do not include the thousands of smaller auction and art houses scattered throughout the world, from London to New York to Tokyo. If all their sales were lumped together, they would add many billions to the $5 billion of Sotheby's and Christie's.

Most of the transactions are by and for the already wealthy. For example, in October 1989, John Dorrance, the heir to the Campbell Soup fortune, sold paintings valued at $123 million. The bidding at Sotheby's is almost exclusively confined to the top percent of the wealth distribution, those beyond the kink.

Our point here is that interest from a bank, even compounded, may not be enough for some of the wealthy, even though it almost certainly perpetuates fortunes. By having enough cash to invest in unusual items like paintings and classic cars, the rich can sometimes beat returns offered through banks by substantial margins. The fortunes of the second generation can grow even faster.

INHERITANCE

So much for the first fortune. Second (or inherited) fortunes are normally regarded as a birthright by those who receive them. For those born to wealth, an entirely different set of incentives or values is possible, compared to those who from birth know they will spend most of their lives in pursuit of the everyday necessities. A fortune, once amassed, takes on a life of its own. The assets produce income for which no personal labor is required. Beyond some point, the income builds faster than most people can spend it.

By its very nature, great wealth has always been associated with power. To be able to designate one or more individuals upon whom you will bestow a lifetime income sufficient to cover all creature comforts, without any personal effort on the part of the recipient, is power. Control over assets to use in any way you please is power.

The aspect of wealth which engulfs all others in importance is this ability to pass on the assets and to affect future generations. For example, consider the duPont family. Of the 1984 *Forbes 400*, twenty derived their status from the original duPont fortune.[21] It had been frozen in huge lumps of wealth. Our weak estate-taxation laws act like a refrigerator, allowing these cubes to be passed down, unmelted, to affect later generations.

ORGANIZING AN ECONOMIC SYSTEM

Before we begin our discussion of inheritance, we need to examine its origin. Consider the ways to organize an economic system. Economics texts recognize three such systems: Tradition, command, and market. The traditional economic system—the oldest and most common throughout history—is represented, for example, by the medieval manor system. It was vital for its preservation that the central organizational element of such a system remain undivided and the responsibility of a single person, the lord. Thus the lord had abundant privilege as the wealthiest and most powerful of the small society he headed.

However, inextricably bound up in the pleasures of reign and wealth was the responsibility and institutional duty to preserve the manor and all its institutions. When marauding armies appeared, it was the lord's duty to command his knights in defense of his manor. He performed many other leadership roles, less dramatic in nature. So with wealth and power came a duty of vital importance to the traditional society. The transmission of the estate intact to the eldest son of the next generation assured the estate remained whole and had one chief at a time. Younger sons and daughters were provided for, but did not gain control of the assets. Estates made sense in this traditional society.

A command economy, such as those of Albania and North Korea, recognizes no usefulness of privately held property, at least officially. Estates and inheritances are never institutionalized. No vast estate exists apart from the government.

In the United States, a free-enterprise market economy, estate inheritance remains, but without a clear rationale. Heirs do not perform a discernible service for the economy. There is no manorial system to maintain. Thus estate inheritance lingers on, but only as a holdover from the traditional past.

From many sources, researchers have come to similar conclusions about wealth and its transmission. Let's examine some of them.

Lester Thurow, dean of the Sloan School of Management at M.I.T., writes:

> At any moment in time, the highly skewed distribution of wealth is the product of two approximately equal factors—instant fortunes and inherited wealth. Inherited fortunes, however, were themselves created in the process of instant wealth in an earlier generation.[22]

But what is the exact proportion of new fortunes and old wealth? To answer that question, we would have to undertake a trek to the thousands of county courthouses to search probate records; a daunting task.

Fortunately, some of the work has been done. Chester finds that gifts and bequests, on the average, account for half of the net worth of very wealthy men, and for most of the net worth of equally wealthy women.[23] Although this study concerns only decedents in the Cleveland area for 1964–65, it is highly likely that it applies to recent data and all across the country. Further, since there are about equal numbers of wealthy men and women, at least to a first approximation, the numbers imply that about three-quarters of the assets of the wealthy are inherited to some degree. Thurow's proportion of one-half is a reasonable approximation, given the fact that data on this subject is not easy to find. The result is so important that we will use it later in our Alternative Distribution System (ADS) to reduce wealth and income inequality.

Inheritance means the transfer of material wealth at the death of an individual to his or her heirs. We will use the word in a more general sense, to mean all transfers of wealth, whether during the lifetime of the wealth holder or at his death. Current tax laws allow generous gifts to pass tax free, within certain specified limits. No record need be made by the donor or recipient of the gift. While quite pleasant for the latter, it makes it difficult to determine exactly how much wealth is passed around in this manner. It's another way in which transfer of wealth is made more of a challenge for researchers.

How important are inheritances for the population as a whole? Survey data indicates that for most people, inheritance is a minor source of assets. Some 80% of the U.S. population claims never to have inherited any assets, and only 1% of the population admits to having inherited assets of $110,000 or more.[24]

In addition, most inheritances are apparently received late in life. While only 8% have inherited by the age of twenty-five, over 40% of those seventy-five or older have inherited. This last sentence applies only to the small proportion who have inherited *anything*. Apparently the scenes from the old movies about the college boy inheriting a great fortune from his long-lost uncle and traipsing off to Europe to become a playboy are only that—scenes from old movies.

WHO GETS WHAT FROM INHERITANCE

What is important in determining who gets what from inheritance? Clearly, the division of the estate, the family size, and marriage patterns. In the United States, equal division among children is the rule. In Britain, primogeniture, or the exclusive right of the eldest child (especially a son) to inherit a family's estate, has been practiced for centuries.

The two systems produce quite different outcomes. Given equal divisions, family size is a major factor in the size of the inheritance received by each child. The third factor, marriage patterns, is much more difficult to trace and analyze. At the top wealth levels, marriages resemble corporate mergers. The impact of who marries who upon wealth is significant, but the lack of data makes any examination complicated.

Only at the very top can this information on marriages be gained. The social pages are a more likely source than financial records. Accountings are made at death, not marriage.[25]

Who gets what from inheritance will depend of course on the level of taxation. The idea of the state taking a cut of the proceeds is a relatively new idea in history. One of the first such taxes was introduced by Harcourt in Britain, in 1894. His assessment of the power and limitations of inheritance still stands up, almost a century later:

> Nature gives man no power over his earthly goods beyond the term of his life. What power he possesses to prolong his will after death, the right of a dead hand to dispose of his property is a pure creation of law, and the State has the right to prescribe the conditions and limitations under which that power shall be exercised.[26]

In the United States, John Brittain, one of the foremost researchers on inheritance and its impact on our society, reports that one's economic status at birth and in maturity tends to be the same. Other things being equal, the stronger the influence of inheritance, the greater the inequality of wealth.[27]

He concludes that the extreme concentration of wealth may confer power on a few that is hazardous to democratic institutions.

To this point, we have been concerned with how fortunes are created. Now we turn to how their owners view their wealth and the necessity to dispose of it at death. According to Thurow, "Once the fortunes are created, they are husbanded, augmented and passed on, not because 'homo economicus' desires to store up future consumption but because of desires for power within the family, the economy or society."[28] He argues:

There is a limit beyond which it does not pay to accumulate more wealth. Every individual has a finite lifetime and must allocate his time optimally across investment, production and consumption activities . . . Since time is necessary to consume and since wealth is stored future consumption, a finite lifespan implies a maximum amount of wealth (future consumption) any individual can use. Because of the time budget constraints, economic man would also start to de-cumulate at some point in his lifetime. As an individual grows older, the probability of dying grows larger. The value of future consumption falls, since the individual is less and less likely to be alive to enjoy it . . . Economic man does not accumulate a fortune he cannot use, yet these individuals have fortunes they cannot possibly use. . . .

The mystery of larger fortunes at time of death is further compounded by U.S. tax law. Under our laws a substantial amount of money can be given to the next generation tax-free if it is given before death, and all of it can be given at much lower tax rates than if wealth is transferred at death and subject to estate taxation. If a person were really interested in future consumption of his children, the tax laws provide a strong incentive to transfer the desired wealth before death. Yet very little use is made of this loophole. Parents do not give their money away before death, even though their children would have much more wealth if they did so. Such actions hardly square with the view of parents sacrificing themselves and accumulating wealth to raise the consumption standards of their children. When given a tax-free or low tax method to take care of their children, they do not use it.[29]

If we could hear the voices of the wealthy from beyond the grave, we might hear the following: "Yes, I know that the taxman got a lot more of my estate than I had planned. But I hadn't expected to go quite so soon. I definitely had plans to give away most of what I owned to the children in a year, or two, or three. But that heart attack happened so suddenly."

What Thurow describes may be accurate enough, but it also may reflect a belief in one's own immortality, a belief not confined solely to the wealthy. Thurow continues:

The motive that has been left out of neoclassical economics is that of economic power—within either the family or the community. Whereas consumption possibilities are finite, subject to diminishing marginal utility and severely limited by time budget constraints, economic power is not subject to the same limitations. Appetites for power are larger and may be subject to increasing marginal returns. Great economic power takes no longer to wield than smaller economic power. If one likes economic power, then one wants to maintain it until death. To de-cumulate assets or to give them away is to give up economic power . . . To give up economic power within the family is to give up one's status and station. Few individuals are willing to give up their economic power, even vis-à-vis their own children.

For similar reasons, individuals do not buy annuities even though they would guarantee consumption expenditures over an uncertain future. To buy an annuity is to give up exactly what the individual wants—economic power.[30]

Do people begin to de-cumulate, or use up or give away, their possessions in old age? This is a question we can check. In 1983 the Bureau of Labor Statistics reported savings rates by ages.[31] The rate increases relentlessly for each group from age twenty-five up. Individuals typically save—storing up for future consumption—right up to their day of death. So Thurow's point seems to be correct. While it is true that older people usually get less income than younger ones, they still do manage to save, as Thurow suggests. They do this by dramatically reducing consumption, and becoming more and more risk averse.

WEALTH IN REVOLUTIONARY-ERA AMERICA

Are we dreaming the impossible dream? Was the distribution of wealth ever less skewed? The research of Professor Soltow shows that at the beginning of the Republic, wealth distribution was probably as equal as it ever gets in a free society.[32] Soltow's estimates of wealth allocation, first shown in Figure 2.1., are reproduced in Figure 4.2.

This graph represents wealth, not income. The vertical axis is in dollar units. About 99% of the population had a total wealth less than $100,000. About 60% had less than $1,000, and so on. The graph paper is the probability type, explained previously. The horizontal axis is then the *cumulative* population up to that point in the distribution. There are two key points to be made. First, the kink at around the top 3% is much less apparent than in other, later, graphs plotting distribution of wealth. Second, the slope of both the lower 99% and the upper 1% is much less steep than in later American wealth distribution graphs. Because the slope is less steep, wealth was much more evenly distributed when John Adams was in office than it is now. And because the kink was much less obvious in 1798, almost all of the population followed the same lognormal wealth distribution.

Was opulence evenly distributed in 1798? Absolutely not. A glance at the graph shows some with over $100,000, and half with barely $500 in wealth. Still, because of the two points we made immediately above, revolutionary-era America was as close to a "starting line" in wealth as we are likely to see in this country.

If 1798 was good for wealth equality, 1698 might be even better. However, the farther back we go, the less data there is. The end of the eighteenth century is probably the earliest time from which some statistical conclusions can be drawn.

Figure 4.2
Wealth Distribution in the America of 1798

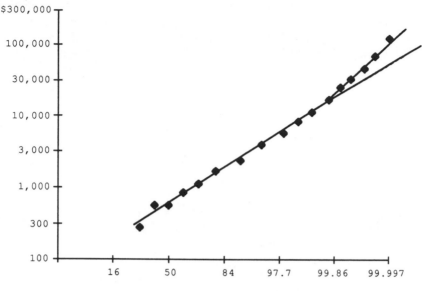

Cumulative percentage of people
(Ordered from smallest to biggest wealth)
Probability Scale

Revolutionary America was a source of hagiography almost as soon as it concluded. After all, two of the four faces on Mount Rushmore are from that period. This adulation led inevitably to a later debunking and skepticism: Washington was a slave owner; Jefferson had a mistress. In terms of wealth distribution, however, if one prefers a more equitable distribution than in twentieth-century America, revolutionary times remain a golden era.

SUMMARY

Wealth is distributed to 98% or 99% of us in a way that can be described lognormally. Beyond that, however, our "kink" shows that there is a distinct and dramatic change in the amount of wealth owned by people in the top 1% or 2%. This is shown in the far right side of the probability-lognormal graph we have been using, vastly different from the rest of the graph. The top 1% of our population controls over 30% of our national wealth. This is in contrast to the income distribution, an annual tally, in which it is the top 3% or so that can be called rich.

Our Alternative Distribution System (ADS) saws away on the chain of wealth at the inheritance link. Our proposal, detailed later, allows a wealthy person to control the distribution of his or her assets to others, as is presently the case. But ADS encourages spreading them to many heirs, rather than just a few. Over time, this would have the impact of bending the kink at the top toward the line of the rest of us.

__ 5 _____

HOW DO WEALTH AND INCOME DIFFER?

Wealth and income statistics frequently come intermingled. One such set says this: In 1983, the top 2% of the income distribution held 30% of the liquid financial assets, 20% of the property, 50% of the stocks, and 33% of the businesses in the United States. Those earning the top 10% of incomes owned 51% of the financial assets, 50% of the property, 72% of the stocks, and 78% of the businesses owned by individuals.[1]

The relationships between income and wealth have been noted by Jan Tinbergen, the Nobel Prize-winning economist:

> Part of the income distribution clearly depends on the distribution of wealth, not only because earned income derives from wealth, but also because wealth constitutes a reserve for its owner and so enhances his maneuvering possibilities. This has been understood ever since Marx, and an enormous literature exists on the various alternative ways in which the impact of wealth on income and power distribution can be reduced. There is no point in even trying to summarize this literature.[2]

It is this relationship which will be examined in this chapter: the profound and often misunderstood processes of accumulating wealth, the mechanisms which perpetuate this concentration, and the effect of the wealth distribution upon the income distribution. We will make explicit the bridges between wealth and income.

Before doing so, we should clear up a few technical points about our numbers. Some of our data refer to the top wealth holders, and some to the top income earners. They are not always the same people. As well, there are about 87 million households in the United States, but about 107 million tax returns were filed in 1987. Data on income and wealth distribution come from three government sources: the IRS (income and estate tax returns), the Census Bureau, and the Federal Reserve Board. Income tax data covers a mixture of families and individuals; estate tax returns are strictly for the latter.

In common parlance, we call "rich" those who have high current income—famous surgeons, entertainers, and chief executives of giant industrial firms. The gigantic sums made by American entertainers and show-business people have always been a source of great public curiosity. In recent years, people like Michael Jackson, Steven Spielberg, and Bill Cosby have had annual incomes ranging up to $60 million.[3]

In other cases, we call "rich" those who have large fortunes in the form of assets—huge land holdings, vast art collections—even though their current incomes are unknown or unknowable to us. These people tend to be prominent in the annual *Forbes, Fortune*, or other magazine lists of "the wealthiest." In recent years, they have included the King of Saudi Arabia, the Sultan of Brunei (an oil-rich Pacific principality), John Kluge (a Virginia media businessman), Sam Walton (the founder of a drugstore and discount chain), Daniel Ludwig, and others. The rise and fall on the magazine lists of these wealthy individuals may only be partially dependent on what they actually own, and partially dependent on the ingenuity of magazine reporters.

WEALTH AND INCOME: SOME CLARIFICATIONS

To clarify such terms as richness, wealth, or affluence, some preliminary qualifications and definitions are required. First, we refer here exclusively to money incomes or implicit money incomes. Enhancement of social position, religious insight, libidinous experience, or other forms of psychic income are not our subject. We confine ourselves to accretions—either real or potential—of solid cash.

Four Types of Income

Money incomes include four subtypes. The most elemental type of income is that received currently for the provision of labor or service. There are wages, salaries, fees, or commissions, among others, paid in the current period for work done by the receiver of the money. This we call earned income.

One step away from earned income is unearned income. This has two aspects. The first is that derived from savings out of past *earned* income. The second arises from assets which were not earned—inheritances, gifts or other windfall gains such as lotteries. This income can be considered double unearned, to coin a phrase. No personal effort was needed to obtain either the assets or the income. Assets such as common stocks, bonds, savings accounts, annuities, or certificates of deposit which provide income without personal effort fall into the first of these two sub-categories.

Total income in a period then is the sum of the above three classes. It is the earned income, garnered through personal effort, plus the unearned income, received as a return on assets—whatever the asset source.

Countin' Pictures on the Wall

There is a fourth type of income which, while not apparent when counting current income, is real nevertheless. The Matisse on the wall, the Fabergé jeweled eggs in the guest house, the diamond rings on the fingers, all are stored income. They do not produce a steady cash flow like a bank deposit, but in many cases, as we have noted previously, their worth can grow faster. Until that time, they can be enjoyed without being consumed.

We noted above that the largest single source of income for the $1 million-and-up bracket was capital gains. It generated an average of $1.06 million for the 94% of this group that had capital gains. We have no idea what proportion of these were due to Manets and Hepplewhites, and what proportion was due to the sale of more mundane items like stock certificates and real estate.

Wealth is then the money value of all assets, whether created through past earnings (savings) or through gifts, inheritances, fortuitous events (finding out that that ugly and worthless picture hanging in the basement was painted over a Rembrandt, for example), or any other source.

STOCKS AND FLOWS

Wealth is a stock, income is a flow. Recall the dam analogy where wealth was represented by the dammed lake, and income by the free-flowing river. Gardner Ackley long ago discussed this important difference in another way:

> It is useful, right at the beginning, to stress some characteristic types of variables and their differences. The most important such distinction (the neglect of which has been the cause of infinite confusion) is between stock and flow variables. A stock variable has no time dimension; a flow does. The weight of an automobile is a stock variable; its speed is a flow variable. The population of cars is a stock variable; traffic is a flow. The weight of a car is 2,200 lbs.; the number (population) of cars is thirty million—not 2,200 lbs. per day or month or thirty million cars per year or minute. To be sure, a stock may be measured at some point in time. The weight of a car may change (by accretion of mud, or by using up of gas or tires); the car population may increase or decrease by the difference between production and scrappage. But the *magnitude* of the stock has no time dimension. A flow, on the other hand, can only be expressed per unit of time. Speed

is 60 miles per hour (or one mile per minute, or 1/60 mile per second, or 1440 miles per 24 hours—all the same speed but expressed in different time units). Traffic is measured as so many cars passing a given point per hour, or so many car-miles per day, or in some other way that inevitably requires the statement of a time unit or else the measurement is meaningless. To say that speed is one mile, or that traffic is fifty cars, is meaningless.

All of this may seem obvious; but almost no other single source of confusion is more dangerous in economic theory—not only to beginners but sometimes to advanced students in economic theory. Money is a stock; expenditures or transactions is a flow; income is a flow, wealth is a stock. *Saving* is a flow ($100 per month); *savings* is a stock ($1000 accumulated as of July 1).[4]

This leads us to the single most telling distinction between income and wealth. It is in the forms of wealth that streams of income can be transmitted from one owner to another. This is a theoretically unending chain, in which recipients have exerted no personal effort but have nevertheless gained an impressive reward. This particular animal, arbitrary unearned income, is one that has bedeviled the philosophers' sense of logic, order, and fairness. We touched on some of their objections in a previous chapter.

It is difficult enough to accept the huge disparities we observe in earned income, between a Michael Milken taking home $550 million in a year and a homeless man eking out a few dollars. It is incomparably more difficult to reconcile the unearned riches gained by inheritance with our sense of justice. When Elvis died, his talent died too. But his daughter, Lisa, still inherited great wealth. The inheritance could have easily gone to a randomly selected name in the phone book.

Old American Fortunes

In the United States, estate taxation provides the rules by which this transmission is governed. The legislation has allowed, for example, John D. Rockefeller (died 1937) and E. I. duPont (died 1834) to pass to their progeny intact fortunes so large that of the *Forbes 400* of the late 1980s, many are still Rockefellers and duPonts.

How have the fortunes of the duPonts, or those of similar families, managed to stay together all these years? The secret is found in the little rate book carried by every realtor—compound interest. We will illustrate how this happens over time with an example.

AN EXPERIMENT IN WEALTH ACCUMULATION

What happens if all current earnings are spent for current expenses? Obviously, there are no resulting savings. Something of this type of consumption patterns seems to be true for most households in the low and moderate range of income in modern-day America. There is a constant drumbeat in the media bemoaning the low savings rate, as Americans seem to spend almost every penny they earn. True, some manage to save a nest egg, but do not look for many in this group to make the *Forbes 400* list any time soon.

The results of this simple fact can have striking effects on the distribution of society's wealth and income. A simple model can illuminate the power of saving and the law of accumulation. By taking an imaginary cross section of households and tracing out their varying "fortunes" over a twenty-five-year period, some important and powerful principles can be demonstrated. Our aim is to show the interconnection between saving, investment, and the distribution of wealth and income over time. In this experiment, let there be 1000 households. At the starting gate, everyone is equal in wealth. Nobody has any; all they have is income.

There are over thirty income classifications used by the IRS. In our calculations, we have narrowed them down to twelve for simplicity. The numbers in each group correspond roughly to the categories used by the IRS. We have 200 households with an average income of $4,000 (group A); 200 with incomes of $12,000 (group B); and 200 with incomes of $21,000 (group C). This accounts for the lower 60% of the population.

There are fewer members in the groups with higher incomes. We assume one hundred with average incomes of $32,000 (group D); one hundred with incomes of $44,000 (group E); one hundred with incomes of $63,000 (group F); and fifty with incomes of $88,000 (group G). We now have accounted for 950 of the 1000 households.

The final fifty comprise thirty with incomes of $115,000 (group H); ten with incomes of $290,000 (group I); five with incomes of $450,000 (group J); three with incomes of $700,000 (group K); and two with incomes of $1.2 million (group L). The income levels have been set to correspond closely to the 1987 IRS figures.[5]

Rules on Saving

How much do each of these groups save? We proceed under the assumption that the more income, the easier it is to save. Our rules are as follows: For an after-tax income of $21,000 or less, 1% is saved. In the following rules on saving, we will consider only *after-tax* income. Lower-income brackets, in our case groups A through C, spend almost all their income on consumption, with few exceptions.

We assume a savings rate of 4% for incomes between $21,000 and $50,000. For example, a household with an income of $50,000 will save $210 from its first $21,000 (= 1% of $21,000) and $1,160 from its next $29,000 (= 4% times $29,000), for a total of $1,370.

We assume a 10% savings rate for $50,000 to $100,000 and 20% for $100,000 to $200,000. At this level, saving becomes easier (or harder to avoid), as obvious consumption possibilities like clothing, food, gadgets, and travel are more readily fulfilled.

Savings are 30% from $200,000 to $500,000, and 50% above $500,000. Thus someone with an after-tax income of $1 million would save, in our example, $210 from his first $21,000; $1,160 from his next $29,000; $5,000 from his next $50,000; $20,000 from the next $100,000; $90,000 from the next $300,000; and $250,000 from the last $500,000, for a total of $366,370. This is about 37% of his income.

The average household savings in 1988 in the U.S. was about 6% of personal disposable income.[6] The total income of this hypothetical group of 1000 households is $38.8 million. The total savings in the first year of this group was $2.43 million, or 6.3%. The result of our savings estimates produces an average savings rate close to recent U.S. experience.

What we call saving above the $500,000 level may seem like extravagant consumption to people other than those engaged in it. But at this level, things bought tend to be in the nature of assets or stored income. Art, rare coins, Arabian horses, other collectibles and vast estates, while being enjoyable "consumer" items, tend also to be investments in stored income. They usually accumulate in value over time, rather than being worn out and thrown away. Thus, in this rarefied atmosphere, one "saves" in spite of himself.

To put it a crude way, at an income of $10,000 a purchase might be an ice cream cone, gone in five minutes. At the $500,000 level, a purchase might be a summer home, enjoyed for years and which can be sold later for a profit.

In the real world, all of us must pay taxes. We have allowed the government its due. We assume an *average* (not marginal) tax rate of 5% for income of less than $21,000; 15% for income between $21,000 and $115,000; and 25% for income above $115,000. For example, those in group A, with incomes of $4,000 would pay 5%, or $200; those in group L, with incomes of $1.2 million, would pay $300,000. While there is some progressivity in present-day income-tax rates, they are not as steep in the higher brackets as they once were.

All of the twelve groups save something. We will assume a *real* (i.e., inflation-free) interest rate of 3%. This has been close to the average real interest rate over the past two or so decades. The bank may pay 8% interest, but if the inflation rate is 5%, the real interest rate is 3%.

The previous paragraph shows that, for simplicity, we are assuming no inflation. The conclusions we draw come out about the same when inflation is factored in, although obviously the money amounts would be different.

The Clock Begins

Now start the clock. The lowest five groups, A through E, have incomes of $44,000 or less. These groups, with 80% of the population, have about 39% of the income. However, they must spend almost all this income to pay their current expenses. It is only above the $50,000 level that as much as 10% of income can be saved.

Consider two simple examples, on groups D and K. Group D has an average income of $32,000 in the first year. Their after-tax income, with a tax rate of 15%, is $27,200. They save 1% of the first $21,000 and 4% of the excess, for a total of $458. At 3% interest, their interest income is $13.74 for this first year. The second year they again earn $32,000 in salary, to which they add $13.74. Tax reduces them to $27,212. They again save at the previous rates, for a second-year saving of $458.50. Their total savings is then $458 plus $458.50, for a total of $916.50. Interest at 3% is $27.50, added to next year's income.

Group K has an average income of $700,000. After taxes of 25%, they have $525,000 left. Their total savings the first year are $128,500, using the rates noted above. Interest at 3% is $3,866. This is added to their second year's income of $700,000, for a total of $703,866. They save $130,270 of this, for a second-year's total saving of $259,190. The interest on this amount is $7,776, which is added to the third year's income.

The calculations go on, year after year. They are laborious, but can easily be performed on a hand calculator or home computer.

A Generation On

After twenty-five years, we stop the clock and look at the results, shown in Table 5.1. They are remarkable.

The top half of the table shows the initial conditions. The lowest five groups—in terms of income, not position in the table—have 80% of the population, but only 39% of the income. The two groups highest in income, K and L, have 0.5% of the households, but over 11% of the income.

The transformation begins with the first tick of the clock. After twenty-five years, the *savings* accumulated by each household are distributed much more unequally than the original *income*. The poorest household has a savings of $950, as shown in the bottom half of the table; those in group L have accumulated $9.1 million. The ratio of the highest savings to the lowest is about 9600. The original ratio of the highest income to the lowest was 300.

The second numerical column in the bottom half of the table shows the final savings per *group*. Since there are far more people in the low-income groups than in the top-income groups, this fact evens out the picture somewhat. For example, there are 200 households in group A, so

Table 5.1
The Power of Compound Interest

Group	Income ($ thousands)	Number of Returns	Cumulative Returns	Percent of Initial Income
A	4	200	200	2.1%
B	12	200	400	6.2
C	21	200	600	10.8
D	32	100	700	8.3
E	44	100	800	11.3
F	63	100	900	16.2
G	88	50	950	11.3
H	115	30	980	8.9
I	290	10	990	7.5
J	450	5	995	5.8
K	700	3	998	5.4
L	1,200	2	1000	6.2

Group	Final Savings per Household	Final Savings per Group	Percent of Final Savings
A	$950	$190,000	0.3%
B	2,860	570,000	0.9
C	5,000	1,000,000	1.5
D	11,600	1,200,000	1.8
E	22,000	2,200,000	3.3
F	44,000	4,400,000	6.7
G	99,000	5,000,000	7.5
H	160,000	4,800,000	7.2
I	860,000	8,600,000	12.9
J	1,840,000	9,200,000	13.8
K	3,700,000	11,100,000	16.7
L	9,100,000	18,200,000	27.4

ASSUMPTIONS: (1) No inflation
(2) Real interest rate of 3%
(3) Average (not marginal) taxes of 5% on incomes below $21,000; 15% between $21,000 and $115,000; 25% above $115,000
(4) Savings are 1% below after-tax income of $21,000; 4% for $21,000 to $50,000; 10% for $50,000 to $100,000; 20% for $100,000 to $200,000; 30% for $200,000 to $500,000; and 50% above $500,000.

the savings of $950 per household are multiplied by that number, yielding $190,000. However, the highest income group, L, still has the largest *total* savings of over $18 million.

The third numerical column in the bottom half shows the fraction of total savings accumulated by each group. The three wealthiest groups, J, K, and L, have 58% of the total savings. Yet they constitute only 1% of the total population. The lowest 80% get 8% of the savings.

Figure 5.1 shows the wealth concentration calculated from Table 5.1. The vertical axis is in thousands of dollars per person; the horizontal axis is in cumulative percent of the 1,000 households.

We see the familiar kink as we approach the top percent. Yet at the beginning of the twenty-five-year period, any line of wealth would have been

Figure 5.1
Wealth Accumulation after 25 Years

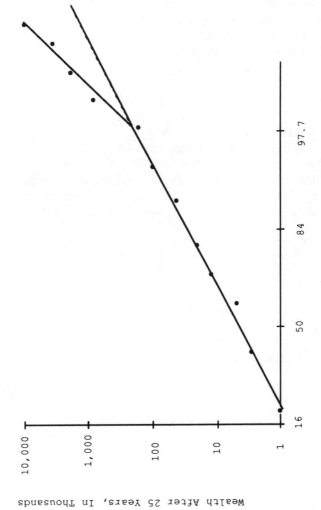

Wealth After 25 Years, In Thousands

Cumulative Percentage of People

perfectly flat. Nobody had any wealth, by our definition. Compound interest produced the kink, not any mysterious or magical law.

Another common way to depict distributions is with a Lorenz curve, as we have done in Figure 5.2. In this scheme, again arrange people in order of their incomes, and then see what percentage of the distribution accrues to the first 20% of the people, If that number were also 20%, the distribution would be equal, meaning that at each level the percentages of people and income (or wealth, if we were considering that aspect) would be the same. The solid line in the center of the graph represents perfect equality. This has never been reached, with the possible exception of early Christians.

However, neither should all the income or wealth be owned by only a handful, as apparently happened under the Somoza regime in Nicaragua some years ago. Lorenz curves tell us how unequal society is as a whole. The Somoza distribution would cling to the bottom of the graph as it moved to the right, and then shoot up vertically as the greedy dictator was reached.

The data from Table 5.1, when graphed in the Lorenz manner, illustrates the unalloyed strength of compound interest. After twenty-five years, those in the top few percent have garnered most of the wealth.

Figure 5.2
Lorenz Curve of Compound Interest

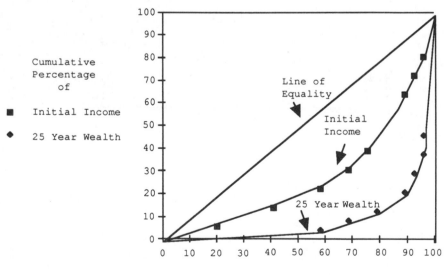

Although we think of the Somoza example as a barbarous example of a typical Third World country, what we show in this graph is not too far from the wealth distribution set up by the late unlamented *caudillo*. Depending on which assumptions are made, the top two individuals—who started with 6% of the income—end up with 27% of the wealth.

Other Latin American countries apparently have not got too much past the Somoza pattern. In Peru in 1989, 50% of the income went to 1% of the people.[7]

Compound interest is the underlying mechanism transforming income to wealth. That is why fortunes, once garnered and competently husbanded, tend to grow over the generations. Even allowing for significant spending on the part of recipients, estates will rebuild after being divided.

GEORGE GILDER'S VIEWPOINT

George Gilder was one of the best-selling economics writers of the 1980s. According to one story, President Reagan, upon taking office in 1981, had a special gift for each of his Cabinet officers. He gave them all copies of one of Gilder's books. Whether or not they were read is unreported.

The climate seems to have changed somewhat since the giddy days of Reagan's first term. President Bush, presumably Reagan's protégé, was not recorded as handing out any books by economists when he took office.

Gilder is skeptical about the wealthy gradually growing richer through compound interest.[8] Why don't the rich keep getting richer, until they own nearly everything? He gives an impressionistic picture of how increasing concentration of wealth does not happen: "Widows . . . traipse off to Europe with their money and marry indigent dukes or such. Fortune hunters abound near the funerals of the rich." Delightful plots for soap operas, but not borne out by the facts. We have not tried to prove that the rich do or could own everything. Rather, unless they are complete bunglers, they can use a goodly portion of their income to build wealth, without producing the miraculous inventions that society is supposed to crown with its gold.

The 3% real interest rate we chose represents a wide range of values. Some of the rich will gain 10% interest if they invest in the right oil wells. Some may have a negative interest rate, by investing in dry wells, stocks that collapse, or properties that are condemned. This implies that they lose rather than gain wealth. But the rather small value of 3% real interest is probably a reasonable depiction for wealth as a whole. Gilder goes on to say: "In recent years, moreover, the magic of compound interest has met its match in compound inflation and taxes. These two forces hit hardest at both the assets and the earnings of the rich, destroying about a tenth of their income whenever the price level rises 2% or more."

At the height of inflation under President Carter, the inflation rate was about 13% annually. Under Gilder's rule of golden thumb, admittedly vague, the rich should have lost about 65% of their income in that fateful year alone. No evidence of panic selling of Monets, Rubens, Canalettos, or country estates appeared in that or any other year since the Great Depression of the 1930s.

And what about the inflation of the other Carter years, some of which lingered into the Reagan administration? Using Gilder's law, the income of the rich should have dropped well below zero. New and surprising faces should have appeared on the hot-air grates around midnight.

In spite of the lack of evidence, Gilder continues: ''Even such families as Mellon, Rockefeller, and Frick, while remaining wealthy, are in steady decline.'' As we implied above, a given Mellon, Rockefeller or Frick may indeed have fallen from the ranks of the wealthy, as a result of bad investments. An average interest rate implies some sort of distribution, with the lucky few well above the average, and the sad sacks with a negative interest rate, or loss. But almost all of the wealthy will have a positive interest rate in the growth of their wealth.

A RATIO BETWEEN INCOME AND WEALTH

Lebergott,[9] in a brilliant piece of analysis, examined the relationship between income and wealth from a different perspective. While his data is from 1970, the analysis is still probably applicable.

Briefly, using IRS and other data, he found the relation between income and wealth for different income brackets. For example, at an average income of $15,000, average wealth (including a house or houses, stock, cash, autos, etc.) was about $47,000. This may sound like a lot of wealth for a relatively modest income, but a good proportion of that is in home ownership.

The simplest way to consider Lebergott's mass of numbers is by means of the ratio between wealth and income. We show this in Figure 5.3. In the example given immediately above, the ratio is about 3.2 (= 47/15). This is about the ratio for most of what is called the middle-income group.

However, the ratio rises rapidly once we get beyond $50,000 income annually. By the time we get to the top income bracket—more than $1 million annually—the ratio is about nineteen. In that bracket, the average income is about $2.4 million, with an average wealth of about $46 million. We can see this trend develop as the upper part of Figure 5.3 rises toward the upper right-hand corner of the graph.

The rising ratio of wealth to income bears out our contention that the distribution of wealth is much more skewed than that of income. To put it in a simple way, the rich get wealthier faster than their income goes up.

Consider how this works by an example. Someone has an income of $50,000. According to the figure, this is a wealth-to-income ratio of about

Figure 5.3
Ratios between Wealth and Income

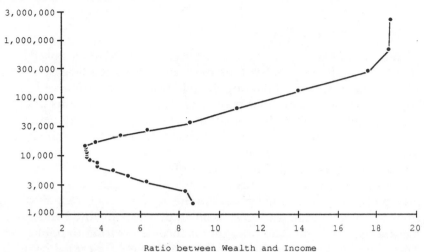

Ratio between Wealth and Income

ten, meaning that a typical net worth in this category is about half a million. Then, over the years, income rises to $100,000. But net worth is *more* than ten times $100,000 or $1 million. The ratio has risen to thirteen, so a typical net worth in this income bracket is $1.3 million.

The ratio of wealth to income in the very highest income bracket—$1 million or more—bears some further discussion. With wealth at $46 million, if it were all invested in tax-free municipal bonds at 6% interest, it would bring an annual yield of $2.8 million. None of this would be subject to federal income tax, other than the alternative minimum tax. If the wealth were invested in 8% savings accounts, the return would be $3.7 million annually. Both the calculated tax-free and taxable incomes are higher than the average income in this bracket of $2.4 million. This implies that some top income earners may be getting bad financial advice. Why otherwise would these very richest have financial holdings that give them less income than they would get from a sure thing like a municipal bond or a bank savings account?

While evidence is sketchy, one conclusion that could be drawn is that the overwhelming proportion of wealth in this lofty bracket is not in the form of interest-bearing funds. Recall the estimates we made in a previous chapter. We calculated that the average of the taxable and tax-free securities for the $1 million-and-up bracket in 1987 was about $4.5 million. Lebergott notes that cash, deposits, bonds, and mortgages—close to the financial instruments we estimated above—were about 10.5% of the wealth of $46 million in the $1 million-and-up income bracket. This corresponds to $4.9 million in Lebergott's estimate for 1970, almost the same as our estimate for 1987.

Capital Gains and Losses

But this correspondence does not answer the question we raised above about the bad financial advice the most affluent were allegedly getting. While there is no way of reading the minds and financial records of the very wealthiest without their permission, one clue is in terms of capital gains. It is well known among accountants that amazing feats can be performed with capital gains and losses that cannot be done with ordinary income like salaries and bank account interest.

One of the most prominent examples of this use of paper "losses" was the case of former President Nixon. He wrote off a substantial "loss" from giving his Vice Presidential papers to the government. The only reason this came to light at all was because an employee of the IRS had a grudge against the President, and brought his income tax form to public view. The returns of those listed in the *Forbes 400*, with the capital gains and losses underlined, are never publicized this way.

Another way one can guess that the answer to our question is tied up in the capital gains systems is by considering the 1987 tax returns. The average capital gain, subtracting capital losses, of those in the $1 million-and-up bracket was about $1.06 million.

Lebergott notes that their wealth, excluding the financial instruments of bank deposits, bonds, and mortgages, averages about $37 million. This then implies an average capital gains rate from this source of less than 3%, which seems very small. At present, there is no way to prove the contention of unusual financial goings-on in capital gains other than by anecdotal evidence, but there seems to be some smoke coming out from under the door.

PECULIARITIES OF THE WEALTHIEST

In a compilation as complete as Lebergott's, there are bound to be a few curiosities and illuminating points. Consider, for example, the case of automobiles. Car values are included in the total wealth for each income bracket. As you would expect, the poor generally have no or ancient vehicles. The middle class have newer and more valuable models. This is evidenced in the data.

In the $1,000 to $2,000 income bracket, the average value of the car or cars in a household was about $220, obviously representing a rattletrap. By the time we move up into the $20,000 to $25,000 income bracket, the average car value was about $3,000, a reasonable value in 1970. The odd aspect of the car values is that the numbers continue to rise with total income and wealth, rather than levelling off at some point. In the $200,000 to $250,000 income bracket, cars are worth $25,000; in the $500,000 to $1 million category, $50,000; and over $1 million, $166,000. Allowing for the fact that a new Mercedes cost only $10,000 to $15,000 in 1970, one wonders how many cars the very wealthiest had at that time—or do now.

The most affluent generally have larger garages than the rest of us— three-car garages are becoming standard in better neighborhoods these days—but the 670 individuals in the $1 million-and-up group in 1970 probably did not have fifteen car garages. One hopes that the data gatherers were not including the value of autos owned by servants and gardeners in the estates of the wealthiest groups.

The Moles of Professor Pen's Parade

The grand parade of Chapter 1 showed that U.S. tax laws can produce strange results in tax returns. We sometimes find wealthy people in low income brackets when it suits the purposes of their accountants. These were the people in the front of Professor Pen's parade, with their heads in the ground.

Some evidence of this is available from Lebergott's data. For example, in the lowest tax bracket (those with absolutely no adjusted gross income or even a loss) the average business equity is about minus $57,000. This implies a giant debt, quite out of keeping with the people expected to be at this income. One would expect them to be those who are virtually destitute, or who have suffered a fire or some such calamity. With their large business mortgages, most of the people in this group are obviously not panhandling. We use the term "most of the people" because we recognize that there probably *are* some poverty-stricken people in this very lowest income group.

By way of proof, two income brackets up (in the $2,000 to $3,000 annual income group) the average business equity is about $400. This is about what we would expect from such a poor part of the population. The bracket with no income at all also had a total corporate stock of about $14,600 in 1970. Those with income from $1,000 to $2,000 had stock worth about $400. In fact, one would have to rise to the top 6% of the population, which in 1970 were those with incomes of more than $20,000, to again reach the $15,000 level of stock ownership.

There are two anomalies in the curve of Figure 5.3. One of them, the bottom of the curve sloping to the left instead of the right, may be due to the phenomenon we have just described. One would think that poor people would have very little wealth, having to sell everything they have to keep body and soul together. Thus one would expect the wealth-to-income ratio for the very poorest to be close to zero. Figure 5.3 shows that the ratio is around eight, and actually decreases as we go up the income scale. We can deduce that part of the reason is that some of the people at the very lowest incomes are not really that badly off—quite the contrary. Their financial affairs have been so adjusted as to tell the IRS that they have little or no income.

The second anomaly, which is demonstrated by Figure 5.3, lies in the upper right-hand corner. From about $12,000 in income to about $250,000, the wealth-to-income ratio rises fairly steadily, from a value of about 3 to seventeen to eighteen. But as income rises above the quarter-million mark, the ratio remains about constant. This is shown in the graph as a vertical line.

Is this the kink we have mentioned on a number of other occasions? We think not. In this context, it has nothing to do with two distributions joining at this point. Rather, we suggest that it may indicate an under-reporting of wealth on the part of the highest income earners. We do not know exactly how this underreporting takes place.

We can make some rough calculations of how much might be under-reported. If the trend from the $15,000 level to the $2.4 million level (the average income of those in the $1 millon-and-up bracket) had continued linearly, it would have reached a value of about 26. The total wealth, by our estimate, in the $1 million-and-up group would be 26 (not 19) times $2.4 million, or $62 million. This implies that about $16 million, or about one-quarter of the *true* wealth of that group, is not described to either the IRS or researchers.

In spite of these and other curiosities, the wealthy almost invariably have high incomes. What is more, the ratio of wealth to income rises the higher you go. The ratio is about six times higher in the top income brackets as it is for those in the middle. With that excess wealth, ever more income can be generated, adding more wealth in a never-ending cycle.

SUMMARY

We have defined wealth, discussed compound interest, wealth allot-ments, and inheritances. Where does all of it lead? Wealth distribution controls a large part of income distribution, especially in the upper reaches. There is a critical point above which compound interest ac-cumulates faster than it can be spent. What brings this process to an end? Death, which allows the capricious transfer of wealth to those designated by the wealth holder. So inheritance is a key link in the wealth cycle.

6

PREVIOUS THEORIES OF INCOME AND WEALTH DISTRIBUTION

Theories of what income and wealth distribution should or could be are legion. We touched briefly on some earlier when we mentioned Lorenz, Pareto, and Gibrat. However, they spoke as economists. Most of the rest of us who consider income or wealth find it difficult to think in these terms. yet our opinions, as expressed in tax laws or other potential infringements on income or wealth, *do* count.

Many of the opinions advocated, in whole or in part, by the public or philosophers are a mixture of ethics, economics, and politics. For some of the following list, we are grateful to Pen,[1] Cowell,[2] and Sahota,[3] who have covered the waterfront of what has been advocated at one time or another. A few of these theories relate primarily to poverty, as opposed to wealth. However, lack of wealth is the main contributor to poverty, so we have a two-sided coin here.

1. *You are completely on the wrong track. Income or wealth do not really matter. Things of the spirit—art, music, literature, and friends—are vastly more important.* Our theories, as well as those of economists in general, can not really address this attitude. If all possessions are either useless or soul-destroying, then their distribution is about as consequential as who is five cars in back of you in a traffic jam, or whether you are listed at the top or the bottom of a page in the telephone directory.

More people have these feelings, or at least some of them, than is immediately obvious. The hippies of the 1960s, with their emphasis on thinking rather than "thinging," were the most recent prominent example of this sentiment. Their communes, however, are now abandoned and overgrown with crabgrass.

The conspicuous consumption habits of yuppies (some of whom may be former hippies) now fill magazines and newspapers. But the ascetic ideal, going back to the early Christian hermits and even beyond to ancient Eastern religions, will be back. It is alive and well, resting on a Himalayan mountaintop.

According to the thought at the beginning of this section, there is little difference between a $1 and a $500 bill, other than the Presidential portraits. Then the number of these pieces of paper in your palm also has little significance.

To our knowledge, the theory that things—by which is included money—are irrelevant has never won over the majority of the people in any extended region or nation in recorded history. If nothing else, our physiological desires for food and shelter impel us to desire material goods, if only the street person's can of beans and a coat to keep the cold out.

Some might point to the Essenes of Dead Sea Scrolls fame, who apparently quit the materialistic world and went off into the desert. Yet there is evidence that at least some of their needs were supplied by others in the world that they despised.

Most of us have a different viewpoint from that expressed at the head of this part. Although we have been taught since we were children that we should not discuss it in polite company, we *do* desire money, mostly for what it can buy.

Some of us are obsessed by it; others are a little calmer when confronted by green. Yet most want, as Oliver Twist said at the orphanage, more. This does not make us better or worse than the ascetics, like monks or nuns; just different. The recluses who forego money will not pay attention to the top 3%, bottom 97%, or any other division of society along what they regard as unnatural lines. This book will not be read in monasteries.

2. *The family is the basic unit of society. Any income distribution that strengthens it is good. Any other type of income distribution should be changed.* Again, this does not bear directly on how rich the rich should be. Helping families stay together in comfort is surely one of society's prime goals, but how does the level of affluence impinge on this?

There are many (perhaps an infinite number) ways to improve family life. One of us (HI) grew up in Canada, where family allowances were a way of life. Their objective was to help out the poorer segments of society, even those who were not badly off enough to qualify for welfare. He can vaguely remember his mother receiving a monthly check for $6, which seemed like a lot of money at the time. In principle, this type of monthly allowance for children strengthened the family.

The taxation that yielded this family allowance presumably affected the upper reaches of income and wealth, in some slight way. However, you would need a microscope to see how this minor tax changed the income of the rich. Family allowances may have been—and may still be—a good idea for poor families, yet they had almost no influence on the higher levels of income distribution.

If we were to propose direct transfer of supposedly excessive income to aid the family, that would be another matter. We do not. An almost endless number of places to spend tax revenues already exist, like so many cubby-holes in a roll-top desk. We are not attempting here to choose into which hole to put the dollars.

3. *Everyone equal*. Short enough, if not always sweet. In principle, it could be done, if we could find someone Draconian enough to make Stalin, Hitler, and Genghis Khan look like Caspar Milquetoast on one of his gentler days. Even in a nation with supposedly one of the most egalitarian—and also bizarre—systems of government in the world, Albania, the highest-paid worker earns twice as much as the lowest-paid.[4] Now if they would not or could not narrow the gap in that country, where the words of the Great Leader and Teacher, Enver Hoxha, were law and delivered in Albanian to boot, you can imagine what problems we would have here.

The sole advantage of such a system would be to make everything neat and tidy. How long it would last is anyone's guess. There is an old French saying that if all money were equally distributed on Monday, by Friday it would be about as unequally distributed as before, though not necessarily in the same hands. In a fast-moving country like the United States, we might not wait until then.

In terms of how rich the rich should be, the answer under a system of perfect levelling is simple: as rich (or as poor) as anyone else. The kink at 3% would of course disappear. The entire distribution on probability graph paper would be a flat line, marching off to the horizon in both directions.

Sahota's masterly survey of writings on income distribution, with over 300 references to the economic literature, concerned itself mostly with "positive economics."[3] That is a technical term to describe those theories that try to explain why we have certain income distributions, and how those distributions might change in coming years. Positive economics is vastly different from *normative* economics, which says what should be, not merely what is. Saying that all should be equal in income is normative economics at its most strident.

The concept that all should be equal goes back into the mists of history. Some of the Biblical statements we quoted in a previous chapter could be taken to mean that all should be equal, although the ancient sages rarely said this in so many words. In more recent centuries, the Levellers in England, prominent at the time of the Cromwellian upheavals, implied that all should be equal in wealth and income. Their ideas were never put into practice.

Probably the most publicized theory of equality in recent years has been that of John Rawls, a philosopher from Harvard.[5] It has been stated of him:

"Few contemporary outsiders [to economics] have made such an impact on economic thought."[3] From our viewpoint, one of his most important statements is that "Social and economic inequalities are to . . . be . . . to the greatest expected benefit to the least advantaged [the maximin criterion]."[6] From this and other simple assumptions about a distribution of human abilities, Rawls deduces that perfect equality is the most logical position for society as a whole to take.

Rawls recognizes that some people in any society are more favorably endowed in intelligence or other skills by environment or genetics. If they improve their economic lot, and still help the poor even a tiny amount, is Rawls' maximin criterion of working toward greater equality still satisfied? For example, some of the Canadian family allowance that one of our mothers received long ago undoubtedly came from wealthy people in Canada. But a few cents from the wealthy, either in taxes or charity, hardly changes the world.

The problem in dealing with these points is that Rawls, being a philosopher, thinks in *qualitative*, not quantitative, terms. If equality is to be reached, it would have to be on a *quantitative* basis.

Let us turn again to a small-change example. John D. Rockefeller was well-known around the turn of the century for handing out shiny dimes to newsboys and other assorted urchins. In a quantitative sense, his fortune was being diminished. In a qualitative sense, nothing of any significance happened, except that the billionaire attracted favorable publicity.

The consequences of everyone having the same size bank account and salary, enforced by law, would be disastrous; lack of initiative and eventual economic collapse would ensue. Even worse, those who wrote books about income distribution would have to hit the streets.

4. *The social safety net should have small holes.* The term "safety net" was popularized during the first days of the Reagan administration in 1981. It was as if the millions of poor were precariously crossing, one at a time, a tightrope slung across economic scaffolding. Exactly what the safety net meant was never made clear, although it presumably was some combination of welfare, Social Security, Medicare, Medicaid, and other programs. This is another of the worthy areas that could be filled with extra revenue from increased inheritance or income taxes on the upper 3%.

Poverty, said George Bernard Shaw, is the worst of all crimes.[7] A rewrite of 1960s-style slogans might then read, given the fact that about one in eight is below the poverty line: "Free the U.S. 30 Million!"

Making sure that the poor receive more money than they do now, either in the form of higher wages and salaries or government programs, is surely a form of income redistribution. However, we continue to be concerned here with what could or should happen to the *rich*, not the poor.

We mentioned above that there are close to an infinite number of ways to strengthen the family by means of income policy. There are probably even more ways to distribute any revenues derived from the rich: welfare to the poverty stricken, a spaceship to Mars, tax reductions for the middle class, improving education, and so on. Trying to enumerate all these options, let alone evaluate them, would put us in the position of writing prescriptions for *all* of society's needs and wants. We prefer to focus on the smaller area.

5. *The rich should pay more taxes than the poor.* They do now, at least on average. The difference is not as great as some would like, we admit. So-called progressive income tax is not as progressive as some think it is. For example, in 1982 2,999 couples and individuals, with average incomes of about $500,000, paid no U.S income taxes.[8] And this took place after years of minimum taxes and other fiscal devices designed by the government to make the wealthiest pay at least some taxes.

The principle of at least some progressive taxation, although not popular with the rich, is accepted in most industrialized countries. One of the major exceptions to this has been the United States after the 1986 tax reform law. Due to a complicated series of surcharges on the top income brackets and partial repeal of those surcharges, those who earned above about $150,000 in the late 1980s actually paid a smaller marginal rate than those below. (The exact rate depended on the number of exemptions and other factors). To our knowledge, this was the first time that richer people paid a lower marginal rate than people poorer than they since the income tax was begun in 1913.

In spite of this peculiarity and the fact that a small number of the wealthy escape all taxation, we *do* have a progressive system for both income and estate taxation. The question then is, how progressive is progressive? Should the rich pay a dime, a quarter, or even 99¢ more per dollar than the poor? All those rates are literally progressive in that the rich pay more than the poor. These examples show that the word "progressive," which once had a noble heritage, has become as soft as newly made dough.

6. *We should at least be no worse than other countries in inequality.* The concept of using a "yardstick" to compare one system to another has a long and distinguished history in America. For example, Franklin Roosevelt, in a 1932 speech in Oregon presaging the Tennessee Valley Authority, proposed using publicly owned electricity systems as a measure against which the efficiency and rates of private ones could be contrasted.

About the same can be done for international equality or inequality of income. In other words, one criterion for the fairness of the United States is that it be no more unequal than Britain, Japan, Sweden, or other nations at about our economic level.

Making comparisons within a country is difficult enough. Devising international ones, given all the unknowns in data and their interpretations, can be downright dangerous.As well, it would take an enormous amount of space to discuss in detail all the international data that has been generated in recent years. In spite of these limitations, our conclusion is that the United States is probably more unequal in distribution than many other industrialized nations, but more equal than most of the Third World.

It is reasonable to use international yardsticks. Yet the problem remains: If the United States is best, worst, or somewhere in the middle, what does that prove?

7. *From each according to his abilities, to each according to his needs.* This is probably Marx's most famous phrase, after one gets past, "Workers of the world, unite!" It is indeed a type of income distribution. Like most of Marx's concepts, it looked good on paper, but not so good once it got up and started to walk around the room.

The first part of this exhortation concerns what individuals—always male when Marx was writing—would *contribute* to society. Since we are concentrating here on income, rather than what people give to their fellow men, we will not analyze the first clause. However, the use of the vague word "abilities" gives an intimation of the trouble to come in the second clause.

The meaning of this second clause, in terms of income distribution, hinges on "needs." Nobody, probably not even Marx himself, knows or knew what that means or meant. According to standard economic theory, we all have unlimited wants. Some of them may be true needs, but who is to decide that?

Suppose Joe and Joan both want $50,000 a year. Joe says that, of this amount, $40,000 is for real needs, and $10,000 is not absolutely necessary. Joan's values are $45,000 and $5,000, respectively. According to Marx, Joan should get $5,000 more than Joe. But suppose Joan had arbitrarily padded her "needs" total, and Joe was being more honest. Should Joe get less?

Marx, being conveniently dead, will never have to answer questions like this. We suggest that even if he were to come back to life, he *still* could not answer them.

Although the United States is about as far from a Marxist society as one can get, there are still vestiges of the concept of "needs" here and there. For example, polling organizations from time to time publish surveys of what the public thinks a family "needs." The survey might say that a household needs $25,000 or $30,000 in today's economy.

Yet a family at that level, unless they included many children and aged dependents, has a certain amount of discretionary income (i.e., money not absolutely essential for keeping life and limb together). In responding to these surveys, people always assume that a family "needs" at least some discretionary or nonessential income, thereby voiding the whole concept of "needs."

A homeless person clearly needs a place to sleep, food, and other amenities. But does he or she "need" $10,000 a year, $50,000, $100,000, or any other amount? We can specify elementary needs easily enough. Once we get beyond that, talking about real income distributions, Marxian analysis soon gets into a swamp.

Marx clearly stimulated a whole new branch of economic thought. To this day, he is probably the most-cited economist in the scientific literature. Unfortunately for his reputation, most of those citations are to contradict, not agree with, him.

8. *Provide the poor with at least a bare standard of living, not out of charity, but to protect the better-off from the poor.* This is sometimes called Kantian justice, after the great German philosopher.[9] The proposal clearly does not require equal income distribution. On the contrary, it is about the most niggardly of the theories we will consider or have considered. In essence, give the poor just enough to keep them from storming the mansions of the wealthy.

By modern standards, this would be rejected by almost everyone, at least explicitly. However, critics of the nation's welfare system say that it is really not very far from what Kant proposed two centuries ago.

In partial defense of the philosopher, he labored under the "constant pie" theory of economics. We have referred to this before. This theory, which described reality in almost all the world until about the 19th century, assumed that there was close to a fixed amount of economic goods to go around. If that is true, someone operating out of self-interest would want to give to the poor, either voluntarily or through taxes, only enough to keep them from breaking into his house. Any more would be a waste.

Kant may seem hard-hearted by modern standards, but his was quite a common philosophy in his era. The last vestiges have not quite disappeared in our times.

9. *The well-to-do will take care of the poor voluntarily.* Economists call this "market-determined distributive justice." In other words, there is a type of market for charity. Some of the wealthy will be moved by the plight of the poor, and will contribute to their relief. Others will avert their gaze and give nothing. One can think of the process, at least theoretically, as intersecting demand and supply curves. Economists use these types of curves to describe much of the way the world works.

The *demand* curve would rise from the very poorest, sleeping in doorways and on grates, to the near-poor who may just need an old clunker to get to work. The *supply* of charity could descend from the likes of Andrew Carnegie, the nineteenth-century philanthropist, who thought that a rich man should give away all his money before he died. It would continue down to Scrooge McDuck of the comic strip, who still has the first dime he ever earned, as well as most of the subsequent ones.

The trouble with this model of income redistribution is that it depends on voluntary giving. With the accession of George Bush, with his "thousand points of light," to the White House, there is renewed emphasis on voluntary charity and helping one's neighbor. There is little question but that this has been part of the American ethic for centuries.

But in a modern society, voluntary giving is likely to be a few percent, at best, of the aid given to the poor. Consider the dollar value of all government programs for the poor and near-poor: school lunch programs, welfare, Medicaid, and so on. Now contrast this with the cash—not the time devoted, but the dollar bills—given to the poor by the middle class and the wealthy. That latter amount is probably larger than in any other country, but it is still minuscule compared to government expenditures.

Even if the wealthy were more charitable than they are now, the criterion at the head of this section does not suggest exactly how income could or should be distributed. It merely says that the wealthy will give some undefined portion of their holdings to the poor. Will it be 1%, 10%, or 90%? And will they do it year after year, or only on a one-time basis? Obviously, giving up 90% of one's wealth can only be done once.

Equally obscure is any definition of the well-to-do. Are they the top 3% in the graphs we have shown, the top 10%, or any other fraction? The criterion is silent on this.

We can conclude that, while charity is one of the most noble of human instincts, we can not rely on it for any measurable income redistribution. Voluntarism can only go a limited way in changing the slope of the line showing the incomes of the top 3%.

10. *Ill-gotten gain must not be allowed*. The problem with this criterion is, what do we mean by ill-gotten?

Suppose you surreptitiously find out where the state is going to run a certain highway, and buy up the land in the right-of-way in advance. You make a big profit. Is this crooked? If you then send Mr. Greasy, the state employee who passed you the information, on a free trip to Tahiti, is his gain equally unscrupulous? Most would say yes, but others would say no. Anatole France once said that all wealth is theft. Like all aphorisms, this one is a corkscrew. It twists and turns, sometimes working, sometimes not.

We can divide the huge mass of possibly unfair gains into two categories: legal and illegal. That is, either one breaks a law or one does not. Even here the definitions are a little rubbery. Selling liquor during Prohibition was illegal. Now it is not.

So to keep the discussion simple, let us assume that all money made legally, at least at the time it was acquired, is fairly gotten. Everything else is ill gotten.

All economic gain is subject to the tax laws. Unless you have hidden your corrupt wealth from the IRS, you have to pay taxes on it. Al Capone served time in a Federal penitentiary not for putting ventilation holes in his fellow thugs, but for concealing his illegal income from the Feds.

Unless we know the distribution of questionable money, how much was involved, and what was declared on Form 1040, we cannot estimate whether confiscating it would significantly affect income distribution. The number runners and bagmen of the 1950s were mostly small time, so if the IRS had taken away their illegal earnings there might have been a small quiver on the bottom of the income heap.

Drug Dealing and Income

Now drug income is by far the largest source of illegal wealth in the United States, far larger than the old-time numbers game. There is little point in trying to estimate how great the total drug take is, because anything illegal is based, in the final analysis, on fragmentary and anecdotal evidence. During the 1920s we had only a vague idea of how many gallons of rum were being smuggled into the country.

Drug use again raises the point: What is dishonest? Drug users would likely say that the money they pay to dealers and importers is not ill gotten by the latter, but given in return for a valued commodity. While the legality of drug use has never been put to a referendum in this country, presumably many drug users would vote to make it legal. The question of ill-gotten gain is vaguer than some of us would like.

If the drug dealers are not caught, then their dishonest gain goes completely tax free. They are then taxed at a lower rate—zero—than the rest of us, rather than the higher, confiscatory rate suggested by the criterion at the start of this section.

Did they fill out the tax forms in the first place? Nobody knows. They probably decided, to avoid detection by the IRS, not to fill out any forms at all. In that case, they would not have appeared in our income distribution graphs, since our estimates are based on income actually declared.

On the other hand, some drug dealers may have decided on a facade, declaring their occupation to be "importers of rare goods," with an income of a few thousand dollars a year. We noted before that there are more people with low incomes than we would expect on the basis of a lognormal distribution. We attributed most of this bulge to part-time workers and Social Security recipients, but some of them may be drug dealers in disguise.

Nobody, by definition, is in favor of dishonorable gain. Yet the examples we have given show how difficult it is to define. It is even more difficult to detect. For many, attitudes are summarized by Mae West: "It ain't no sin to crack a few laws now and then, just so long as you don't break any."[10]

11. *Don't even think about income distribution. It would just upset the apple cart, and all of us would be worse off.* This attitude is perhaps transferred from the Heisenberg principle in physics. According to that theory,

whenever you want to measure the position of an electron or other subatomic particle, the very act of measurement introduces an uncertainty about where it is. You can never know its position exactly. Measurement alters matters.

If we apply the Heisenberg principle to income or wealth distribution, then just the fact of plotting a graph or adding up numbers introduces some type of disturbance into the system. Somehow, in an as yet unknown way, this stimulation will make all of us worse off economically.

Could this be true? It sometimes seems that everything, thought of and unthought of, is possible in economics. We therefore can not rule it out. But some more proof has to be supplied, beyond the words: "watch out, it could happen".

Have the physicists given up on measuring electrons and other particles since Heisenberg's principle was announced? No physics labs have emptied in discouragement because the limits of nature have been reached. The Nobel prizes in physics are still being handed out. Scientists today use Heisenberg's principle to estimate what is or is not knowable, rather than shut down their particle accelerators.

Probably the best-known advocate of not peering too closely into the mysterious mechanisms that govern income or wealth distribution is George Gilder. We described some of his thoughts in Chapter 5.

At first glance, the concept of declaring certain branches of economics off limits might seem peculiar. Because Gilder's opinions have been persuasive to many, we will take the liberty of an extended quotation of his reasoning:

> [Adam Smith's] followers, beginning with David Ricardo, quickly became bogged down in a static and mechanical concern with distribution. They were all forever counting the ranks of rich and poor and assaying the defects of capitalism that keep the poor always with us in such great numbers. The focus on distribution continues in economics today, as economists pore balefully over the perennial inequities and speculate on brisk 'redistributions' to rectify them.
>
> This mode of thinking, prominent in foundation-funded reports, bestselling economics texts, and newspaper columns is harmless enough on the surface. But its deeper effect is to challenge the golden rule of capitalism, to pervert the relationship between rich and poor, and to depict the system as a 'zero-sum' game, in which every gain for someone implies a loss for someone else, and wealth is seen once again to create poverty.
>
> As Kristol has said, a free society in which the distributions are widely seen as unfair cannot survive. The distributionist mentality thus strikes at the living heart of democratic capitalism.[11]

Some of these outbursts resemble a fireworks display, in which rockets are shot off in all directions. A few give us a little illumination, but most end up in the bushes or burrowed into the ground. Gilder is saying that when it comes to income distribution, we are like children playing with a complicated watch. Open the case to poke around, and it will never work properly again.

Are we striking at "the living heart of democratic capitalism," like criminals who disrupt a bypass operation? Our publisher is a capitalist of sorts, with stockholders, a board of directors, and all of the trappings of late twentieth-century industry. If he thought that by some insidious scheme we are proposing both the demise of him and the system of which he is a part, he never would have allowed us to darken his doorway.

Kristol's idea is a reworking of Harold Davis' mathematical interpretation of history.[12] According to Davis, if the income distribution becomes too uneven, there is liable to be a revolution led by the left. If it becomes too flat (i.e., wealth is fairly evenly distributed) the right will overthrow the government.

Kristol takes this concept one step further by attaching a psychological twist. If the people *think* that income distribution is unfair—regardless of whether or not it really is—then the state will fall. He does not say whether the revolution will come from the left or right of the political spectrum, but presumably it would come from the left or levellers.

Cowell, one of the leading theorists of income distribution, describes Davis' theory as "mildly bizarre . . . seeking the mainspring of the development of civilization in the slope of a line on a double-log graph paper does not appear to be a rewarding exercise."[13] Davis had tried to predict such events as the French Revolution by how much the nobles of the day raked in from the long-suffering peasants.

But then again, Cowell himself is tainted irrevocably. He has actually studied income distribution himself, becoming one of the "baleful economists" that Gilder decries.

Has income distribution in the United State been *perceived* to be unfair? Here the evidence is unmistakable. The answer is yes. The first peacetime federal income tax, passed nearly a century ago in 1894, was based in part on the assumption that there was an unfair distribution of income. The fact that all federal income tax systems, without exception, have been at least somewhat progressive in their rate structure indicates that Congress has thought that the wealthy could and should "pay more." If it were widely thought that the present income distribution—or that of 1894—is or was "fair" in some sense, there would not have been even an attempt at progressive income taxation.

If Kristol's aphorism is put under a microscope, it becomes a tautology. If income distribution is regarded as unfair, a free society in which this occurs cannot survive. If a free society *does* survive, it proves that income distribution was fair in the first place.

But this is just another way to state a tautology: If something you claim is caused by maldistribution of income does not happen, then there *is* no maldistribution. It just doesn't wash, Mr. Kristol.

Suppose we change the cataclysmic term "survive" to "remain in about the same form." Then Kristol's statement would say: If the income distribution in a free society is widely perceived as unfair, it cannot stay in the same form.

Now consider the situation in the United States in 1894, when the first peacetime income tax was passed. After the enactment of that law—it did not go into effect until 1913 after a constitutional amendment—American society was no longer the same. In other words, if income distribution is regarded as unfair, a law, tax, or another regulation is automatically passed, and the free society is altered in some way. But this says nothing other than laws reflecting public sentiment are enacted from time to time.

Gilder warns about tampering with income distribution. It could lead to unpleasant problems, even the overthrow of capitalism. But Kristol's statement is that income distribution is self-correcting. If society regards it as unfair, it will be taken care of in due course. The two approaches are contradictory.

Leaving aside any inconsistency between Gilder and the philosophers he quotes, is there validity to his argument? Not really. Perceptions about income distribution in the United States have had their ups and downs over the decades. During the 1920s, very little was written on the subject, as the nation enjoyed the pleasures of the second Gilded Age. That rapidly changed in the 1930s, as the Depression inspired many "baleful" economists to look again at income distribution. Their theories were eventually reflected in income redistribution through taxes and other means.

Whether economists are interested in income distribution or not, society goes on. The catastrophes predicted by Gilder simply do not happen. The economists of the 1930s, poring over tax tables, cannot be accused of upsetting any apple carts. The carts were upset before they came on the scene. The economists of the 1920s who generally ignored income distribution cannot be tagged with producing the Great Depression. Gilder attaches more power to economists than they really have. By studying income distribution, we may be rearranging the apples on the cart and maybe giving a few to hungry people. We certainly could not knock it over, even if we wanted to.

12. *The rich deserve what they have. They are the elite.* (Gilder again.)[14] The rich have demonstrated their sterling qualities, so they *should* own whatever they own.

The thesis might be true if we could agree on who these "elite" are. Is it traceable to intelligence, energy, entrepreneurship, other factors, or some combination of all the preceding? The media often define the elite indirectly as those who are already wealthy or who have high income.

But if the rest of us do that, we are creating yet another tautology: The elite are elite because . . . well, they just *are*.

Are the rich really smarter than the rest of us? Any detailed study is complicated by the fact that no widespread measurement of the IQs of the rich has ever been carried out. The faces of those portrayed in the *Forbes* or *Fortune* list of the wealthiest *seem* intelligent enough. But is it just a trick of the photographer?

All we can say with certainty is that many intelligent people have never had their faces appear in *Forbes'* pages. Einstein, whose IQ was alleged to be over 200, never was in any list of the nation's wealthiest. The same could be said of most scientists, engineers, professors, and others reputed to be highly intelligent.

Are the rich really an elite? Of course they are, if you define an elite as being wealthy. Once we get into the realms of intelligence or other admirable human qualities, the evidence is far from certain.

13. *Mobility into the classes of the wealthy is the key attribute to look for, not what anyone earned in a given year*. This thesis is due to Cowell.[2] In this view, the fact that some are wealthy is accepted as an economic given.

What is objected to is a *perpetuation* of wealth. As long as people can move into the land of the wealthy, then the situation is satisfactory. What is to be avoided is the European model—or at least the pre-World War I version —where movement from the lower or middle class to the upper ones in terms of wealth was close to impossible. We still see that ancient model in working order in some parts of the Third World today.

Exactly how would one measure "mobility," the key to the point being made? If 1% of the top wealth holders are new each year, is this adequate mobility? Or would it take 5% to satisfy the criterion?

We have been assuming that mobility is only upward. But downward mobility also exists. Is the criterion satisfied if 1%, 5%, or any other specific percentage of the wealthy are stricken from the list in a given year? How much downward mobility do we want? Are we assuming that the total number of top wealth holders is more or less fixed, so that new recruits can only fill the place of those who have been cast overboard? Or is the list open-ended, so that new names can enter without having to crowd anyone out?

The word "mobility" implies to some a Horatio Alger story, with a newsboy rising to the top and eventually taking the place of William Randolph Hearst. Is that what we mean by mobility? Suppose someone in a specific year is a few dollars below the ranks of the top wealth holders. The next year, due to good investments, she makes the list. Do we count that as mobility? How many years do we allow for mobility to take place? An oil gusher can produce upward mobility in hours. Others may require more than a generation to get to the top ranks. Do we count these two cases as equal in terms of mobility?

Mobility, especially the upward variety, has been a fundamental goal of American society ever since it began. Yet our calculations in the previous chapter show that, once high income or wealth is attained, it is relatively easy to build and hang onto a fortune, generation after generation. It takes a lot of skill to produce downward mobility from such a lofty pinnacle.

Mobility exists and always will continue to exist. Rockefeller, Ford, Hunt, Getty, Ludwig, and Walton were once just names of ordinary folk. The names and the families were upwardly mobile. But until we know more about what mobility is and how it can be measured, the criterion at the head of this section will remain hollow.

14. *Raising the taxes on the wealthy will encourage even more luxurious living by them*. (Gilder yet again.)[15] The idea is that the wealthy spend a certain portion of their income and wealth on productive investments such as starting new businesses. The rest is presumably spent on luxuries like fast cars and trips to Antarctica.

If taxes on the wealthy were raised according to this thesis, the wealthy would cut back on productive investments, but continue to spend on extravagances. The nation would soon face unemployment and a possible depression. So do not tax the wealthy more than now.

But what is a "luxury?" A large diamond ring may be a nonnecessity to most of us, but a requirement for Elizabeth Taylor. Economists, with few exceptions, do not divide goods and services into luxuries and necessities. There has never been, and never will be, a sharp dividing line between the two.

Some portion of income and wealth of the affluent goes into so-called productive investments, and some into what could be called luxuries. However, the exact proportion between the two is not well known. Furthermore, the production of luxury goods requires investment as well. For the wealthy to have large mansions and Mercedes in the driveway, someone had to invest in the construction industry, architects, and the auto business.

So it is far from clear that changing the proportion between "good" and slightly shady consumption and investment would change society all that much. Since luxury goods are, by definition, a small portion of our gross national product, boosting or decreasing their production somewhat will change GNP little. If Elizabeth Taylor had gotten two—or none—of the fist-sized diamonds that Richard Burton was said to have given her, the world would still have rolled on.

The statement appeals to the prude in many of us. We already regard the wealthy with some suspicion about their sybaritic ways. Too much laughter is coming from the tiled swimming pool. Their redeeming feature is the money they lend to build new factories.

If taxes on the wealthy were to increase, this last saving grace would disappear. The wealthy would become total hedonists, contributing nothing to society. This would be a *bad thing*, according to the upright. Therefore, why take the chance? Better the wealthy should be half selfish, rather than yield to indulgence completely.

While the proposition is appealing to those who want to squelch unnecessary pleasure, there is no evidence anywhere for its validity. If taxes on the wealthy are increased, it is likely that the proportion of money they spend on "wasteful" and "useful" pursuits will remain about the same. Spending solely on luxuries will eventually lead the wealthy to the welfare office, a prospect they probably relish even less than the rest of us.

15. *Do not worry about pre-tax income or wealth; it's what happens after taxes that counts.* We have, with few exceptions, dealt in this book with pre-tax income and wealth. Taxes surely change the distributions. However, the present level of taxation does not change our conclusion about the 3% and 97% distributions, and the cut-off between them.

The statement is accurate, as far as it goes. But it does not tell us what level of taxation to impose, how progressive it should be, or how it can avoid loopholes. Until it does, it will remain only a general description.

16. *Set the maximum income at a fixed ratio to the minimum income.* This concept has been around for decades, if not centuries. One of the most recent proponents has been Herman Daly.[16] He proposes an upper-income limit 20 times a lower-income base.

These schemes at least possess specificity. This has been lacking from most of the criteria we have evaluated above.

Problems still lurk. What would be the minimum income that society would either give or allow to the poorest? Would it be the welfare level now achieved, or would it be higher? Should it be 2080 (the number of working hours in a year) times the minimum wage, $3.35 in 1989?

Questions like this are not simple. Until we get answers, we cannot begin to evaluate the lower limit of income, let alone the upper limit.

Why should the upper limit be 20 times the lower? Is the value based on the number of fingers and toes we have, or is there a more fundamental reason for its choice? We suspect, without any proof, that the truth may lie in the fact that our numbering system is decimal.

Putting a lid on income will lead to economic inefficiency. Highly valued members of society will work to that limit, and then cease their efforts. The extra skills and expertise they could have supplied will be lost. In what we advocate, we set no upper limit on income, merely requiring that the upper 3% distribution conform to the lower 97%. This will preserve the economic efficiency we need for a productive society.

17. *Turn back the clock to 1980, to 1971 to . . .* Whatever the distribution is now, it was better in 1980, 1971, or whenever. Any tax or other measures should turn back the clock to that time.

Those who were not happy with the economic policies of the Reagan years want to go back to the Carter Administration, in terms of income patterns. For example, Mortimer Zuckerman[17] notes that the income of the top 1% of the nation rose by 74% from 1977 to 1988, in constant dollars, but that of the lowest 10% dropped by almost 11% in that interval. Zuckerman holds up the Carter years as better than the Reagan era in terms of income distribution.

Those who want to favor the poorest of the nation might favor turning back time to the late 1960s or early 1970s. Inflation was low by later standards, and employment was full due to the Vietnam buildup. The poor were in as good shape in terms of income distribution as in recent memory.

Conservatives might wish a return to the distribution of 1929, when the top few percent held a concentration of income and wealth not equalled in the six decades since. What else sparked the boom of the 1920s?

All these people and groups can't be right simultaneously. The point of these examples is that, depending on one's individual leanings and sense of history, a "golden" year will be chosen as the one with the optimum distribution. But there can be no rule generally used for choosing that year, so the matter is close to arbitrary. Because it is, the criterion at the head of this section is essentially unworkable.

18. *It does not matter who gets what, as long as minority or disadvantaged groups get a chance at wealth or high income.* In the United States, Jews, Japanese, and other groups, who once had an average income far lower than the majority WASPs, have in some cases caught up and even surpassed them. Is this cause for celebration? Yes. Anytime the tables of history are turned, or even rotated a few degrees, it gives some hope that the mistakes and discrimination of the past will not be repeated forever.

What does this have to do with income distribution? As far as we are concerned, little or nothing. If an Irish Catholic family like the Kennedys makes it above the 3% kink, thereby displacing a WASP who tires of life's rat race and drops below that point, the overall distribution remains the same. We are seeing faces of different colors and minds of different religions above the kink these days, but the shape of the curve remains about the same, year after year.

The fact that the upper 3% is more multihued than it used to be is a cause for celebration in some quarters. According to George Gilder,[18] a new American upper class, "consisting largely of Jews, Italians, Orientals, Germans, and Poles" is forming. As has been said, this is one of those propositions that is more interesting than it is true.[19] A look at the luncheons of the boards of directors of the top dozen or so corporations in the nation would show few eating sukiyaki, matzo ball soup, or lasagna. In any case, it does not change the distribution to have wealth in the hands of Cohen rather than Connally, Walesa rather than Walsh. Someone with enough energy and access to IRS files could make up income graphs for each ethnic group. We believe that the shape for each of the curves would be about the same as for the entire nation.

Even if the ascent of some non-WASPs were a cause for rejoicing, the largest racial minority in the country is still waiting for the doors to open. The black community lags far behind the rest in terms of average income, high income earners, and possessors of wealth.

Consider a few examples.[20] In 1983, about a third of nonwhite families had no liquid assets—savings and checking accounts and so on—*whatever*. Of those that did, their assets were between a third and a quarter that of whites, depending on which statistical measure was taken. Of those nonwhite families that did have liquid assets, half had less than $1,000. Total financial assets, including stocks, bonds, trusts, and the like, were about one-quarter that of whites. It will take many Michael Jacksons to make that up.

19. *Lifetime earnings should be equalized, or at least reduced in inequality.* A good point. The vast majority of data on income and wealth deals with numbers for only one year. If that year were truly representative of all the years in someone's working or earning life, there would be no reason to advocate this criterion.

But life is not quite that regular. Even a highly paid professional can be unemployed due to a company shakeup, or to a temporary physical disability. The uncertainties even extend to the higher ranks. The *Forbes 400* compilation conveniently provides a list of those who have departed its exalted ranks, or who have cleared the hurdle.

Women have by far a more variable income from year to year than men. One season a woman may work in the home. A few years later, having brushed up on some old skills, she may be in a well-paid position.

If we were diligent enough to keep our tax returns since the first one we filed, upon checking them we would almost certainly find variations in income over the years, in addition to those induced by effects of inflation. For some of us, the variations could be big: we took a new job, or lost the old one. For others, they would be small: we either did or did not get a promotion, or suffered a one-time loss.

So the rationale is clear. It is not enough to consider only one year in evaluating income or wealth disparities. We should consider those quantities over an entire lifetime.

Here is another case where principle clashes with practicality. When we referred to all the tax returns you ever filed, you may have gotten a little nervous. If you are like almost everyone else, you did not have enough room in the filing cabinet to hold them all, along with the various receipts and schedules. The less organized among us may not have had a filing cabinet in the first place.

We suppose that the IRS could keep lifetime totals on each taxpayer via their Social Security number. They may already do so. Yet with the public's sensitivity to invasions of privacy, to the best of our knowledge the IRS has never released statistical analyses of lifetime earnings, and they may never do so.

If and when lifetime earning figures are made public, they will likely show about the same shape, kink and all, as the annual curves do now. The slopes may be a littler different and the kink may not be in exactly the same place, but the overall shape will be the same.

Why should this be so? A well-paid missile engineer may be laid off for a few months if Congress cancels her project. But she almost certainly will start again on another missile or weapons systems shortly afterward. If we looked at a graph of her earnings year by year, we would probably see a steadily rising line at a high level, with a few brief drops for unemployment.

Now consider a ghetto dweller, poorly educated and with few if any job skills. He gets some employment from time to time, but usually subsists on unemployment insurance and welfare. Consider his earnings over the years. On a graph, they would be at an almost uniform level, with occasional spikes as he got decent employment.

For most people, earnings curves are fairly constant, allowing for inflation and the fact that experience on the job is often rewarded with higher salaries. So taking one year's income as representative is not too far from the truth. And anything we advocate to reduce income inequality for one year will, in most cases, do the same for lifetime earnings.

There are exceptions to this, of course. Consider the arts. The star of today may be walking the streets tomorrow. For many years, *Newsweek* had a feature entitled, "Where Are They Now?", reflecting in many cases the fall from glory that the famous had suffered. One of the members of the Supremes, the best-known all-female singing group, was found at one time to be receiving welfare.

Those in the arts form only a tiny portion of the population. In this small group, only a few have achieved enough stardom to be later listed, on their way down, in "Where Are They Now?" These rockets of income, rising and falling within a few years, do not strongly affect our conclusions of lifetime vis-à-vis annual income.

We never know lifetime income until death. This may seem so obvious as to be hardly worth mentioning, but it should be. With annual income, we can come to conclusions rapidly. If we evaluated them over a lifetime, we might take decades to decide anything.

People also spend different times on earth. How do we compare the lifetime earnings of a teenager killed in an auto accident with that of a top executive who dies at the age of ninety, after drawing large pensions for a quarter century? There is no rational comparison.

Reducing inequality in lifetime earnings is similar, for most people, to reducing this inequality for year-to-year earnings. The exceptions are not taken into account in the IRS filings we have been using as a data source. We still suffer from the defect that has sunk, or at least capsized, many of the other ethical formulations in this chapter—lack of data.

20. *Income distribution should be accepted by the people*. At first this criterion seems as substantial as a cloud. Since there are no rioting masses protesting income inequality, this implies some degree of acceptance. Yet the fact that most people want more money, or the things it can buy, suggest that few truly accept, in the ordinary sense, what they earn.

We can turn these vague thoughts on what is or is not accepted or acceptable into a specific transaction, at least on paper. The technique is proposed by Jan Tinbergen, the famous economist.[21] We do not know if Dutch, the language in which Tinbergen wrote, has an expression for it, but the system he described may be based in part on the common phrase in English, ''I wouldn't take that job for a million dollars!'' Sometimes the term is applied to a position with tremendous responsibility, like being President, mayor of New York City, or the head of a large corporation. Other times it denotes something inherently risky, like being a professional wrestler, coal miner, space shuttle pilot, or window washer on the World Trade Center.

Tinbergen says that we have some sort of rough justice or equality if I know your work and income, you know mine, and we can make adjustments both ways until the two of us are satisfied. For example, consider yourself in a small room with the chairman of General Motors. He has an income, with assorted bonuses and stock options, of several hundreds of thousands annually, if not millions. We will presume that he works hard for it.

You and he will remain locked in the room until both of you are satisfied with the two annual incomes or salaries. This is a zero-sum game in terms of money, in that the chairman and you can exchange cash until the two of you are ready to leave the room. He cannot leave until you are satisfied, and vice versa.

For purposes of illustration, we will make the reasonable assumption that the chairman makes substantially more than you. He starts the session by telling you of his tremendous work schedule, with reports piling up on his desk. The welfare of hundreds of thousands of employees rests on his shoulders.

''Yes,'' you say, ''but look at the gigantic income you get from that job. It's much bigger than mine. If I had your income, I wouldn't mind having your job.''

The chairman then peels off, from a huge roll, thousand-dollar bills and gives them to you. He keeps doing so until your new annual income, which is your old one *plus* the thousand-dollar bills, is high enough that you would not trade places with him because of all the pressure he undergoes. Before he pulled out his wallet, many of us would have been glad to switch with him because of his enormous paycheck.

Consider a hypothetical example, in which the Chairman has an income of $500,000 annually, and you have one of $50,000. Suppose he piles cash on you until you have an extra $150,000. At that point, he might be interested in trading places with you because you now earn $200,000. This begins to be a substantial amount from his viewpoint. Your interest in his job has diminished somewhat because it now comes with only $350,000.

The amount of money transferred increases until at some point, a deal is struck. The Chairman retains his job, but at a salary lessened by the amount he has added to your income. Your job is much more attractive to him because it now comes with that stack of thousand-dollar bills he has given you. Both of you would now trade jobs and income without hesitation.

What would this do to income distribution? Without actually going through these dramas in miniature—they've never been attempted in practice, to our knowledge—it is impossible to tell.

We can foresee evening out of income in some cases. Suppose Frank G. Wells, the president and chief operating officer of the Walt Disney Company, walked into a room with a derelict. According to a nationally publicized article in the fall of 1989, he earned a profit of $74.2 million in exercising stock options that year, adding to his 1988 salary of $400,000 and a performance bonus of $3.3 million.[22] In this confrontation with the ne'er-do-well, Mr. Wells might transfer part of his salary, stock options, and performance bonus to the other person even if the poor devil did not want any of the money or the responsibility. This might be done out of a sense of charity, not because of an abstruse economic theory. So in cases like these, the top 3%—and Mr. Wells is certainly a part of it—would drop toward the lognormal distribution of the other 97%. Whether they would drop down enough to make the two diverging lines converge would depend on their sense of giving and how clever those beggars *really* are.

Yet if all these uncounted billions of transactions took place, income distribution might not be any flatter than it is right now. It could easily become more uneven. Let us suppose that H. L. Hunt, J. Paul Getty, and other legendary oilionaires were as convincing as stories say they were. When you went into the room with them you might emerge clad only in your underwear, but at the same time pleased with the opportunity to contribute your income to these hard-working gentlemen.

Tinbergen's proposal, while seemingly valid on paper, turns out to be one of those pipedreams that occasionally float through economics texts. Extend his concept to an apartment building, and we are talking about an enormous number of sessions, one on one. So large, in fact, that very little other business could get done. Everyone would spend their time negotiating, and the money that theoretically would be passed back and forth would never be earned in the first place.

And all of this would be based on perfect rationality between the pairs that entered the little rooms. Unfortunately, this type of rationality is not very common. What is needed, as the economist Jan Pen[1] points out, is millions of little Tinbergens.

We have spent considerable time on Professor Tinbergen's idea partly because he is one of the greatest economists of our time. It describes one of the few mechanisms which can theoretically determine income distribution in a "fair" way, satisfactory to everyone.

Two other major methods of setting incomes are of course the market— letting economic forces work their will—and government intervention by means of taxes or other mechanisms. While Tinbergen's one-on-one negotiation is in principle different from and superior to these two major systems, in practice it is simply unworkable. Back to the economic drawing board.

SUMMARY

We have considered philosophical and economic theories and sayings, bearing in some way on income and wealth distribution and redistribution. On the face of it, many of these statements make some sense. When we analyze them more closely, we find ourselves in a disappointing weather forecast: considerable cloudiness. Although many purport to tell us how income and wealth should be distributed, in reality they offer very few precise guidelines.

An analogy could be drawn with the federal legislative process. At the beginning of most laws are "findings" by Congress: There are too many homeless, AIDS is a dangerous disease, people are starving in Africa, and so on. These findings are usually general and noncontroversial.

After the findings at the start of a bill, Congress gets more specific. So many millions are allocated to the homeless or starvation victims in Africa, a research program for conquering AIDS is proposed, and so on.

Yet in spite of the complexity of many federal laws, it is often found that the directions given have been too nebulous. This vagueness is then cured by regulations published in the *Federal Register*. This official publication contains tens of thousands of tightly typed pages each year.

Leaving aside questions about the overall efficiency of the federal legal system, we see three levels of detail: findings, laws, and regulations. The criteria for distribution we have considered are analogous to legislative findings—general in nature, and in some cases noncontroversial.

But in order for a broad thought of Congress to be translated into an action that affects us, it has to get down to the regulation stage. This is where most, if not all, of the criteria fail.

In this book, we are somewhere between the law and regulation, continuing this legislative analogy. We have been specific why we have come to the conclusions that we do. Our final line is buttressed by the graphs—not simple ones, admittedly—we have drawn and the tables we have compiled. As such, we are on much firmer and supportable ground than the above twenty criteria.

This does not mean that the criteria should be abandoned. Many contain a grain of truth, if only a grain. But if they are to be put into effect, to paraphrase an old statement of the late Senator Hubert Humphrey, they must get out of the clouds of obscurity and walk forthrightly in the sunshine of arithmetic.

7

WHO ARE THE RICH?

It is tempting, in any book about great wealth, to list a long series of anecdotes and stories about the affluent. Certainly there are far more stories about them *per capita* than there are about poor people.

We have refrained from doing so until this point. This is not because we are unconcerned about the wealthy as people. They are undoubtedly as interesting as any other group. Many would claim that they are more so, because their money has allowed them to do things that the rest of us cannot.

But our object in this book is not to pass judgment on who is interesting and who is not. Rather, we estimate how rich is too rich. This transcends the question of how clever, famous, sincere, charming, or friendly the rich have been, are, or could be.

THE RICH TALK ABOUT A CUT-OFF POINT

In the rest of this book, we give our opinion of how rich is too rich and how a cut-off point might be chosen. But the rich have their own opinions. They naturally are less analytic, so their estimates of what constitutes true wealth vary all over the map.

The thoughts of the affluent on the position of the cut-off point or line tend to be collected in anecdotes and sayings, rather than graphs or tables. Thorndike[1] collected many. One of the most celebrated is attributed to Gene Fowler, a newspaper columnist of the 1920s. He supposedly overheard Henry Ford talking to William Randolph Hearst, the newspaper magnate:

> "Mr. Hearst, have you got any money?"
> "I never have any money, Mr. Ford. I always spend any money that I am to receive before I get it."

"That's a darned shame, Mr. Hearst. You ought to get yourself two or three hundred million dollars together and tuck it away."

This alleged conversation so tickled readers that it has been reprinted in dozens of anthologies and stories on the rich. But it is unlikely to have taken place, at least in the form described.

Hearst was a wealthy man most of his life. It is true that he spent more money publicly than most of the wealthy, most notably on his world-famous mansion in California, San Simeon. But many other wealthy people spent at an even *faster* rate than he did. The difference between them and Hearst was that their purchases and expenditures did not get into the tabloids. The statement that Hearst was alleged to have made was in agreement with public perception of him at the time, which makes it suspicious. What the public thinks about rich people often does not accord with reality.

By the time of the story, sometime in the 1920s, Ford had accumulated between $600 million and $1 billion.[2] He was one of the richest men in the nation, if not the world, and clearly had more money than Hearst. Thus it would have been reasonable for Ford to pick a figure or range of figures well below his own accumulation for Hearst to shoot at.

If the conversation was held exactly as reported, was the level of $200 to $300 million for achieving a reasonable degree of wealth appropriate? According to Lundberg,[2] around the time of the conversation only eleven families (or groups of associates) had a total wealth above the $200 million level. The number of *individuals* who had wealth above that level is difficult to determine. It probably was within a factor of two, up or down, of the number eleven. That is, a case can be made that the individuals over the $200 million level in the United States in the 1920s numbered between five and twenty-two.

So if the story was accurate, Ford was almost certainly picking dollar values out of the air. If he had close to $1 billion, something like a quarter of that amount might have seemed like a plateau where "real" wealth began.

But there is no theoretical basis for Ford's alleged estimate, other than the fact that Hearst was talking to Ford. If the newspaper tycoon had held exactly the same conversation with John D. Rockefeller or Andrew Mellon, he might have suggested a much larger number for him to "tuck away." If he had been chatting with Bernard Baruch or Julius Rosenwald (a major stockholder in Sears, Roebuck), with fortunes of the order of $30 million, he probably would have been quoted a much smaller figure. A judgment about how rich is too rich, or where the cut-off point of wealth exists, cannot be made on the basis of who William Randolph Hearst ran into at a dinner party.

OTHER ESTIMATES OF "RICHNESS"

If we take the Hearst-Ford conversation at face value, then what Andrew Carnegie was alleged to have said at J. P. Morgan's death makes some sense. The financier's estate was valued at $68 million, excluding his art collection, later valued at around $50 million. Recalling Morgan's enormous influence in the financial corridors of power, Carnegie was reputed to have said, "And to think, he was not a rich man!"

By this criterion, $60 or $70 million at the time was "not rich." Again, this is because it was Andrew Carnegie, with a fortune of perhaps $400 to $500 million, speaking. To the vast majority of Americans, J. P. Morgan was the word "rich" personified.

The H. L. Hunt Standard

Other wealthy people have had different attitudes. In the 1950s, H. L. Hunt, allegedly the richest man in the world at that time, was supposed to have said, "A man who has $200,000 is about as well off, for all practical purposes, as I am."

Note that we use the word "allegedly" in describing Hunt. The most affluent are rarely in the habit of giving newspaper interviews or writing articles for the public. To our knowledge, of the many estimates of wealth made in the annual *Forbes* or *Fortune* compilations, few if any came directly from the wealth holders' accountants. All the other estimates are made by financial journalists, as best they can.

Because of the fog surrounding both what the wealthy say and the size of their wealth, almost all the words attributed to Hunt have a mysterious and unverifiable background.

We presume that Hunt was referring to wealth and not income, although the context is not clear. If he indeed was talking about income, his comment would have made some sense. Even in the late 1980s, an annual income of $200,000 would have put a recipient in the top ½%, or one out of 200, of the population. In the 1950s, when Hunt was supposed to have spoken, an income of that size would likely be that of someone in the top one in a thousand.

If Hunt were referring to wealth, that would have been another matter entirely. By 1962, shortly after the date of the Hunt quotation, the top 1% of the population (1.87 million people) had a net worth of about $487 billion.[3] This then is an average net worth of about $260,000.

Then about two million people, according to Hunt, were "about as well off" as he was. Were they? The true size of Hunt's fortune was one of the best-kept secrets in the financial world, although he sometimes presented himself as the world's richest man. Observers said it was of the order of hundreds of millions, if not billions.

Were the two million or so Americans truly as well-off as Hunt? On a strictly financial accounting, obviously not. But if Hunt lived simply, not building real-life castles in the sky as Hearst did, he may have felt as well off as two million of his fellow citizens.

Hunt apparently lived fairly frugally. According to stories he may have planted himself, he supposedly brought his lunch to work in a brown paper bag. One claim is that when he came to Washington for a Congressional hearing, he parked blocks away from Capitol Hill to avoid paying for parking. Some of this may be the stuff of press agentry. Many suspect that Hunt himself concocted these stories to develop a public *persona*. Certainly he had definite, forceful, and highly conservative views on public policy. An image of riotous living and wasteful spending would have made his views less acceptable to the public.

In any case, how H. L. Hunt felt about his wealth and relative standing in the company of the wealthy is ultimately irrelevant to the question of how rich is too rich. He may have thought that a fortune of about $200,000 could enable someone to be about as well-off as he was. There is some truth to this. A car can be only so long; a house only so big.

But with his excess over the $200,000 level, Hunt was able to do things that the other two million Americans supposedly about "as well-off" as he was could never do. Hunt was able to buy and sell enormous oil properties. He could, and did, propagandize his political views—with little success—over hundreds of radio stations. Very few of the other two million with accumulated wealth over the $200,000 level could do those things.

Who Did You Speak to Last?

In terms of the rich themselves, how rich is too rich apparently depends on who you last talked to. Henry Ford seemed to believe that one becomes reasonably rich at the $200 to $300 million level. H. L. Hunt thought that it could be done for perhaps one-thousandth of that amount, at $200,000. Andrew Carnegie's story doesn't specify a figure, but the implication is that the cut-off point is somewhere above $68 million.

All of these stories, numbers, and personalities have one factor in common: nobody knows. For all their skill in accumulating wealth and ability to manipulate numbers, these gentlemen, and the protagonists of many other similar stories, have clearly not devoted too much thought to how rich is too rich.

If they did spend any time on the subject, their conclusions were highly changeable, depending on their mood and circumstances. In 1868, Andrew Carnegie[4] wrote (we have retained his punctuation):

> Thirty three and an income of 50,000$ per annum. By this time two years I can so arrange all my business so as to secure at least 50,000 per annum. Beyond this never earn—make no effort to increase fortune, but spend the surplus each year for benoevelent [sic] purposes. Cast aside business forever except for others.

An income of $50,000 in the early 1990s would have been only enough to put someone in the middle class. Shortly after the end of the Civil War, it would have put the young Carnegie into the equivalent of the $500,000 and up bracket, that is, near the very tip of the income pyramid.

Yet that was not enough. As Thorndike[4] writes, "During the next thirty years, he went on to build the world's greatest steel company and to make a fortune that by the end of the century was probably second only to that of John D. Rockefeller."

Carnegie's views on what was a reasonable level of income and wealth obviously changed. We do not fault him for this. Depending on the context, the attitudes of the wealthy alter on what level real wealth begins.

Only by an analytic process, along the lines we have suggested, can the question truly be answered. We do not claim that our approach is the only conceivable one. Rather, relying on what the wealthy may have said from time to time leads to contradictions and a logical dead end.

A BRIEF HISTORY—THE MIDDLE AGES

"How rich is too rich?" and "How many people should be rich?" are questions that have persisted through history. We have already dealt with what has been said about them in the past, but only in a general way. Now we will reconsider these and related questions from a much more specific viewpoint. In so doing, we should remember the cautionary note of Jan Pen[5]: "Not a single theory has so far succeeded in sorting out exactly how the high incomes come about." In other words, what follows—in line with most economic histories—is a description of *what* happened, rather than *why* it happened.

Let us go back to the sixteenth century. Braudel,[6] in his masterly economic story of Europe between the fifteenth and eighteenth century, rarely discusses the distribution of wealth in a quantitative way, saying only that it was uneven. But he spends considerable time evaluating the distribution of power.

Claudio Tolomei,[7] from Siena, Italy, wrote in 1531:

> In every republic, even a great one, in every state, even a popular one, it is unusual for more than fifty citizens to rise to the posts of command. Neither in ancient Athens nor in Rome, neither in Venice nor in Lucca, are any citizens called to govern the state . . . although these states govern themselves under the name of Republic."

In sixteenth century Venice, the nobility numbered perhaps 5% of the population. In Genoa, the corresponding nobility numbered about 700 out of about 80,000 citizens. With families, this was about 4% of the total. Braudel notes that this proportion was high compared to other cities in the Middle Ages. In Nuremberg, power was restricted to perhaps 150 to 200 people out of a total of 40,000 in the region. This corresponds to 0.5%, or one out of 200, in the ruling group. Braudel shows a painting of the assembly room of the Nuremberg Town Hall in the Middle Ages, an impressive chamber with a painted ceiling. The nobles of the town are shown dancing with their wives. They are almost lost in the room's vast spaces. Braudel sardonically observes that the room "is not exactly over-crowded."

How did someone get into that tiny group? Braudel[8] says,

> [O]ne condition towered above all the others: A good start in life. Men who rose from rags to riches were as rare in the past as they are today. And the recipe given by Claude Carriere, writing about 15th century Barcelona— 'The best way to make money in big business . . . [was] to have some to start with' applies to every period in history.

Another account[9] had early seventeenth-century London, around the time of Shakespeare, ruled by fewer than 100 wealthy merchants. In the Netherlands around the same time, the aristocracy was about 10,000 out of a population of perhaps two million, or about 0.5%.[10] In Lyons, Le Mans, Antwerp, and a host of other towns, municipalities, states, regions, provinces, republics, and areas not enumerated by Braudel, the situation was about the same. Sometimes the small group held power because of wealth, and sometimes because of being in a noble class. Frequently the two were combined.

MONEY AND WEALTH IN THE MIDDLE AGES

The research done by Braudel and others is useful, but does not really address the question of wealth distribution. Some of the aristocracy mentioned above undoubtedly had high incomes and wealth; others may have lacked one or the other.

At first glance, reconstructing past incomes and wealth appears hopeless. How can we determine who was rich in the mists of history? Today we have W-2s, 1040s, and computers to calculate and digest numbers. Many transactions long ago were carried out by barter, not cash. Even if past scribes wrote down the numbers, the slips of paper or parchment have long been lost, or so we imagine.

Fifteenth-Century England

But there *are* some numbers available, giving us a picture of income distribution long ago. Return now to the year 1436 in England, two generations before Columbus.[11] Table 7.1 shows annual incomes for the top classes at the time. The groups considered—a collection of major landowners and lesser gentlemen—numbered only about 7,000 out of a population of millions.

The annual income, by today's standards, is low. Much commerce in those days was by barter, so little gold and silver changed hands. The low incomes are also a testament to the inflation of the last five centuries. Five pounds today would not buy a meal at many English restaurants, let alone provide an annual income for a gentleman's family.

The table shows a distribution of sorts, although for only a small part of the populace. If we plotted the numbers on probability graph paper, and took the logarithms of the money amounts, we would get close to a straight line. This means that the incomes are lognormally distributed. However, we do not see the kink we have come to expect. There very well may have been one in fifteenth-century England. The numbers are confined to such a tiny portion of the population that it does not show up graphically.

The Seventeenth Century

Turn ahead two-and-a-half centuries, to the Glorious Revolution of 1688. England has been racked by religious strife for well over a century. It is about to put an end to it by calling in a Dutch Protestant prince to replace a Catholic king. As James II, the last of the Stuarts, flees the country, data are being gathered on most, if not all, of the nation. It will later be summarized by Gregory King.[12] The descriptions of the population classes are often so delicious that we have reproduced them in their entirety.

The 1688 data shown in Table 7.2 have far more classes than that of 1436, partly due to the differentiation of society since that time. Some

Table 7.1
English Family Income in 1436[11]

Class	Families in Class	Annual Income (pounds)
Barons	51	865
Knights	183	208
Lesser knights	750	60
Esquires (three classes)		
gentlemen	1,200	24
merchants	1,600	12
Artisans, etc.	3,400	5 - 9

Table 7.2
English Family Income in 1688[11]

Families in class	Class	Family Yearly Income (in pounds)
160	Temporal lords	3,200
26	Spiritual lords	1,300
800	Baronets	880
600	Knights	650
3,000	Esquires	450
12,000	Gentlemen	280
5,000	Persons in greater offices and places	240
5,000	Persons in lesser offices and places	120
2,000	Eminent merchants and traders by sea	400
8,000	Lesser merchants and traders by sea	198
10,000	Persons in the law	154
2,000	Eminent clergymen	72
8,000	Lesser clergymen	50
40,000	Freeholders of the better sort	91
120,000	Freeholders of the lesser sort	55
150,000	Farmers	42½
15,000	Persons in liberal arts and sciences	60
60,000	Shopkeepers and tradesmen	45
50,000	Artisans and handicrafts	38
5,000	Naval officers	80
4,000	Military officers	60
35,000	Common soldiers	14
50,000	Common seamen	20
364,000	Laboring people and out-servants	15
400,000	Cottagers and paupers	6½
30,000 (persons)	Vagrants, beggars, gypsies, thieves and prostitutes	2 (per head)

remain the same—baronets (called barons in 1436) and knights (combining knights and "lesser knights" of 1436). But all the millions not tabulated in 1436 now appear in 1688—farmers, military officers, seamen, merchants, clergymen, and so on. Even what the popular song called "gypsies, tramps, and thieves" appear on the bottom line, although their income is traditionally difficult to estimate. At that time they supposedly earned about two pounds a year, the lowest of all the classes enumerated.

The highest income in 1688 (3,200 pounds) was about four times the peak in 1436 (865 pounds). Part of this is due to intervening inflation. There is also more cash in the economy, as barter gradually faded away.

We will make no effort to define the exact meaning of the descriptions in the table: persons in greater or lesser offices, freeholders of the better or lower sort. Obviously the statistician who prepared the table engaged in a number of moral judgments. Some of the terms, such as soldier or seaman, have come down to us almost unchanged. Others, such as "persons in the liberal arts and sciences," meant something different three centuries ago than it does today. The total number of families, not counting the vagrants and beggar class, is about 1.3 million. This probably encompassed most of the English. So if we plot this information on probability graph paper, we are including by far the largest proportion of Englishmen and women of the late seventeenth century.

The Kink Appears

We *do* find a kink in the graph (not shown) at the 0.02% level. This is in the lofty realm of what were known as the lords spiritual and temporal, roughly corresponding to the House of Lords. Even though there was vast inequality—baronets received about 135 times more than cottagers—incomes followed roughly a lognormal distribution. It was only at the doorstep to the House of Lords that the Pareto distribution began.

In modern times, the kink between the two distributions is usually between 1% and 5% of the nation. Regardless of the reasons why the kink was so close to the top of the income pyramid in 1688, it *did* exist three centuries ago.

U.S. WEALTH DISTRIBUTIONS

Now let us turn to the United States. Information on the prerevolutionary era is scattered at best. But by the time shots rang out at Concord, conditions were radically different from those in Europe:[13]

> Visiting contemporary observers were unanimous in describing colonial America as a utopian middle class democracy, where economic opportunities were abundant and egalitarian distributions the rule. After his 1764 visit to Boston, Lord Adam Gordon remarked: 'The levelling principle here, everywhere operates strongly and takes the lead, and everybody has property here, and everybody knows it.' A French writer . . . viewed Boston in 1788 and 'saw none of those livid, ragged wretches that one sees in Europe . . . ' Of colonial Philadelphia, visitors pronounced that 'this is the best poor man's country in the world.'

So much for the word pictures. If Braudel and others are correct, in addition to these glowing scenes of economic opportunity and lack of poverty, there should have been an elite of some type. This elite should, in turn, have been reflected in income distributions. Was it?

As far as we know, there was no income data gathered at the time of the young republic. The first income tax was passed as a Civil War measure in 1862. Until then, there was no legal requirement to state your income to any official. However, in 1798, about a decade after the new government got started, the Secretary of the Treasury, Oliver Wolcott, instituted a direct tax on real estate. Nowadays that type of tax is confined to states and their subdivisions. But it provided much-needed income to the new republic. It also generated data on the more than one million free adult males.[14]

We have already shown the resulting graph in previous chapters. Part of it confirms the observations of foreign travellers in the revolutionary era. Yet most of these observers thought that Americans had about the same level of possessions. The graph, showing wealth, clearly contradicts this. Of the 1.7 million adult males—any wealth owned by females at the time apparently was not counted—about 1.2 million had real estate worth less than $200. About 130 men had valuations of more than $50,000, an enormous sum in those days.

The foreign observers were right on one point. The graph in Chapter 2 has little or no kink between two distributions. There are clearly some who are much wealthier than the masses, but we do not see an elite whose wealth distribution rises more sharply than the lognormal or Gibrat distribution.

The numbers were based on real estate, not cash, factories, stock, or other belongings. Most of eighteenth-century wealth was concentrated in land, so leaving out other forms of wealth does not affect the results too much. For example, George Washington was one of the richest men of his day. He owned no factories. Almost all of his wealth was in land—and slaves.

Mid-Nineteenth-Century America

Fifty years later, things had changed. Moses Yale Beach, owner of the *New York Sun*, compiled a list of wealthy people.[15] His 1845 numbers differed from the 1798 information in three ways. First, they were not based on any government tax or census. They were similar to the annual *Forbes* list.

Second, Beach considered only the wealthiest people, as does this modern magazine. He does not show the level of wealth from the richest to the poorest, so we cannot tell if a kink in the wealth distribution had formed in the five previous decades. Third, the list applies only to New York City, not the entire country. Some of the largest fortunes in the nation were there, but there were wealthy men in Boston, Philadelphia, and other places.

Perhaps the most striking aspect of Beach's list (not reproduced here) is the size of the fortunes he details. In 1798, the largest fortune was around $300,000, for the entire nation. By 1845, in New York City alone, John Jacob Astor headed the list with $25 million. The estate of Steven van Rensselaer, an old Dutch landowner, came next at around $10 million. Beach described its source: "One son owns Albany county, and the other Van Rensselaer county."

The quarter millionaires of the turn of the century had been replaced by multimillionaires. Astor, who had started as a furrier, soon abandoned that odiferous profession for real estate. Van Rensselaer also had the bulk of his holdings in land.

De Tocqueville had noted the growing inequality in America[16]:

> I am of the opinion . . . that the harshest manufacturing aristocracy which is growing up under our eyes is one of the harshest that ever existed. . . . The friends of democracy should keep their eyes anxiously fixed in this direction; for if a permanent inequality of conditions and aristocracy . . . penetrates into [America], it may be predicted that this is the gate by which they will enter.

THE CIVIL WAR AND AFTER

In most history books, the great explosion of U.S. fortunes happened after the Civil War. Referred to as the "Gilded Age" by Mark Twain, it was when fortunes were made on a a scale unprecedented in the nation's history.

Not so, according to some academic historians. The kink between the lognormal and Pareto distributions had already appeared by 1860.[14] This means that the elite, almost nonexistent in 1798, had shown up even before the Civil War broke out. Americans had read de Tocqueville assiduously, but paid little attention to his warning about aristocracy.

By the 1890s, the fortunes made after the Civil War were being consolidated. The general attitude found voice in preachers and ministers. The Reverend Russell Conwell of Philadelphia went around the country delivering his lecture on "Acres of Diamonds." In it, he said:

> Money is power. Every good man and woman ought to strive for money, to do good with it when obtained. Tens of thousands of men and women get rich honestly. But they are often accused by an envious, lazy crowd of unsuccessful persons of being dishonest and oppressive. I say: Get rich, get rich! But get money honestly, or it will be a withering curse.

William Lawrence, the Episcopal Bishop of Massachusetts, had this to add: "[I]t is only to the man of morality that wealth comes . . . Material prosperity is helping to make the national character sweeter, more joyous, more Christlike. . . . Godliness is in league with riches."[17]

We will refrain from comment, not being cruel by nature.

The Gay Nineties

In 1892, the *New York Tribune*[18] published a list of 4,047 American millionaires (i.e., those possessing a net worth of $1 million or more). This was by far the most comprehensive list published till then. Because it was produced by a newspaper and not a government bureau, it suffered from the same defects as lists published by *Forbes* and *Fortune* a century later.

Some of the 1892 results are shown in Table 7.3. Rather than a detailed analysis, we focus on one aspect: How *nouveau* were the *nouveau riche* of the day? We have pointed out at various points that much of today's top fortunes are inherited. But in 1892, things were different. The proportion of newly rich was about 82%.

While the exact amount that each of the millionaires listed in the table owned may never be known, the overall results make economic and historical sense. By 1892, the United States had completed one of the largest national expansions in the history of the world. (The depression of 1893 loomed on the horizon.)

Much of the wealth created since the Civil War had gone into private fortunes. It was then logical that most of the millionaires in 1892 had made acquaintance with their money fairly recently. For some locations, such as Chicago, almost all—98%—of the millionaires were new to the block. Again, this fits history. A generation before 1892, Chicago was a relatively small city, with little of the manufacturing and financial clout it later acquired.

By 1892, the United States had spread from sea to sea. It was a far different country from 1845, the year of the *New York Sun* survey. But almost 60% of millionaires were concentrated in only three cities: New York, Philadelphia, and Boston.

ESTATE AND INCOME TAXES ARRIVE

Debate on whether an income tax should be imposed filled about two decades before it was accomplished by constitutional amendment in 1913. Before the law went into effect, Congress gathered data on the top wealth holders of the day.[19] Some of the results are reproduced in Table 7.4.

The founder of the Rockefeller clan, John D., heads the list. Carnegie, the steel magnate whose dreams we described earlier, comes in second. Another Rockefeller, William, is in third place. But fourth place goes not to a living human, but to an estate. Marshall Field, the Chicago department

Table 7.3
The Nouveau Riche in 1892[18]

City or State	Millionaires	Nouveau Riche	Inheritors	% Nouveau Riche
New York State				
New York City	1,103	763	340	69
Rest of state	405	324	81	80
New Jersey	123	81	43	65
Boston	217	172	45	79
Philadelphia	209	175	34	84
Chicago	316	309	7	98
Rest of U.S.	1,673	1,497	176	89
Total	4,047	3,321	726	82

Table 7.4
Top Wealth-Holders in 1913[18]

Name	Wealth, in $ millions
John D. Rockefeller	500
Andrew Carnegie	300
William Rockefeller	200
Estate of Marshall Field	120
George F. Baker	100
Henry Phipps	100
Henry C. Frick	100
William A. Clark	80
Estate of J. P. Morgan	75
Estate of E. H. Harriman	68
Estate of Russell Sage	64
W. K. Vanderbilt	50
Estate of John S. Kennedy	65
Estate of John J. Astor	70
W. W. Astor	70
J. J. Hill	70
Isaac Stephenson	74
Estate of Jay Gould	70

store founder, found a way to pass on his wealth without dividing it—at least for a time. The business of setting up trusts to prevent estates from being broken up was burgeoning.

George F. Baker of First National Bank comes next, with about $100 million. Two partners of Andrew Carnegie—Henry Phipps and Henry C. Frick—follow. J. P. Morgan's trust is on the list. The Vanderbilts, for many the epitome of wealth, also appear.

The leaders of 1845, the Astors, also show up, but they are far behind the Rockefellers. The enormous fortunes that can be made from oil have far outstripped the money from real estate, the Astors' favorite investment. Three-quarters of a century later, oil is still the way to mind-boggling wealth. The two richest men in the world according to a recent survey, King Fahd of Saudi Arabia and the Sultan of Brunei, have made their fortunes exclusively from petroleum.

Even though the list was compiled about eight decades ago, some of the names still have resonance. The Harriman clan was personified for a long time by Averell, adviser to many Presidents and Ambassador to the Soviet Union. The Jay Gould trust commemorates one of the classic robber barons of the Gilded Age. And J. J. Hill is still remembered in the Northwest as one of the great railroad builders of his age.

Some names have yet to appear on this wealth list—Henry Ford, for one. The original list went on down to $25 million, but he still did not make it. His turn would come.

The *Forbes 400* and *Fortune* lists of the early 1980s had a cut-off point of around $100 million. By that criterion, only about seven of the 1913 wealth holders would make it to modern lists.

AMERICAN INCOMES

All the information we have compiled on the United States so far has been about wealth. But where there is wealth, there is income. Table 7.5[20] shows the top *incomes* in 1918, the fifth year the income tax was in effect. Those shown in the table constitute a tiny elite, being about 380,000 taxpayers from a total population of about 100 million. In those days, only the top income earners paid income tax. In our day, perhaps 80% to 90% of income earners, depending on the exemptions in a given year, pay at least some tax.

Because the 1918 group was so small, we cannot use it to determine if there is a kink between two income distributions. That type of analysis had to wait until more recent times.

A curious feature about the table is that it has two categories for those earning above $1 million annually: $1 million to $5 million, and above $5 million. A total of 206 taxpayers fell into these two rarefied brackets. In recent years, the IRS has condensed these two classifications into one: $1 million or over. This is in spite of the fact that the number of income millionaires has risen from 206 in 1918 to 36,300 in 1987.

The year 1918 was the final year of World War I. Many people had made gigantic fortunes in supplying war equipment to the military. Once the war was over, military orders dried up. The number of millionaires dropped from 206 to 33 by 1920, only two years later.[21]

Their number rose to perhaps 100 in the late 1920s, the height of the golden boom. The Great Depression drove the number down again to a low at the end of the 1930s. Few of those in the fabled *New Yorker* cartoon who were "going to hiss Roosevelt at the Trans-Lux" were millionaires.

Table 7.5
U.S. Income in 1918, Based on Tax Returns[20]

Annual Income, $	Number in Class
3,000 - 4,000	85,100
4,000 - 5,000	72,000
5,000 - 10,000	150,000
10,000 - 25,000	30,900
25,000 - 50,000	23,700
50,000 - 100,000	10,500
100,000 - 200,000	4,180
200,000 - 300,000	1,153
300,000 - 1 million	1,085
1 million - 5 million	196
More than 5 million	10

SHOCK AND HORROR IN THE *NEW YORK TIMES*

Imagine that you are a high-income earner in early September, 1925. The Presidential campaign of the previous year was finally receding into memory. The Democrats had battled themselves into exhaustion in the fight between William McAdoo and Al Smith for the Presidential nomination. As Frederick Lewis Allen wrote[22]:

> So much emotional energy had been expended by the Westerners in hating the Tammany Catholic, Smith, and by the Tammanyites in singing 'The Sidewalks of New York' that the Democratic party never really collected themselves and the unimpassioned Calvin [Coolidge] with his quiet insistence upon economy and tax reduction and his knack for making himself appear the personal embodiment of prosperity was carried into office by a vast majority.

And in case President Coolidge had a fit of absent-mindedness and wandered off the reservation, there was his Secretary of the Treasury, Andrew Mellon. He was already being hailed as the "greatest Secretary since Alexander Hamilton." The two would make the world safe for those with drive, initiative, and financial skill.

Do Not Open that Newspaper!

Imagine, then, your shock and horror as you start reading the *New York Times* on that warm September 1, 1925. There, in black and white, is your name—along with many others—listing your income and the federal tax you paid last year. You just about choke on your coffee as you splutter over this massive invasion of your privacy. True, there are other names there—you did not know that Henry Ford paid about $2.6 million in taxes in 1924—but your own name seems to glow on the page, as if it were written in neon.

A direct call to Andy must be made right after breakfast, along with a telegram. Those damn fool Bolsheviks on Capitol Hill must be stopped before this happened again. This is precisely what took place. As Lundberg[23] wrote:

> The legislation enabling the publication of the figures even in jumbled form was understandably very unpopular with the rich, who were able to get it repealed before the 1925 figures were issued; public opinion would be greatly embittered, to be sure, if the monotonous yearly recurrence of stupendous individual revenues would be observed.

In the over six decades since the income tax returns of the wealthiest were splashed over the newspapers, it has never been repeated. This has been in spite of supposedly more openness in government, Freedom of Information Acts, and a host of other measures designed to feed government information to its citizens. The door was opened a crack in 1925, and almost immediately afterward shut tight.

It is true that we can occasionally peer through a keyhole. When a wealthy man or woman gets involved in a lawsuit, from time to time tax forms are made part of the public record. We mentioned Mortimer Zuckerman, the real estate magnate who paid no federal income taxes, earlier. He was one of those in that unfortunate position. The world learned about Michael Milken's $550 million annual compensation through yet another lawsuit. The sons of H. L. Hunt, the late oil baron, have been party to so many lawsuits and Security and Exchange Commission filings in the last decade or two that much of their sources of former wealth is in public print. Finally, those running for President (and sometimes Governors of larger states) often make their tax returns available to the press. This is a custom, though, and not required by law.

Jack Kent Cooke and Child Support

These cases are the exception, not the rule. For example, consider a lawsuit that unfolded near Washington, D.C., in early 1990. Jack Kent Cooke, the owner of the football Washington Redskins and possessor of a large fortune, was being sued by a former wife. The battle was over child support for a baby he had fathered during the marriage. In many child support cases, the father has to produce income tax returns to the court, so it can determine how much he can pay. But if any motions to this effect were made in the Cooke case, they did not get very far. His assets remained a secret. Wealthy people can generally keep their tax returns and listing of assets out of the public domain.

What did the open door in 1925 reveal? We show some partial results in Table 7.6. The second column shows the actual taxes paid in 1924 by the individuals listed on the left.[24] These are the only amounts about which we are sure.

If we compare the listing of the top tax payers in 1924 to the top wealth holders in 1913, as shown in Table 7.4, we see some familiar names. A Rockefeller heads the list in 1924, but it is not the same one as in 1913.

There are probably reasons why the elder of the Rockefeller clan, John D., Sr., did not appear on the 1924 list. He lived till 1937, so at least he had the possibility of showing up. There were a total of twenty-one Rockefellers in the lists prepared by the Bureau of Internal Revenue (predecessor to the IRS) and printed in the *Times*, with a total income of $7.3 million. Thus about $1 million in taxes were paid by the twenty Rockefellers other than John D., Sr.

Table 7.6
Top Income Taxpayers in 1924[24]

Name	Taxes Paid (thousands)	Estimated Family Fortune (millions)
John D. Rockefeller, Jr.	$6,278	$1,077
Henry Ford	2,609	660
Edsel Ford	2,158	660
Andrew W. Mellon	1,883	450
Payne Whitney	1.677	322
Edward B. Harkness	1,532	450
R. B. Mellon	1,181	450
Anna R. Harkness	1,062	450
Mrs. H. E. Dodge	993	
Wm. Wrigley, Jr.	837	
Frederick W. Vanderbilt	793	360
George F. Baker	792	210
Thomas F. Ryan	792	108
George F. Baker, Jr.	783	210
Edward J. Berwind	722	150
Vincent Astor	643	114
James B. Duke	641	156
Cyrus H. K. Curtis	584	174
J. P. Morgan	574	728
Claude H. Foster	570	106

The main difference between the 1913 and 1924 lists is the appearance of Henry Ford and his son, Edsel, in the latter compilation. They now ranked second and third. Andrew Carnegie, second on the 1913 list, had passed away. Before his death, he had given away almost all of his fortune.

Andrew Mellon, the Secretary of the Treasury, appeared fourth on the list of 1924 taxpayers. If the fact that the head of the Bureau of Internal Revenue reported to Mr. Mellon implied any leniency to the latter in terms of taxes, there is no hint of it in the record. In fact, the Mellon family as a whole paid more of their income in taxes than many others on the list.

Some of the names in the 1924 list were not familiar to many in the contemporary audience, and are even less so today. The Harknesses and Whitneys owed much of their wealth to the original Standard Oil group set up by John D. Rockefeller. This group was probably the biggest money-making organization in the history of the United States, and perhaps of the world. One estimate[25] is that the wealth owned by the Rockefellers was a quarter of that generated by Standard Oil.

New names, generated by the 1920s boom, appear on the 1924 list. The Dodge car-making family and Wrigley of the gum-making empire still, to this day, are recognizable to most Americans. But some of the old names—almost hallowed by time at that point—also appear. The Vanderbilts and the Astors, after a century, have not vanished. They no longer head the list of income earners and fortunes, but they still occupy a respectably high position.

The table reveals some peculiarities. J. P. Morgan was long gone by the time it was drawn up, but he is listed. What is shown are the taxes on his estate or trusts, not his personal income.

The middle column of the 1924 table tells us what taxes these affluent individuals paid, but what were their incomes? Lundberg[2] estimates that the rate of tax for this group ranged between 30% and 45%, so the numbers in the middle column should be multiplied by between 2.2 and 3.3 to yield total income.

For example, the twenty-one Rockefellers paid tax of $7.3 million on estimated income of $17.9 million, or 40.7%. The two Fords paid tax of $4.8 million on an estimated income of $11 million, or 43.3%. The lowest tax rate among the very top earners was paid by 28 members of what Lundberg called the "Standard Oil Group" (Archbolds, Rogerses, and so on, not shown in the table). The highest was that of the two Bakers connected to the First National Bank. The three Mellons paid among the highest rates, at 43%.

High Tax Rates

One of the historical curiosities about these tax rates is that they are so high. We tend to think of the 1920s as a time when the rich paid little or no taxes, due to their influence in Washington. This does not seem to be the case. In fact, an argument can be made that the late 1980s and early 1990s are closer in reality to our mental picture of the 1920s, at least as far as the very wealthiest are concerned.

It was only in the late 1980s that the custom of the very wealthiest paying substantial amounts of tax changed. For example, in 1981, those with an adjusted gross income (AGI) of between $500,000 and $1 million earned a total of about $9.8 billion, on which they paid $4.1 billion in taxes. Their rate was then 42%. The top tax bracket, above $1 million, earned $11.1 billion and paid $4.9 billion in taxes. Their tax rate was 44%. Both these rates were comparable to those paid by the very wealthiest in 1924.

By 1987,[26] all these numbers were radically different. Those in the $500,000 to $1 million bracket earned $51.9 billion, an increase of 430% over 1981. They paid $15.3 billion in taxes, for a rate of 29%. Those in the highest tax group, above $1 million, now earned a total AGI of $87.2 billion. This was an increase of 685% over 1981. They paid a total of $25.6 billion in taxes, for an equal rate of 29%. The rates for both these tax brackets were substantially lower than they were for the very highest income earners in 1924.

The 1924 Fortunes

The third column of Table 7.6 represents estimates of the total fortunes of the families of the top income earners. Since Lundberg did not have access to a listing of their assets, he followed a crude procedure. He merely multiplied their estimated income by a factor of about 15. Since the income tax was about 40% of total income, this calculation implies that the income tax in the middle column is multiplied by about 37.5 (= 15/0.40).

This form of estimation says that the ratio of accumulated wealth to income is about the same for all top income earners. This is obviously not true. On the other hand, this form of estimation may not be, on average, much worse than the "guesstimates" made by *Forbes* or *Fortune* in determining top fortunes. Until such time as the wealthiest publish their complete assets, we will always be somewhat in the dark.

Note that the fortunes listed in the third column represent that of a family, not an individual. Thus the listing of the two Fords is exactly the same. The third column of the 1924 table can then, in principle, be compared to the 1913 table. In the interest of brevity, we will only note that while some names in the later table are new, others carry on from generation to generation. The mechanical power of compound interest, to which we alluded in Chapter 5, is clear.

And so the door closes. The wealthy can and will be discussed in the following six decades, but never again will we be able to associate with precision a specific name with a public tax return.

THE *FORBES 400*

In 1982, *Forbes* magazine published what it thought was its first list of the wealthiest people in America.[27] Four hundred were chosen, that being the number invited to a memorable party in nineteenth-century New York City.

The magazine editors thought they were blazing a new trail. However, they soon determined that the founder of *Forbes*, B. C. Forbes, had had the same idea in 1918,[20] 64 years before. Good ideas are obviously worth repeating.

We have already mentioned the reservations attached to any listing of this type. Wealth can often be hidden, especially when tax collectors loom. Liabilities are often concealed, both by the affluent and not-so-affluent.

Given these and other caveats, what can we deduce from a typical *Forbes* (or *Fortune*) listing? Canterbury[28] was one of the first to draw some conclusions. The rest of this section deals with his analysis.

First, the basic facts: Where do the 400 live? Many of them have more than one residence, but the listing gives one principal place of business or retirement. New York State again heads the pack, as it did in 1892 (see Table 7.3). But it has dropped considerably in prominence. Ninety years previously, it held 37% of the wealthiest people; by 1982, it had only 21%.

The 1892 listing encompassed 4,000 millionaires. The 1982 list, analyzed in Table 7.7, is much smaller, at 400. To get onto it required about $100 million in wealth. As a result, the two lists are not comparable. As well,

Table 7.7
Statistics from the 1982 _Forbes 400_ [28]

State of Residence	Number	Percent
New York	85	21
Texas	66	17
California	53	13
Florida	22	6
Other	174	43
Total	400	100

Industry		
Manufacturing	133	33
Oil	73	18
Real Estate	67	17
Publishing	47	12
Shipping	4	1
Other	76	19
Total	400	100

in determining places of residence, we are merely counting heads, not dollar bills. It may well be that, when all the bank accounts, stocks, and bonds are totalled, New York has not declined at all in almost a century.

Other states came up rapidly. Texas, by 1982, ranked second only to New York, with 17% of the elite group. Much of this boom was due to oil wealth, which was a only a tiny factor in 1892. However, the crash in oil prices in the mid-1980s pushed Texas farther down the list.

The third state of the _Forbes_ list was California. This was another area that did not make the city-by-city listing in 1892. By 1982, it had about 13% of the nation's centimillionaires. Although it had had a larger population than New York for almost two decades, it still lagged behind it in financial power, at least by this measure. Florida came fourth on the 1982 list, a fact that would have astounded the makers of the 1892 listing. At that time, Florida had the lowest population of any of the Southern states, being widely regarded as a particularly unhealthy place to live.

About half the U.S. millionaires in 1892 were concentrated on the Eastern Seaboard states of New York, Massachusetts, Pennsylvania, and New Jersey, even though these states had only about one-quarter of the nation's population at the time. By 1982, the wealthiest people were more spread around the country, although New York was still a major center for them.

Forbes 400 Industries

What are the sources of all this money? Table 7.7 shows the five major industries. At least one title, publishing, should probably be changed. John Kluge of Charlottesville, Virginia, has been at or near the top of a number of _Forbes_ listings, with assets well into the billions. (The average 1982 holdings were $231 million.) His fortune was made in what is now called "media"—television and radio as well as print.

In specifying which of the centimillionaires belong in which industry, no distinction was made between those who inherited their money from an industry, and those who are working in it. For example, the original Rockefeller wealth derived from oil. Most, if not all, of the heirs are in other areas. Jay Rockefeller is the Senator from West Virginia. Congress may be a form of service industry, but Senator Rockefeller's wealth derives from his oil-based inheritance. The table cannot take account of this.

Because the United States was only in the middle of its rapid transformation to a service-based economy by 1982, manufacturing headed the list of industries as a source of major wealth. By now, with John Kluge, the media magnate, and Sam Walton, the drugstore domo, vying in recent years for the title of "Wealthiest Man in the United States," service industries such as communications and retailing may assume a larger role.

Industries can rise or fall in importance. In 1982, the United States was still feeling the effects of the fall of the Shah of Iran and the subsequent run-up of oil prices. By the mid-1980s, the price had dropped precipitously. Savings and loans in the Southwest were raising white flags. The proportion of centimillionaires in the oil industry also declined. Much of their wealth lay in oil deposits in the ground that had fallen in value, rather than bank deposits that continued to draw interest.

Self-Made or Inherited?

One of the key questions we ask about the wealthy is how much of their wealth derives from inheritance. A problem in answering this question is that the *Forbes* list says only that an individual inherited wealth or not. We do not know if the person inherited a million or a billion. We also do not know if, through that person's skills or carelessness, his or her original inheritance has gone up or down in value.

Canterbury checked the effect of inheritance on the wealth of the 400 listees. He found that an inheritor was about $100 million richer than a self-made man or woman, all other factors being held constant. This does not mean that the inheritors got $100 million at birth. Some may have received much less. The exact amount they got is unknown, as we noted above. Yet the fact that they received an inheritance gave them the freedom to watch their holdings grow under the power of compound interest, or take risks in developing business. Noninheritors never had that freedom.

Inheritance explains 43% of the mean wealth of the sample. The other 57% is explainable by other variables: Age—older people generally have more wealth than younger; source of wealth—those in shipping or oil generally have more wealth than those from other industries; and so on. The value of 43% of total wealth explicable by means of inheritance is close to the 40% of the 400 who were inheritors.

Lester Thurow, in *The Zero-Sum Society* [29] said, "If one examines the very rich, about 50% of the great fortunes are gotten through inheritance." The empirical evidence suggests that Thurow was close to the mark. The 1989 *Forbes 400* lend their support to his thesis: 40% inherited their way to the top, 54% were self-made, and the other 6% parlayed a small inheritance into a major one. [30]

Compare this to the situation in 1892, as shown in Table 7.3. Of the 4,000 millionaires at the time, only 18% were described as having an inheritance. It is true that the 1892 listing was for all millionaires, not the 400 top wealth holders. Yet the growing influence of inheritance, as opposed to building a fortune with one's hands, is clear. The proportion of inheritors among top wealth holders has doubled in less than a century. Will it continue to rise indefinitely, until the United States reaches the position of Britain?

SUMMARY

We now have a better idea of how the rich have changed through history, and who some of them are in the modern era. We are in a better position to specify how the two-segment income distribution, partly based on wealth inheritance, can be modified to a one-segment distribution.

__ 8 _____

IF YOU'RE SO RICH,
WHY AREN'T YOU SMART?

In this chapter, we will deal with how inherent ability relates to inequality in income and wealth. Are rich people really better endowed by their Creator, in some sense, than the rest of us? Suppose we could determine that Joe, who lives down the street, had ten times the ability of Max, who lives around the corner. Some of us think that it would be reasonable that Joe had ten times the income or wealth of Max. But how do we measure that ability? Is it intelligence, drive, or some other factor?

TWO THEORIES OF INCOME AND INHERENT WORTH

Sahota,[1] in compiling his massive fifty-five-page summary of the scientific papers on income distribution, evaluated over 300 studies. There was no end of theories within theories on the relation of inherent worth, however defined, to incomes. He sorted out the confusion by dividing all the concepts into two categories:

1. *It is in our grasp.* People can make their own fate in terms of income and wealth. A corollary of this says that societies, by way of government, can alter income distributions if they wish; and

2. *It is out of our grasp.* Inequalities are largely preordained. This may be done by a Supreme Being through genetics, luck, or just the way that economic transactions take place.

Liberals and Conservatives

When these two major philosophic beliefs are arranged in this way, the terms "conservative" and "liberal" tend to lose their meaning. For example, Lester Thurow, the prominent MIT economist, has advocated taxation to reduce the differences between the rich and the poor. He is thus labelled as liberal, if one takes the first of the two categories as indicating belief in government actions to relieve society's problems. Yet he is well-known for the random walk theory of wealth accumulation. Briefly, this suggests that the laws of chance govern building of fortunes.

In the view of Thurow, and many other economists, the laws of luck rule much of the rise of personal affluence. This belief would tend to put Thurow into the ranks of converts to the second category. This is ordinarily the realm of conservative economists, who do not think much of government interference.

Both sets of theories appeal to our gut instincts. Must one prevail over the other, or can they both be true at the same time? We like to think that we are masters of our ships, but we realize we can be sunk by an unexpected iceberg. This dichotomy in our minds about how much power we personally have over our incomes accounts for the two sets of theories.

Some conservative economists are attracted to the first theory. In their minds, a high-school dropout makes his or her own decision, and thus deserves to have low income the rest of his or her life. The reverse of the coin, still within the same theory, is that if one person can make a choice about his future income, society collectively can do so as well. It can levy taxes on high incomes, wealth, or both. Thus conservatives and collectivists find themselves as uncomfortable bedfellows in this theory.

The "Beyond-Our-Control" Theory

The second theory, that distributions are somehow preset by forces beyond our control, has some subtheories. One of them is that income and wealth are genetically determined when a baby enters the world. This is the subtheory that we will be exploring in depth in this chapter.

A second subtheory of the second category is the random walk of Thurow and others. According to these economists, income distribution is caused by chance, luck, and other noncontrollable factors.

If you believe in the second category of income distribution theory, then any action by the government to change income distribution is doomed to failure. Set high marginal tax rates, levy huge penalties on large estates—all will come to naught, according to this philosophy. The old income and wealth distributions will return, sooner or later. The wealth may be in different hands—the good-for-nothing son of a brilliant and wealthy investor may dissipate his father's fortune—but the overall disparities will continue.

Where do the two authors stand on the two basic theories? Obviously, we believe that government action can make a difference. We will later describe our Alternative Distribution Scheme for inheritance taxation. Only government can tax.

On the other hand, at what type of income distribution are we aiming? The lognormal (or Gibrat) type was described earlier. This seems to be close to a universal distribution, persisting in diverse industrialized societies, almost a "natural" allocation of income. This then puts some of our philosophical orientation in the *second* category of income distribution theory.

The two basic schools of thought are analogous to how many religions are constructed. By definition, religions are always based on belief in a Supreme Being (or Beings). The Being can and will do wondrous things under the right circumstances. Yet the work of the religion based on this Being—the care of the hungry, the clothing of the poor, the paying off of the building mortgage, collecting the minister's salary—must be performed by mere mortals, as best they can.

Our personal attitude toward the two categories of philosophy paraphrases an old saying: "Accept income distributions as if they came from some mysterious and inscrutable force; act as if changing these distributions depended on fellow citizens."

EDUCATION AND INCOME

One of the first factors that will be brought up to explain discrepancies in income will be that of education. "He's gone to medical school (or law school, or graduate school, or management school). It's no wonder he makes so much more money than his twin brother, who never got beyond high school."

Education is a major factor in the allocation of income in this country. This was summarized in a *New York Times* article,[2] which in turn was based on a 1984 report entitled *What It's Worth: Educational Background and Economic Status*.

The average professional—graduates of law, medical, and dental schools—earned an average of $3871 a month. High school dropouts, on the bottom of the education ladder, earned $693. Second on the list were those who earned doctorates, who earned $3265 monthly. Next came those with master's degrees, averaging $2288 monthly, and so on down the line. The report also classified incomes by professions, starting with law, at $3726 monthly. It concluded with home economics, at less than one-third of lawyers, at $1063 monthly.

Most of this is well-known. Why yet another expensive report on the obvious? Yet there are a few points that are not quite that obvious:

1. The report says nothing about the top reaches of the income ladder. The maximum reported for either degrees or professions was $3871 monthly, or about $45,000 annually. This would put the recipient of such income well below the 3% kink we have described previously.

2. The report is *descriptive* in terms of fields, but does not *explain*. Why should those specializing in home economics earn the smallest salaries of the professions considered? Are they inferior beings, in terms of IQs or other supposedly objective measures of talent? Or, as is more likely, is it because they perform what is traditionally "women's work," in the past often completely unpaid?

Go up the list of professions, and take away one word from the home economists. That word is "home." Economists are among the highest paid, at $2824 monthly, or almost three times what the home economists earn. Can one word in a title make all the difference? Apparently it does.

3. The relations between incomes of doctoral recipients and those who graduated from professional schools deserves some comment. Most professional graduates spend four years in formal education beyond a bachelor's degree, although in some medical specialties the period is longer.

While the average length of time in graduate school to achieve a Ph.D. can vary from field to field, a typical period is six to seven years of full-time study. This means that a Ph.D., on average, has spent longer in school than a professional school graduate.

All other factors being equal, we would expect that the longer someone is in school, the higher that person's income. This is the implication of what we have been told by our parents. But in the case of doctoral versus professional degrees, the opposite seems true.

The Census Bureau says that "holders of doctoral degrees, while having extensive professional training, are scattered over a wider variety of fields, and thus, on average, earn less than professionals, who are concentrated in the high-paying fields of law and medicine."

This describes but does not explain. If all the holders of doctorates were in chemistry, for example, would they have higher salaries than lawyers and physicians? We doubt it.

4. Another implication of the listing by salaries by period of education is that those who succeed in completing long periods of education are more intelligent than those who do not. Granted, the word "intelligence" is not used in the news report, but it is suggested between the lines.

The length of time in school has only a partial correlation with intelligence. Those who go to graduate or professional schools have, on balance, higher IQs than those who do not. But the differences are not enormous. The variations in earnings between those who get advanced degrees and those who do not are much more substantial.

Is the difference in earnings due to the inherent intelligence of the people who obtain advanced degrees, or to the educational process itself? Or, most likely, is it due to a combination of the two?

THE LOGNORMAL INCOME CURVE AND EDUCATION

How does the number of years of education relate to the V-shaped income distribution, divided into lognormal and Pareto? If there is no correlation between the two, then years of schooling may not describe the upper part—the Pareto distribution—of the income curve. We can show that it does not.

Consider two examples. The first deals with the largest part of the income distribution, the lognormal or Gibrat distribution. The second deals with the super-high-income earners.

We showed in the previous section that the relationship between length of time in school and earnings is inverted compared to what it should be for professional and graduate school graduates. (The relationship *does* hold for master's and bachelor's degrees, though.) But even if there was a strong relationship between years of education and earnings on the lognormal or Gibrat part of the income distribution, it does not hold for the very highest earners, in the Pareto region.

Suppose, for simplicity, that the average level of education in the United States is about 13 years of schooling. This would allow 12 years for high school graduation. About one year in addition would be added for the proportion of the population that went on to some type of higher education, either graduating or not. This average also allows for the fact that a significant group does not graduate from high school.

Suppose further that this average level of education corresponds to about the 50% level of the income distribution, as displayed in our previous income graphs. In 1987, this was about $17,000 for the median—50% above, 50% below—tax return.[3] In that year, the top 2% of tax returns had an average income of at least $132,000. The top ½%, or one in 200, had an average gross income of at least $286,000. The ratio of these incomes to the average income of $17,000 is then 7.8 and 16.8, respectively.

Then these groups of high-income earners would have to spend 7.8 and 16.8 times the period in school of the average person. That is, *if* there is a linear relationship between education and income.

Simple calculations show this can not be so. Multiplying the average education level of 13 years by 7.8 and 16.8 yields 101 and 218 years of education, respectively. Methuselah might have attended school that long, if there had been colleges in his time. For the rest of us, it is well beyond any conceivable lifespan, let alone interest in continuing our education.

In our previous section, we saw that the amount of annual earnings for professional and doctoral degrees were well below the highest few percent of the population. When we related typical earnings for lawyers and Ph.D.s to the years they spend in college, we were dealing with that part of the income curve below the 3% kink. Even there, we do not see an exact relationship between years in the classroom and earnings.

So while education has some relation to income, it explains only part of the spectrum. The upper part of the income curve is simply inexplicable on the basis of education. And since in this book we are mostly concerned with that upper part, the educational theory of income differences leaves us as dissatisfied as a thirsty man when the well runs dry.

HUMAN CAPITAL AND EDUCATION

When a businessperson decides to build a new factory, he (or she) has to raise capital to construct it. The capital can be in the form of money from retained earnings from previous operations, borrowing, or some combination of the two. All of this is well-known to every economist.

About the same approach can be taken with respect to education. When someone goes to college or professional school, he is, in effect, making an investment in himself. Leaving aside the question of learning for the love of learning, the student has to make the decision: If I forego earnings for five or ten years, as well as pay tuition, will I come out ahead financially?

High School or College?

The answer to this question is shown graphically in Figure 8.1. The dotted line represents someone who left high school and went to work. His income rises gradually over the years as he gains seniority on the job. It reaches a peak just before retirement at age sixty-five. We are assuming an *average* income curve, without unemployment, changes in jobs, and large promotions.

The solid line in the graph represents someone who went to and graduated from college. In 1984, the difference between those who left education after high school and those who obtained a bachelor's degree was about $10,000 annually. This is reflected in the middle part of the graph, since the $10,000 figure is an average over all ages.

The initial part of this line, from age eighteen to about twenty-one, shows negative earnings. Some young people have to borrow to pay tuition and living expenses. A loss is represented as negative income in the graph. Others, more fortunate, have their expenses paid by their parents. What is shown on the graph is a rough average; the exact amounts are not of great consequence here.

Many college students earn small amounts during the school year. This is also shown in the graph by a small positive income in the sophomore through senior years.

Finally, the first day on the job dawns. Although some MBA and law graduates may earn over $50,000 annually in their first employment, few

Figure 8.1
Earnings of a High School and College Graduate from Ages 17 to 65

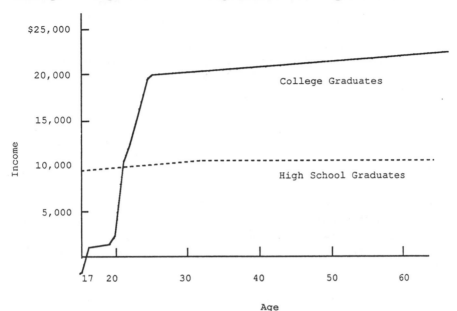

holders of bachelor's degrees earn anywhere near that sum. We see, however, their salary level rising above that of the high school graduate.

The extra income that the college graduate earns over his lifetime compared to the high school graduate has two components. The first part is the difference between the dotted curve and the solid one from age twenty-one to sixty-five. This first part is positive. It is the extra money the college student made compared to his high-school friend.

The second part of the calculation is the difference between the dotted curve and the solid one between the ages of seventeen and twenty-one. It is negative. The area represents the extra amount of money earned by the high-school graduate compared to his college-bound friend, while the latter was hitting the books.

Gains versus Losses

To determine the overall financial gain to the college graduate, we subtract the negative area from the positive one. The graph shows that in this example, it *does* pay to go to college, at least economically. The positive area is much bigger than the negative one.

We are not considering factors such as job satisfaction, which are not measurable in dollars. The college graduate may be extremely unhappy in his job, while the high-school graduate may count the hours till Monday morning. If this happened, the college graduate might quit his job and look for another. We do not know if he would rise or fall on the economic ladder.

The rosy picture for college as compared with high-school graduates may not apply to all. For example, consider the home economists to whom we referred. Their positive areas may not be much bigger than the negative ones. If they are not, the home economists have a *negative* rate of return on their scholastic investment.

The term "investment" suggests why the entire subject is called "human capital theory." In effect, human beings are treated, at least on paper, like little machines or factories. For buildings or hardware, we can perform investment calculations to determine whether or not they should be built or bought. For people, we do the same calculations in terms of whether they should go to college or professional school.

There is one major aspect of human capital theory we have not yet considered—the interest rate. A businessperson makes his investment decisions in part on the prevailing interest rate. The same thing happens in terms of human capital. Suppose a businessperson has $1 million to invest. If the interest rate is 8%, in principle he could put his money in the bank and draw $80,000 annually forever. If, after doing his calculations, he finds that he cannot make a profit of more than $80,000 annually from his new factory, he should not build it in the first place.

About the same can be said for a high school graduate contemplating college, or a college graduate thinking about professional or graduate school. During that period of extra education, with forced absence from the workplace, his compatriots who go to work will earn money. If the interest earned on that money is more than the extra income he gets from his extended education, the prospective students should not register for more classes.

This then is the basis of the human capital theory. As Blaug[4] points out, "the potentialities of [this] theory turned out to be so vast that among the developments in economic thought of the past two decades . . . human capital theory perhaps dwarfs all others."

Imperfect Information

The word "guess" goes to the crux of human capital theory. It assumes that people have close to perfect information on the likely return to their investment. In reality, they do not.

For example, at present college graduate chemical engineers are the highest-paid majors among bachelor-degree holders. A 1990 survey put their average starting salary at around $33,000. Someone who was interested in earning the highest possible salary after four years of college would naturally be attracted to this field. However, there would be two gaps in their information.

First, will they succeed? If she takes two or three years in that field, and then fails the course, time and money will be wasted.

Theorists of human capital will say, chances are that budding chemical engineers will have taken some chemistry and science courses in high school, and thus will have some idea of how good they are in these subjects. It is fair to say that those who do well in high school chemistry will likely do the same in college. Yet there will always be uncertainty until the sheepskin is awarded.

Second, market forces, over the forty or so working years of a graduate, can drastically change the value of a degree in a given specialty. This may be an even greater unknown than the first.

In the last decade, chemical companies have been stymied from building many plants in the United States, due to local concerns about pollution and accidents such as Bhopal. Building these facilities in the Third World has become more attractive, as those countries build up a cadre of chemical engineers willing to work for a much smaller wage than American ones. U.S. microchip makers have moved much of their production to Asia and the Third World because of lower wage rates.

Is it too much to believe that the same can happen to chemical plants, due to the factors mentioned above? Neither of us being chemists or chemical engineers, we do not know.

But if it does happen, the wages of new chemical engineers will fall with respect to other academic specialties. We mention this not to alarm those studying chemical engineering today. Rather, it is done to point out the many uncertainties that anyone planning to invest in his or her human capital must consider.

EDUCATION IN THE HUMAN CAPITAL THEORY

At least one economist[4] has said that the hard core of human capital theory is educational costs. These numbers are easily tabulated and are issued by governments and public agencies. For example, we know how much is spent, by school district, on elementary and high schools nationwide. Even private colleges make their tuition charges public.

But consider job searching, another component of human capital costs. All who are unemployed or just looking for a job incur these costs. Yet few people add them up for themselves. As a result, there is no reliable data on what these costs are, even though they may be substantial in some cases.

So when we talk about spending on human capital, we may mean all types of outlays to improve skills and earning power. But as a practical matter, we are talking about educational costs.

RESULTS OF HUMAN CAPITAL THEORY

Using human capital theory, we should be able to predict both the shape of the V-curve describing income, and the slope of the two lines on probability graph paper.

In one study, Mincer,[5] one of the main proponents of the theory, found that formal schooling accounted for only 7% of the differences in earnings among individuals. Any theory that can explain only 7% of an effect is obviously weak.

Mincer refined his work, taking into account on-the-job training and other factors. He then found that half the variations in earning could be attributed to the distribution of school and postschool investment.

But even with these assumptions, it is far from clear that human capital theory can predict the super-incomes in the Pareto region (i.e., in the top few percent). While the theory can probably predict incomes for 90% to 95% of the population to a reasonable degree of certainty, the last 10% or so seem elusive. Are they just the lucky ones, the recipients of some prize from a cosmic lottery, or are there other factors involved?

MOTHER TERESA AND EINSTEIN

There *are* likely aspects other than years of education involved in explaining spectacularly high incomes. Can we deduce what they are in evaluating their opposite—spectacularly *low* incomes?

What do we mean by "spectacularly low incomes?" No, it is not that pittance that the homeless receive from handouts. Rather, it is the extremely high incomes that some people could receive if they wanted to—but do not.

Look at Mother Teresa and Albert Einstein. As far as we know, the personal incomes of these world-famous figures were and are small, although above the level of the penniless. Yet few would doubt that with little effort on their part, they could have garnered great riches for themselves. Their incomes were and are spectacularly low, compared to what they might have been.

These two had either the drive or the penetrating intellect granted to few on the face of the earth. We do not know Mother Teresa's IQ, but her organizational ability and courage in tending to the needs of the poverty stricken in Calcutta was almost unheard of. If they existed in a business executive, most would say that that executive would reap enormous rewards. Mother Teresa's personal financial benefits? Close to none.

Einstein was one of the great intellects of the century. Some claimed that his IQ was of the order of 200. If earnings correlated with inherent worth as measured by objective tests, Einstein should have been one of the wealthiest men on earth. He was not.

He did live above the average, on a professor's salary at the Institute for Advanced Study at Princeton. If he was at all interested in high salaries and accumulating wealth, he managed to keep it well-hidden from the rest of the world.

Einstein was clearly deficient in what the economist Lydall[6] called the D-factor—drive and/or determination. That factor was and is highly evident in Mother Teresa, regardless of her IQ.

There is almost certainly a factor in human money-making ability other than performance in standardized tests. But that factor does not always operate in the direction of ever-bigger salary checks and larger bank accounts. For some people endowed with the D-factor, it can work in just the opposite direction.

IQ AND ALL THAT

What is inherent worth? While opinions vary on whether it can be measured at all, one almost-standard yardstick is the IQ test. In principle at least, these tests should measure native ability. But what do these tests mean in terms of income or wealth? This broad question in turn poses a number of subquestions.

How is Intelligence Distributed?

Many of us vaguely remember that IQ test results are supposed to be normally distributed, that is, the curve representing the distribution will be bell-shaped. IQs are then symmetrical around an average value of 100.

For every person with a score of 110, for example, there will be someone with a score of 90. An example of what the symmetrical or bell-shaped distribution would look like is shown on the left-hand side of Figure 8.2, about which more will be said later.

There are two problems with this model of IQ testing. First, people who have significant mental problems are not generally given IQ tests. An IQ of 140, while rare, does exist. This implies a corresponding person with an IQ of 60. While the latter person also exists, he or she will not often be tested in this way.

The second, more fundamental, problem with the bell-shaped distribution of IQ is that it is an artifact of the way the scores are compiled and graded. That is, the scores are scaled to an arbitrary normal distribution, presumably because most phenomena in nature are normally distributed.[7] The *true* distribution remains unknown.

Many readers will remember teachers or professors who "graded on a curve," that is, gave out predetermined proportions of As, Bs, and so on, regardless of how bright or dull the class was. About the same happens when IQ tests are made up. The tests are graded in such a way that we get scores that are distributed in a bell-shaped way.

Figure 8.2
Combining Intelligence and Drive into Overall Earnings

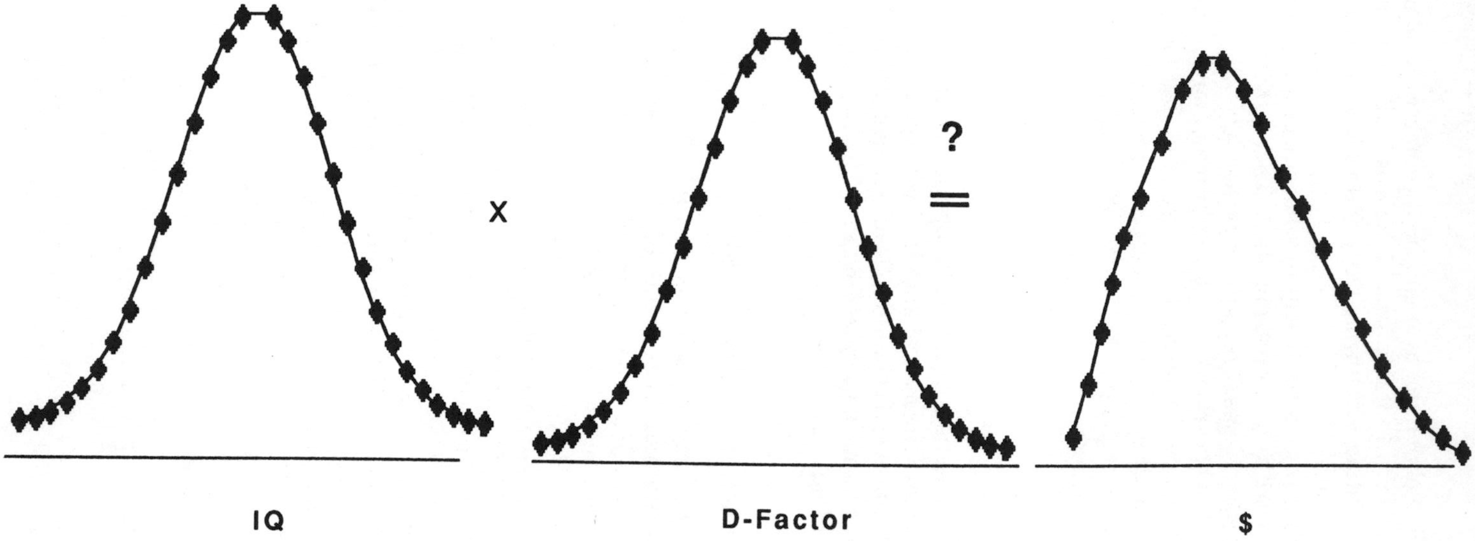

What is the *True* Distribution of Mental Ability?

Stamp[8] and Davis[9] argued that it was not symmetrically distributed around an average at all. Rather, they claimed that it was highly skewed, like the right-hand side of Figure 8.2. If this is true, we then have a clue as to why the income distribution is the way it is. The skewed distribution on the right-hand side of Figure 8.2 looks remarkably like the lognormal or Gibrat income distributions we discussed previously. Recall that this distribution applies to the lower 97% or so of the population.

If the distribution of mental ability is indeed lognormal, it would explain the lower part of the two-line income distribution. Income would then be allocated according to the brains you were given at birth. What could be fairer?

The upper or Paretian part of the income distribution—the top 3%—poses more problems from an IQ viewpoint. This part of the income curve, above the kink, rises very rapidly. In terms of IQ, this would mean a very small number of people with extremely high IQs, perhaps putting Einstein in the shade. Is it possible that they exist?

Mandelbrot[10, 11] argued that each mental ability *did* follow a Paretian distribution. That is, they would fit the upper part of the income distribution curve.

At this point, we stop. We are sinking so deeply into the swamp of social science theories that we may be losing sight of the goal. The problem is that we are dealing with little more than speculation about the shape of the ability curve, not real and basic knowledge about it.

Still, there is a mouse bearing a small, truthful message in the maze of tests and their interpretations. The tests are probably more accurate for most people than merely saying, ''Yes, she's a good student,'' or ''No, he's not very clever.''

Supply and Demand

IQ measurements do not take account of supply and demand. They are solely a measure of the *supply* of certain human abilities.

Suppose one of the portions of the IQ test dealt with the ability to do complicated arithmetic problems in one's head, such as multiplying 1,234 by 5,678. A very small number of people have this ability. It seems natural to them, and unteachable. Curiously enough, it is often found in *idiot savants*—people who suffer from mental disabilities yet can perform amazing mathematical feats (see the movie *Rain Man*).

In the nineteenth century, there might have been a demand for such people to do the calculations of the railroad age. If that had been true, the students who did well on this section of the test would have had well-paying careers. There would have been a *demand* for their services.

With the coming of the mechanical calculator and later the computer, virtually all demand for these mental feats would have disappeared. Yet the basic human ability would have remained the same. The scores on this portion of the hypothetical test should not change over time.

Similar statements can be made about other sections, real or proposed, of any IQ test. Assuming that they measure some facets of human ability fairly accurately—and even here there is controversy—there is no way to predict the demand in the market place for these abilities. Without knowing this demand, we find it difficult to relate IQ scores, wholly or in part, to the dollars of salary they may generate.

Nature versus Nurture

Any mention of IQ and what it means brings to mind the ancient battle over nature *versus* nurture. As a wise man once said, we will need an 11-foot pole to touch this one, since we would not touch it with a 10-foot one.

Scientific estimates of the proportions of ability due to heredity or environment have been put forth. Unfortunately, these seemingly reasonable estimates are frequently demolished, using the same scientific tools used to build the original estimates. As a result, it is close to impossible for us to say anything useful in a quantitative way on this subject.

In 1889, Francis Galton said,[12] "Each peculiarity in a man is shared by his kinsman, but on the average to a less degree." Since IQ tests were in the future, his statistician friend, Karl Pearson, devised a simple test. He measured the heights of fathers and sons. Pearson found that although tall fathers have tall sons, the average height of sons of a group of tall fathers is less than their fathers' heights.[13] In other words, there is a regression, or going back, of sons' heights towards the average heights of all men. What does this have to do with IQs, income, or anything in particular?

Many of us know affluent suburbs around our cities and towns. Let us assume that there is a relationship between IQs and income, and thus many of the adults in these well-off suburbs have high IQs.

If the law of regression is true, their children should have *lower* IQs, on average, than their parents. But in almost all regions of the country, we notice a curious phenomenon. The high school graduates with the highest scholastic honors (e.g., National Merit Scholarships or Scholastic Aptitude Test [SAT] scores close to the maximum)—tend to be concentrated in these well-to-do suburbs.

Yet if the regression rule holds, these students should do *less* well than their parents had in school. We can conclude that while the regression to the mean works for heights, over which one's environment exerts little control, it does not seem to apply to scholastic achievement or even IQ. Score one more point for environment.

PUTTING IT ALL TOGETHER

About all we can say to this point is that there are a number of factors that could, in principle, predict income. They include native ability, length and quality of education, family background, and others. They blend in a complicated way, the details of which are not known. How they combine to predict incomes for the very highest income earners is even murkier.

The crude analogy we can draw is that of a massive computer that will try to predict our personal incomes for the rest of our lives. It asks us for thousands of bits of information, some of which seem relevant, and others which do not: how long we went to school; our coat size; the names of our parents; what we were doing on the night of January 25, 1954; our grades in English; how much we have in the bank; and more. It puts all this information together in a detailed equation, and prints out the answer. Yet we have only a vague idea of what the equation is, or which of the scraps of information we supplied were actually used.

One of the major studies to try to sort out all the variables was by Jencks.[14] In the words of Sahota[1]:

> The general conclusion of the study was that neither family environment nor cognitive talent [reasoning ability] nor school quality determines significant proportions of educational inequalities; and that none of these factors nor educational attainment nor occupational status significantly alters income inequalities . . . Apart from inheritance of property, economic success is largely the result of 'luck and peculiar competencies' over which government has no control. . . . Education cannot achieve non-educational [economic] goals.

What fraction should go to nature and what fraction to nurture? According to this massive study, no more than 45% and no less than 55%, respectively. While the proportion ascribed to heredity (less than 45%) may not seem that much, it is by far the largest component of all the influences on future earnings. Like the Prime Minister in the British cabinet, it is *primus inter pares* (first among equals).

What can we learn from these and other comprehensive studies? The complex of factors that determine the future earnings of a small child seem, at least in our present state of knowledge, to be analogous to a spider web. Some of its threads are stronger and thicker than others, and help to hold it together. These correspond to ability, family background, and other major factors. Some threads are thin; they correspond to lesser quantities such as the child's place of birth, perhaps the university attended, and so on. The threads are joined in a way which yields only a little to our probing. But one factor can overwhelm the entire structure: a strong gust of wind, corresponding to the unknown variable of luck.

MATHEMATICAL EXPLANATIONS

The economists who formulated the theories noted above approached the subject via the front door. They wanted to find the factors that determine future earnings, regardless of the exact shape of the income curve. But others looked through the back door. They desired to see why the income curve (or rather two curves) was skewed or nonsymmetrical. Explaining the two curves at the same time in terms of heredity and/or environment poses a supreme challenge.

Perhaps the simplest way to approach the problem is shown in Figure 8.2. The left-hand side shows a normal distribution for IQ or ability. We noted above that the *scores* for IQ are distributed normally. But the true measure of intelligence or ability may be lognormally distributed, or have an entirely different distribution.

The middle graph of Figure 8.2 is the Lydall D-factor, representing drive, determination, dynamism, and doggedness. Measuring human energy is not simple. If the distribution of IQ is obscure, that of the D-factor is even more so. We all know people who have the oomph of a mashed potato. A few are acquainted with people who hold down full-time jobs, are marvelous parents, and who write books in their spare time. There is thus a spectrum or distribution of the D-factor. We have represented it as a normal or symmetric distribution. But it may not really have this shape.

How do we combine the IQ and D-factor to yield a lognormal distribution of incomes like that on the right-hand side of Figure 8.2? If we merely combine two normal distributions together, as we have indicated with the X, we get *another* normal distribution, not a lognormal or Gibrat distribution. Because of this, we have added a question mark above the equals sign in the "equation" we have devised.

Finding the Pareto or Upper Income Distribution

The uncertainties of Figure 8.2 show that we have to devise a different approach to formulating the upper Pareto distribution. Lydall[6] and Champernowne[15] were able to derive this distribution—applying to the top 3%—from basic principles.

In a typical industrial organization, a supervisor has a fixed number of employees reporting to him or her. For purposes of our argument, the exact number is not important; call it X. Now suppose that each supervisor has an income in a fixed ratio to the employees he supervises. For example, if the lowest level of supervisor has a salary of $20,000, the next highest $30,000, the next $45,000, the ratio would be 1.5 in this instance. The exact ratio will depend on the industry and other factors; call it R.

By using only the two quantities X and R, Lydall found that in this hypothetical industry, income will follow a Pareto distribution. To avoid equations, we will not go into his derivation of this result.

The actual Pareto distribution in the United States is made up of about three million taxpayers. Of these, some will be industrial managers of the type that Lydall describes. Others will be physicians, lawyers, entertainers, and the like, who are definitely *not* at the top of an industrial structure. Within the three million, the exact proportion of those within and outside industrial pyramids is not easy to determine. If most are outside, then Lydall's hypothesis would not work.

Lydall's algebra works only for an industry where the quantities X and R are fixed. They almost certainly vary between industries, and within them. For example, there is no particular reason why Roger Smith (head of General Motors) and Lee Iacocca (head of Chrysler) would have exactly the same number of people reporting to them. Because GM is so much larger than Chrysler, chances are that Roger Smith has more divisions and vice presidents asking for his ear.

The salary ratios also vary from one industry to another, and from one level to the next. For example, all the many vice-presidents at IBM are theoretically at one level in that firm's structure. Yet their salaries will vary considerably, depending on their responsibility. To add to the complications in terms of Lydall's theory, some of the vice-presidents will get large bonuses, others small ones, and yet others will have empty Christmas stockings. Even if all their salaries were equal, the bonuses would throw Lydall's equations off.

Nonetheless, Lydall's theory is one step in predicting a Pareto distribution of income. But to now, it remains only an interesting theory.

Randomness of Income Distributions

Champernowne[15] was one of the first to take account of the randomness of the income process. Someone may meet an old college classmate at a party, be hired by that classmate's company, and receive a large increase in salary. Conversely, someone may work very hard and imaginatively for a company that goes out of business because nobody wants their products. Unemployment results, with a sharp drop in income. These matters of luck are generally not recorded in resumés.

Many economists have stressed the importance of luck—good and bad—in determining income. But how does one take it into account in a theory?

Champernowne assumed that proportional income ranges were the initial conditions. Then he applied "shocks" to these ranges, moving them up or down the income ladder randomly. The random numbers to perform this process can be summoned up on a scientific hand calculator or a computer.

To take a specific example, consider someone with a starting income of $30,000. The first random number we obtained on our hand calculator was 0.901. The numbers are always between 0 and 1. (Readers will almost certainly get a different one themselves.)

Multiplying the original salary by this number, we obtain $27,300. The second random number we got was 0.642. This time, we will *divide* the last salary by this number, yielding $42,500. On and on it goes. Obviously, the three salaries we assumed and calculated do not mean much by themselves. However, if the process is repeated many times, the final group of incomes converges to a Pareto distribution. Champernowne had found a way of incorporating the randomness of life to yield an income distribution close to reality.

But these calculations produce a Pareto distribution for *all* incomes, not just the top few percent. As a result, they cannot describe the entire income distribution. What we need, when it comes to incomes, is a complete horse. Existing theories give us either the head or the tail. None gives us the complete animal.

IF YOU'RE SO RICH, WHY AREN'T YOU SMART?

We *still* do not have a clear and foolproof answer why some people earn more than others. We are still in the dark about why income at the lower level is in a lognormal distribution and then goes into the Pareto region.

Obviously, inherent ability, drive, being in the right place at the right time (the latter two may be the same thing) are interwoven. But how is it done?

We are observing a piece of fabric from across a room. We know that the threads we have mentioned, and yet others, make up the cloth. We inch forward, using the theories of the economists we have described. We are able to make out specific threads, but the exact way they are woven together still eludes us. If someone would just turn up the lights!

9

"WE DON'T PAY TAXES.
LITTLE PEOPLE PAY TAXES."

The lognormal and Pareto income distributions we evaluated in previous chapters were based on a major assumption: Income and estate tax returns are accurate. This chapter presents evidence that some tax returns do not tell the whole truth and nothing but the truth. These facts tend to *reinforce* our conclusions about how rich is too rich, not diminish them.

OVER- AND UNDERREPORTING

When it comes to reporting of income, there are only two streets down which we can travel. Income can be over- or underreported.

It is possible that some taxpayers may have, on occasion, overreported their earnings. A zero added by mistake to a column of figures, an accountant adding when she should have been subtracting—this can all happen.

While most of us are concerned about the federal deficit that has persisted for so many years, few are willing to wash away the red ink by deliberately overestimating our incomes and thus paying higher taxes. If overestimates have occurred, they almost certainly have taken place on a random and rare basis. No tax accountants are employed to overestimate income. No lobbyists work Capitol Hill to have the lawmakers write in anti-loopholes.

This leaves us with only one alternative. Some, perhaps many, taxpayers *underestimate* income to save on taxes.

It is at least theoretically possible that this underestimation does not affect our conclusions about the kink between the lognormal and Pareto distributions. One way in which this could happen is shown in Figure 9.1.

In this graph, we have reproduced the original two-curve income distribution from a previous chapter. The kink represents the division

Figure 9.1
Underestimation of Income by (a) Everyone and (b) Mostly Those with High Incomes

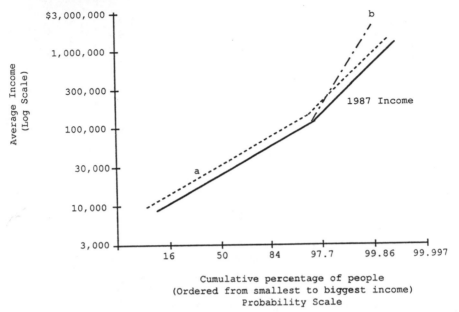

Cumulative percentage of people
(Ordered from smallest to biggest income)
Probability Scale

Source: Hostetter and Bates, Individual Tax Returns, p. 19

between the lognormal (or Gibrat) distribution to the left and the Pareto region on the right. The division occurred around the $110,000 level in 1987.

There are an infinite number of ways in which underreporting of income can happen. Let us consider three possibilities. At this stage, we won't use specific data, only degrees of plausibility.

1. *Tiny underestimation.* Taxpayers underestimate their income by only a few dollars. If this were true, the graph would not change, at least to the naked eye. A magnifying glass would be needed to see the difference. While this is possible for some taxpayers, it would not be widespread. Why bring down the IRS on your shoulders for the price of a steak?

2. *Substantial underestimation by all.* Each taxpayer underestimates his or her income by a large amount. The difference between this example and the previous one is that, in this instance, the underestimation is a fraction of the total reported income. For example, suppose that the fraction is 20%.

In this case, we would see a curve like the dashed one (a) above the solid line. The solid line represents what was actually reported to the IRS.

If *everyone* underestimates by the same fraction, our conclusions would be exactly the same as before. The kink, crucial to our argument, would be in exactly the same place as a percentage of the population. The only difference would be that the entire curve would be shifted upward.

3. *High incomes underestimated more than low.* It is entirely more reasonable to assume that high-income taxpayers underreport their earnings *more* than those in the lower brackets. To make this statement quantitative, we show this graphically as a broken line (b) in Figure 9.1.

This does not mean that those in the upper income regions are basically less law-abiding than poorer people. There is absolutely no evidence to denigrate high-income people in this way, although millions believe it. Rather, this third possibility is based on the assumption that opportunity breeds action. Consider two workers, one in a diamond factory and another making rhinestones. Which of the two is more likely to make an unexpected appearance on the walls of a post office?

Many of us would like the IRS not to know about all our earnings from our company or bank account. But there is no way we can prevent that from happening. On the other hand, if we were to *own* that company or bank, there may well be methods of keeping the IRS from finding out our secrets.

This was precisely the technique used by Leona Helmsley, the New York hotel billionairess. When she told a housekeeper who worked for her, "We [presumably the owners of property] don't pay taxes. The little people pay taxes,"[1] she was summarizing the beliefs of much of the nation in nine little words.

Mrs. Helmsley was found guilty of tax evasion and sentenced to four years in jail. After the trial, we saw no news reports saying that the results were so convincing to other tax avoiders that the IRS was closing down its tax fraud division.

The third possibility we described, that high incomes have greater tax evasions than low, is plausible. But that does not make it true. We will spend this chapter trying to estimate just how valid it is.

Our conclusions? We have, if anything, *underestimated* the difference between the two distributions. That is, the two "nations" are even more distinct than we had surmised.

GHOST STATISTICS

By definition, tax avoiders do not tell the world how much income they have underreported. Yet in news stories on tax evasions, we often see specific numbers on just how much income has been hidden from the IRS. We will use some of those numbers ourselves. How can these two facts be reconciled?

We can answer this by using two examples, the first one from a well-known book on statistics. The authors had heard various estimates of the number of murders committed by the Mafia, and wanted to determine the statistical validity of the estimates. They started off with a few newspaper clippings, stating that Police Chief X or FBI Assistant Director Y had said that there were a particular number of Mafia murders. The statisticians then phoned or wrote those who had made the statements, asking from where their numbers derived. When they did get a reply, it was almost invariably that the speaker had "heard it said," or they were referred to yet another news clipping. When all the clippings, statements, and hints were tracked down, the statisticians found that all were based on one or two extrapolations from simple data. There were really just a few facts on which the elaborate apparatus of references and cross-references rested.

There is no doubt that the Mafia had murdered people. Yet finding accurate estimates of activities which are illegal, shady, or secret is almost never done with certainty.

A second example is the destructive force of nuclear weapons possessed by the major powers. We often read in newspapers or see on TV statements to the effect that "the United States and the Soviets can destroy each other's cities 14 [or another number] times over."

But the reliability of the warheads, and where they are pointed, are highly guarded secrets, the most important in the intelligence arsenal of the two powers. The numbers we see in print are estimates made by independent think-tanks. They may be true. Then again, they may not. The President and the General Secretary of the Soviet Communist party are not talking.

All of this is by way of introduction to the often murky world of income-tax evasion and avoidance. Some of the numbers we will quote in the rest of this chapter are accurate to within a few percent. Others, because of the secret nature of the information involved, are based in part on what they do not allow in courtrooms—hearsay.

LORDS OF THE LOOPHOLES

The Johnson administration was leaving office in January 1969, run down by the Vietnam War. It was a time when cabinet officers did little but clean out their files and look for new jobs. Wave-making was left for the new cabinet.

Not so with Joe Barr, the outgoing Secretary of the Treasury. In Congressional testimony[2] three days before Lyndon Johnson headed back to the ranch in Texas, Barr noted that in 1967, 155 taxpayers with incomes over $200,000 had paid no federal taxes whatever. Twenty-three, or about one in seven, of these skillful tax avoiders had incomes of over $1 million.

People were incensed, and wrote Congress on this issue in unprecedented numbers. And, of course, things changed. the voice of the citizen was heard in the land. Congress passed the Tax Reform Act of 1969, based in part on this wave of indignation. It has amended its handiwork on at least a half dozen occasions since then.

Part of the 1969 law specified a minimum tax to encompass those who, by using existing tax exemptions and deductions, would otherwise have paid no tax. That part of the statute still stands.

Sisyphus and Tax Reform

But have matters really changed all that much? Congress, at least in this area, looks like the ancient god Sisyphus, known for rolling a huge boulder up a hill. When he got the rock to the crest, after tremendous effort, back down it would roll. He would have to start again.

Consider some numbers of citizens who escaped paying taxes on a lower income, of at least $50,000.[3,4] In 1969, before the passage of the Tax Reform Act, 301 fell into that privileged group; in 1979, over 8,000; in 1982, over 10,000.

In all fairness, the value of the dollar dropped from 1969 to 1982. As a result, there were more tax returns with an income of over $50,000 in 1982 than there were in 1969. (Growing national income also contributed to this effect.) Nonetheless, an increase of *thirty times* the number of individuals in that income group escaping all federal taxes cannot be blamed solely on inflation. Congress rolls the rock up the hill. But somehow, the force of gravity, in the form of tax shelters, manages to roll it down again.

Readers at this point might say, "This book is obviously about income and wealth distributions, not taxes. How do the taxes paid—or unpaid— affect your conclusions?"

The answer is simple. The income data we have gathered and presented in the previous chapters is based on the "adjusted gross income" (AGI). Before a taxpayer gets to that line in IRS form 1040, he or she can deduct the various amounts allowed by Congress. If the AGI is not a reasonable depiction of how much *real* income someone takes in, then the income graphs we have drawn will present a distorted picture.

Mr. TS and His Income

Let us see, with actual numbers, how this problem in income data might arise. In the 1970s, the Congressional Joint Committee on Taxation presented data on an unidentified individual. Let us call him Mr. TS, for tax shelter.

In 1974, he had a total income of $182,000 from wages, dividends, capital gains, farming, and oil.[5] If he had had that income in 1987, he would have been in the top 1.5% of tax returns, according to Figure 9.1. In 1974, Mr. TS would have been in the top few tenths of a percent.

While Mr. TS's bank account saw an income flow of $182,000, Congress did not see it that way at all. They allowed depletion and drilling deductions of $34,000 on his oil income. Even more importantly, he had a "loss" of $133,000 on his oil drilling partnership. We use the quotation marks around the word "loss" advisedly.

After these deductions, Mr. TS's AGI was only $9,000. (His economic income of $182,000 less the sum of $34,000 plus $133,000 equals $15,000; the difference between this latter figure and $9,000 is accounted for by yet other itemized deductions.) From being in the top percent of all incomes, Mr. TS dropped well below the average. He fell beneath even the middle class.

Mr. TS was assessed no direct income tax. All he had to pay was $1,000 as a "minimum tax." He ended up sending less than 0.5% of his total income to the IRS. For purposes of tax data, Mr. TS's real income of $182,000 did not appear in the IRS tables. As far as the IRS was concerned, he was just another below-average person with an AGI of $9,000.

Mr. TS may be a rare taxpayer—or, in his case, a nontaxpayer—who just happened to strike it rich with his deductions. In that case, our conclusions in previous chapters will not change much.

But suppose Mr. TS is representative of a large class of high-income taxpayers who, through legal means, have a much larger income than their reported AGI. In that case, our conclusions would be even *stronger*. That is, the Pareto region (above about the 97% level in Figure 9.1) would be approximately that shown by a broken line. The break between that region and the lognormal region below it would be even greater.

We doubt that Mr. TS is alone in his counting room, counting all his money. Just how many Mr. TSs there are, and where they lie on the income curve, will be the subject of much of the rest of this chapter.

INITIAL AND FINAL INCOME-TAX REPORTING

We should mention one curiosity of IRS tables. When they are issued, they are based on the forms as sent in to the IRS. After the forms are evaluated by the agency, they may ask for more taxes to be paid. Occasionally the IRS may send back overpayments, but we believe that this is not common.

In some cases, tax battles over large amounts can last for years. It is no wonder that all we generally have are what the IRS itself labels "preliminary" data.[6]

All this would be of concern only to accountants if we were sure that the final income data was almost exactly the same as the preliminary information. They are not.

Few people are going to argue with the IRS over a bill for $100 or $200. Many would over an assessment of $60,000. This is what faced William

Casey, former head of the Central Intelligence Agency, as he battled the IRS in tax court.[7]

Consider these two facts: (1) The IRS rarely gives back money (we are not counting refunds for initial overpayments); and (2) The biggest IRS extra assessment will be sent to the wealthiest people, all other factors being equal.

If the final income data were available after the IRS got through its handiwork, there would be even more taxpayers at the upper end of the scale than is recorded in the preliminary income results. In turn, the incomes in the Pareto region would be even higher. We would again see something like the broken line on the right-hand side of Figure 9.1.

THE IRS 595

In late 1989, the IRS published data on high-income taxpayers who paid little or no taxes in 1986.[8] There were 595 who paid no tax, in spite of incomes of over $200,000. It is not clear if these people paid an alternative minimum tax, or no tax whatsoever.

The year to which the following numbers apply was 1986, the last year before the 1986 Income Tax Reform Act went into effect. Some changes in that law, lowering substantially the marginal tax rates of the wealthy, were supposed to cut down on the attraction of tax shelters and other forms of deductions. Whether or not they really did so will only be found by later IRS reports.

About 529,000 couples and individuals reported total income of more than $200,000 in 1986.[6] The 595 who escaped tax-free are only a tiny fraction, so at first glance it hardly seems worthwhile to analyze them.

We discuss them because they are only the tip of the iceberg. An additional 33,800 of those who earned over $200,000 paid an effective tax rate of less than 15%. This fraction is less than that of a typical middle-income family.

These 33,800 high-income taxpayers had deductions that their brethren did not. The average tax rate for taxpayers earning over $200,000 in 1987 on their taxable income (somewhat less than AGI) was 33.4%.[6] The fortunate 33,800 paid less than half that rate.

The 595 tax-free individuals in 1986 can be contrasted with the 155 non-taxpayers at the same income level castigated by Secretary Barr in 1969. Allowing for an approximately three-fold increase in income levels in the intervening years, the number of tax-free individuals has not lessened. It might even be said to have risen. These 595 individuals had an average income of about $600,000. Two out of three had capital gains averaging $490,000 apiece.

A total of 453,000 taxpayers reported AGIs of more than $200,000 in 1987. This is less than the value of 529,000 couples and individuals with *total* incomes of more than this amount noted above, since total income is almost always greater than AGI. For these 453,000 taxpayers, the average capital gain (net loss) was about $155,000. Thus most of the IRS 595 had capital gains much greater than their fellow high-income earners.

Of the group, 118 had state tax refunds averaging $21,000. Of the 294,000 taxpayers with income of over $200,000 who received state income tax refunds, the average was $4,800.

The rest of the data on the IRS 595 is shown in Table 9.1. Almost all received some interest, averaging $133,000. Alimony alone, for the nine who received it, would be sufficient to put them into the above-$200,000 bracket.

Few, if any, of this group have what most people would call a zero-income year. But because of the way that the tax code is written, as far as the IRS was concerned, it *was* a zero-income period for this select group.

A LOOPHOLE IS NOT A LOOPHOLE

Perhaps the most common term used by journalists to describe the drafting of a tax bill by Congress is "loophole." "Giveaway" is a close second. A story in late 1989 in the *Wall Street Journal*[9] had a typical headline: "Senate's Tax Panel Measure is Jammed with Billions of Dollars in Giveaways."

A loophole implies something shady or mysterious, like a secret crossing through a mountain range. Yet the so-called loopholes created by Congress or other legislatures are as explicit as laws ever get.

It is true that many loopholes are devised behind closed doors. Yet when the *Wall Street Journal*, the largest-circulation newspaper in the United States, can report on them in great detail, the loopholes may not be as secret as they are often pictured.

Table 9.1
The IRS 595—Income and Deductions[8]

Source of Income or Deduction	Number Claiming	Average Income or Deduction
Wages	457	$232,000
Capital gains	394	490,000
Unemployment compensation	3	not available
State tax refunds	118	21,000
Social Security	33	6,000
Alimony	9	267,000
Dividends	373	136,000
Rent	115	140,000
Home mortgage interest	275	68,000 ($5600 per month)
Medical deductions	25	110,000
Casualty, theft and other losses	19	688,000

None of this is to justify their existence. If any tax code is to be considered fair, it should be written in a general way, applicable to all taxpayers. Special provisions dealing with just a few individuals or corporations should not be included. Yet they continue to be.

Consider some examples from the October 1989 proposed revisions. Fortunately, not all of them were passed:

1. Multi-millionaires with grandchildren could pass on up to $2 million to their grandchildren tax free. The income from this money would accrue to the grandchildren tax free as well. This measure was proposed by Senator Bentsen of Texas, himself a millionaire and grandfather of five.

2. A tax credit for ethanol-based gasoline would save Archer-Daniels-Midland Co. more than $170 million over three years. This was pushed by Senator Daschle of South Dakota. The agricultural crops in that state would be a prime beneficiary of the provision.

3. Pennsylvania is a center of tuxedo manufacture. Senator Heinz of that state proposed that tuxedos be fully depreciated for tax purposes in two or three years, rather than the five years that the present tax code requires. The cost of this change to the government was not estimated.

These provisions are loopholes in the sense that a particular industry, company, or tiny group of individuals (millionaire grandparents) has been favored. They are *not* loopholes in the sense of being completely secret until a clever tax lawyer, burning the midnight oil, stumbles across them.

GIMME SHELTER—A BEGINNING

Tax shelters did not spring up like mushrooms after a rain in the 1980s, with the start of the Reagan administration. Shelters go back to the beginning of the first primitive tax systems. It is only the name that has received all the publicity in recent years.

By the administration of Franklin Roosevelt, even with a Federal government revenue less than a hundredth of what it is today, shelters were common. The president, in a 1935 press conference, referring to one wealthy family that had 197 trusts (one type of tax shelter prevalent in those days) said, "They are a very thrifty family."[10]

In the same press conference, the president gave a definition that still holds up: "Tax avoidance means that you hire a $250,000-fee lawyer and he changes the word 'evasion' into the word 'avoidance.'"

What They Are

Briefly, shelters are an investment in a business arrangement that generates more tax losses—translated into deductions for an investor—than profits. These losses, which should exceed the investor's cash outlay, are subtracted from his or her income when tax time comes around. This transaction should leave the taxpayer with fewer taxes to pay—in some cases, nothing. And after all this, he or she owns part of the investment.

The range of these shelters is staggering. Meyer[11] lists shelters, at one time or another, in citrus farms, duck farms, oyster farms, jojoba beans, llamas, Arabian stallions, and billboards.

Energy Shelters

Tax shelters for oil drilling go back about the farthest of energy shelters. First passed in 1918 by a Congress trying to stimulate what was thought to be a small energy resource, the fabled depletion allowance has withstood assaults for over seven decades. However, it was only in the last decade or two that tax shelters built financially on these allowances were sold to investors who would not know an oil-field Christmas tree from the green ones that go up at the end of December.

More curious have been the shelters built to take advantage of enthusiasm for renewable energy systems. This surge of interest began with the oil crisis of 1973, and has abated only slightly since. The main tax shelters have been in wind energy. Charles Ebinger, director of the Energy and Strategic Resources unit of the prestigious Center for Strategic and International Studies at Georgetown University, writes[12]:

> [The wind industry's] growth has resulted not from energy or cost advantages, but from tax advantages that make wind—in the words of *Forbes* magazine—'perhaps the juiciest tax shelter in the land.' A windmill salesman in California told *Renewable Energy News*, 'A project can generate a 122% return in the first year, even if the machines don't produce power.'
>
> The unparalleled tax preference has led to inevitable problems. The wind industry is worrying about unsound 'windfarm' deals designed only as tax shelters. One industry official recently said, 'One-third of California investment is complete technical garbage or poorly designed projects.'
>
> The 'windrush' in California is costing taxpayers as much as $500 million a year in tax credits and other incentives.

Ralph Nader, the consumer activist, has denounced the conventional energy companies, such as those that produce coal, oil, and nuclear power, for assorted transgressions. However, that has not kept one of the groups he founded, Public Citizen, from criticizing the tax shelters that sprung up around one of the energy industries he favors, wind.

Matthew Cooper, writing in one of Public Citizen's publications,[13] notes that in 1980, Congress gave wind farm investors a 15% tax credit in addition to the standard 10% investment tax credit. California coughed up a 25% tax credit of its own. Wind farms became, according to Cooper, "the stuff of which tax shelter dreams are made." He writes:

> Suppose the investor puts up $120,000. . . . The first benefit is the basic 10% investment tax credit, for a tax savings of $12,000. . . . Then comes the 15% energy tax credit, good for $18,000 . . . and a depreciation deduction which can save $7,875 in taxes for investors in the top tax bracket. [This last value has dropped since the article was written]. The net federal benefit is, then, $37,875. But California chips in with its own 25% tax credit (which actually becomes smaller than 25% once all the math is completed). Add state depreciation and bingo—the total tax benefits for the first year are as much as $59,475 on a $120,000 investment.

One advertisement described in the article made it crystal clear to any investors who still did not get the point: "Reduce federal withholding by earning $52,750 in tax credits with just a $6,000 down payment."

If a tax shelter involving llamas or oyster farms collapses, not much harm is done except to the investors involved. In the case of wind farms, the shelters built around them may have served to retard the eventual introduction of the devices into the nation's energy system. Cooper writes:

> The juicy tax breaks allowed in current tax laws for the first few years of a windmill's operation offer no incentive for well-designed, long-lasting windmills. Investors collect simply by slapping up a windmill whether it works efficiently or not. 'No one cares about it working,' complains James Carabina of the securities division of the Massachusetts secretary of state office. 'We're rewarding the unsuccessful.'

As a coda to the strange affair of the windmill tax shelters, apparently the financing for many of them was done through savings and loans institutions already on shaky foundations. When some of these S&Ls collapsed in the late 1980s, the windmills came into the possession of the Resolution Trust Corporation, a federally owned agency designed to effect a bailout of the S&Ls. So when some windmills in California spin, they are cranking out federally owned energy.

Farm Shelters

We have mentioned curiosities like oyster and jojoba farms serving as tax shelters. But ordinary farms, growing the usual crops of corn and wheat, also can sprout shelters. Paper losses are generated for investors who have never seen a manure pile.

How much do these city-based shelters cost the taxpayers? The Congressional Joint Committee on Taxation estimated a loss of $2.6 billion between 1985 and 1987.[14]

Do these benefits go to real farmers, or to city slickers? Need we answer? A Department of Agriculture study[15] found that 12,000 taxpayers claimed farm losses of $50,000 or more. It turned out that these big losers had not had their farms washed away by floods nor were long-lost refugees from Tobacco Road. Their average off-farm income, from salaries, investments, and other sources was $122,000. The study was conducted in 1976. In that year, an income of $122,000 would have put a taxpayer in the highest few tenths of a percent of the nation.

The average farm loss of this group was $104,000. (Recall that only those with losses of more than $50,000 were included in the study.) Finally, the average adjusted gross income of the group was about $18,000. From being in the top few tenths of a percent of real income they descended to just above average, at least on what was reported to the IRS.

These farm shelters were roaring along in 1976, well before Ronald Reagan took office. The trees may have flowered during his administration, but the seeds were planted earlier.

REAL ESTATE SHELTERS

We mentioned earlier that Mortimer Zuckerman, a member of the *Forbes* 400 list, paid no income taxes between 1980 and 1985. As far as we know, this was done legally. He, along with many others, was able to take advantage of laws encouraging real-estate tax shelters.

Mr. Zuckerman was brought to attention because his tax returns were made public in a legal dispute over his ownership of the opinion magazine *Atlantic*. For almost all others using real-estate tax shelters, tax returns remain locked up in accountants' safes.[16]

While we do not know Mr. Zuckerman's real or economic income during the first half of the 1980s, we can make some rough calculations of his economic position. According to *Forbes*, his net worth by 1986 was about $250 million. If he suddenly became Mr. Cautious and decided to put all his assets in tax-free municipal bonds (another shelter), he might receive an annual income of perhaps $15 million. This assumes an interest rate of around 6%; the rate will vary over time.

All this would be tax free. If he were an ordinary entrepreneur in the top tax bracket of 28%, this tax-free income would be about equivalent to a taxable income of around $21 million.

It is a reasonable assumption that his economic income would be of that order, give or take $5 million. Whatever it is, Mr. Zuckerman's real income is certainly higher than the goose egg he legally reported to the IRS.

Is Mr. Zuckerman a financial genius, who has found a provision of the tax code overlooked by everyone else? Not likely. Joel Kozol, his attorney, has said that due to paper losses allowed by the IRS, a zero tax liability "is true of almost every substantial real-estate developer in the country."

Many of those in the *Forbes 400* are real-estate based. Of this group, fifty-nine made real estate their primary business, and thirty-two have it as a major sideline. This is then about 22% of the total.

What seems to be happening in real estate, as contrasted with other business ventures like drugstores or machinery, can be described by the laws of classical economics. According to these laws, to a first approximation all types of business should be about equally profitable in the long run. Suppose that a business like diamond mining generated huge profits for its entrepreneurs, as it has in the past. If the market works as it should, others will rush into the field to garner some of the profits. The earnings per unit of capital invested will eventually be about the same as in other industries.

This has not happened in real estate, because of government intervention. In 1981, the tax laws were changed so that buildings could be fully depreciated in 15 years. But in reality, commercial buildings last far longer than that. They often *increase* in worth over time, until they are extremely old, rather than the reverse. This depreciation is the basis of tax shelters. The great concentration of real estate developers on the *Forbes* list suggests that normal market forces are not working properly, due to government actions.

Defining a Shelter

When is a shelter a shelter, and when is it a normal part of the tax system? One definition was given by Richard Wollack of Consolidated Capital, the nation's third-largest real estate investment fundraiser in 1983[17]:

> Once you start approaching a 50 percent writeoff in the first year, it starts smacking more of being a tax shelter—when the writeoff becomes one of the more significant investment objectives of the transaction. Certainly if you approach a 100 percent writeoff, I think these are tax shelters. That is, if someone puts in $100,000 and they get a $50,000 deduction in the first year, it is starting to take on a little bit of what I would call a tax shelter perspective, although not nearly as much as the deal that has a 100 percent writeoff or more than 100 percent.

Whoever defines a tax shelter can run into the same fog as those who used to say how rich was too rich without having probability graph paper in front of them. If a 50% writeoff in the first year is not a tax shelter, does 51% make it one? Without a cut-off point of some kind, we are liable to wander around in the usual definitional haze.

OTHER INCOME EXEMPTIONS, DEDUCTIONS, AND GENERAL SUBTRACTIONS

Two examples above, wind and farming, are often instances of syndicated or marketed shelters. But there are many more exemptions and deductions built into the tax codes for those with enough wealth and income to take advantage of them. There are dozens or hundreds scattered through the 2100 pages of the tax codes.

Let us return to the grandparents shelter proposed by Senator Bentsen. In 1986, Congress passed its Tax Reform Act, closing down many shelters. But like a drunk who needs just one more for the road, Congress just could not bring itself to quit cold. For many years before 1986, part of the law was the "generation skipping transfer,"[18] whereby wealthy people shifted assets to their grandchildren without paying taxes. This cut out one level of estate tax, namely, assets shifted to children as opposed to grandchildren.

Congress was apparently influenced by the wealthy wine-making Gallo family of California to keep this provision for three more years. It was to expire at the end of 1989, but not if Senator Bentsen had his way. Under the "Gallo exemption," $2 million per grandchild could be transferred tax-free. Jack Porter of the accounting firm Ernst & Whinney noted that this might save about $1.6 million in taxes for each grandchild.

There are other ways to keeping one's estate from paying taxes upon death. A married couple can give away $20,000 per recipient annually, free of gift tax.[19] This procedure can continue indefinitely. While it would take centuries or millennia to exhaust the fortunes of a John Kluge or Sam Walton this way, many moderately wealthy individuals can avoid paying gift taxes this way. And since Congress raised the tax-free limit on estates to $600,000, well beyond the assets of most Americans, that part of federal taxes is avoided by almost everybody.

Most of the deductions that are argued about are taken by those near the top of the income pyramid. The following two examples show this.

A Cliffhanger Legal Decision

Ben Heineman, chairman of Northwest Industries, deducted the cost of a summer office in Wisconsin from his income.[20] The office was a quarter-million dollar one-room building suspended from the side of a cliff. He said that the office was necessary to avoid the distractions of Chicago (his regular office) and its heat.

In a decision that the *Wall Street Journal* described as a "cliff-hanger," the judge to whom Mr. Heineman appealed allowed the claim. He said that the one-room structure was "appropriate and helpful" to Heineman's duties.

The amount of Heineman's income was not given in the news report. Yet the cost of the office, $250,000, was substantial. Is it unreasonable to assume that his annual income was at least the cost of the office? This would put him well within the Pareto range, in the top ½% of all taxpayers. Assuming that the IRS did not reverse the decision on appeal, Mr. Heineman would have had greater real income than appeared on his tax form.

Solid Gold Cadillac

Our second example deals with luxury cars. In 1983, Congress voted to limit deductions that business people and professionals, like lawyers and doctors, take on these vehicles.[21] According to the American International Automobile Dealers Association's president, Robert McElwaine, about half the 73,000 Mercedes-Benz cars sold in 1982 were to corporations, lawyers, and doctors for use in business operations.

Fred Chapman, a spokesman for the Mercedes-Benz company, was unhappy about the proposal to limit the deductions for business autos to the first $15,000 of cost. "Why cars, why isolate this product? What about first-class air fares? What about Lear jets? . . . What's this penalty for trying to achieve excellence?"

Why and what indeed. While the incomes of the taxpayers who receive these deductions is not known, most are in the Pareto part—the upper 3%—of the income curve. There may be a few relatively poor people who scrimp and save to buy a Mercedes, but we think they are in a small minority.

The deductions of such items as expensive cottages and luxury cars makes the economic income of the wealthy higher than is reported on their tax forms. In turn, it makes the slope of the Pareto region in Figure 9.1 even steeper than shown on the solid line.

'TIS A PUZZLEMENT—COMPLICATED TAX LAWS

One of the reasons why the wealthy are able to show less income on their tax forms than they really garner is only indirectly connected with tax rulings or lawyers. It is based on the sheer *complexity* of the tax laws.

Just before the first proposal for what eventually became the 1986 tax reform act was published, Bernard Shapiro spoke on this.[22] He was national director for tax policy for Price Waterhouse & Co., a leading accounting firm, and a former staff director of the Congressional Joint Committee on Taxation. He said, "Much of the complication would remain even if a 'flat' tax proposal were enacted . . . the tax system will still be complex even if reasonable simplification efforts are successful."

So it has come to pass. The number of tax brackets after 1986 was much less than before, but the tax code itself is not much smaller.

What does this have to do with how rich is too rich? As the old saying has it, "it takes money to make money." If someone wants to challenge the IRS, it will take the services of a tax lawyer and accountant. While the success of the appeal cannot be guaranteed, one thing is for sure: A goodly amount of cash will be required to penetrate the subparagraphs and sub-subparagraphs of the tax code. Few people have this cash on hand, even if they think the IRS did them wrong.

So the imposing length and complexity of the tax code benefits the well-to-do, regardless of what that code contains. It is usually only they who can afford to challenge any adverse rulings, or probe for hidden deductions.

THE CHEATERS

What does the public think of tax cheats? Who exactly are the cheaters?

The public is of two minds on tax cheats and frauds. On one hand, there are severe penalties for cheating on taxes, as Leona Helmsley and others have found. These laws are obviously based on public opinion as reflected in legislation.

However, many people find the tax system unfair. If a large part of the nation thinks the tax system is unjust in some way, they will not be overly concerned about tax fraud.

This is reflected in a *USA Today* survey.[23] About 74% of the respondents thought that people cheated because the system is "unfair." Not, mind you, that only born thieves cheat or because the cheaters want to increase their bank account. Since the system is unjust, according to three-quarters of those asked, the tax cheats have some justification. An even more surprising result was that 36% actually approved of, or were undecided about, tax cheaters.

For many years, income tax officials in this country pointed with pride at the system. "Look at Italy, with millions of income tax cheaters. That's why they have to collect most of their government revenues by sales taxes, gasoline taxes and the like," the IRS might say. "But *our* tax system is supported by almost everyone. Nobody in any country likes paying taxes, but the incidence of cheating here is small. That is why the government here can collect such a large proportion of its revenues from income taxes, and such a small proportion in excise levies."

This may have been true at one time. But the survey quoted above shows that support for the tax system is crumbling. If one-third of the population approves of or condones tax cheats, it will prove increasingly difficult to convict anyone of that crime. Leona Helmsley may be one of the last big-time tax cheats to hear the word "guilty" in court.

The survey did not categorize cheating by the *size* of the offense. Far more people are willing to condone making off with $5 or $10 than are ready to overlook stealing millions. Jean Valjean may have been sentenced to prison for stealing a loaf of bread. Today, he would not see the inside of prison.

There is a certain logic to cheating. The greater the opportunity, the larger the chances that the IRS will not get its due. Someone in an office mail room may purloin a paper clip or two. An accountant in a paper clip factory can doctor the books to pay for a BMW.

The IRS found that taxpayers report 94% of their income.[24] But taxpayers in a more independent position, not as restricted by W-2s stating their wage income, had different results. This latter group, including professionals, owners of small businesses, self-employed people or others likely to itemize deductions, reported only half of the previous proportion, or only 47%, of their income. In other words, half the income of this large group went unreported.

There are those who pay more than they should. About 8% of taxpayers fell into that unfortunate group. But that proportion is far outnumbered by the 43% who did not pay enough. The IRS estimated that this group of scofflaws cost the government over $64 billion in lost revenue in 1987. Other estimates are higher. Note that this is lost *taxes*, not the underreporting of income.

How many people actually cheat, as contrasted to the about one-third that approve or condone it? Separating out cheating from just making mistakes is not simple. Obviously, the 8% of taxpayers who paid too much were not cheating. Or were they? Perhaps they cheated, but *still* paid too much.

About one-quarter of taxpayers actually own up to cheating. Social scientists say the *true* fraction is closer to one-third. Some people will never admit cheating, even when promised anonymity in a research project.

This last fraction sounds remarkably like the 36% who approved or condoned cheating in the *USA Today* survey. Whether those who condone actually do the very deed is not known.

A study in the *Journal of Personality and Social Psychology* described tax evaders in the Netherlands. They are highly competitive, as well as placing a high value on "being better" than other people. Russell Weigel, a psychologist who did some of the research, said, "Their search for opportunities for personal advantages goes hand in hand with a lack of regard for legal and moral standards. They have the attitude, 'Don't lecture me about what's right.'"

Dr. Weigel said this was the first direct psychological examination of law-breaking tax cheaters. This makes it quite different from the self-identification studies often done in the United States. Someone who loudly proclaims on April 15 that he did the IRS out of hundreds or thousands of dollars by a few tricks may or may not be a true cheater. For all we know, he may be one of the 8% who *overpay*, in spite of all his finagling.

Weigel did his work in Holland because the list of tax cheaters there is public. In the United States, that dossier is secret. When someone like Mrs. Helmsley makes the headlines, it is the exception, not the rule.

Cheaters see the collection system as basically unjust. This is also the view of three-quarters of Americans, so the cheaters are not that peculiar in this attitude. However, they think that *everyone* cheats on taxes, in contrast to the three-quarters who claim that they do not. As Dr. Weigel puts it, the inveterate tax cheaters say, "Others get away with it, so why shouldn't I?"

GOING UNDERGROUND

From tax cheaters, who report some of their income but obscure the rest by various tricks, we go to the underground. That part of the economy never shows up on the account books in the first place.

Some of this underground economy may be perfectly innocent and legal, but not reported to the IRS because it is too much trouble. The young people mowing lawns or babysitting around the neighborhood may not realize that they are part of the underground. They generally do not expect to have their meager earnings reported to the IRS, or fill in a form 1040.

Another part of the underground may be completely *illegal*, such as drug dealing, prostitution, and other criminal activities. Nobody expects people who engage in this to fill in forms.

Yet other segments of the underground economy are deliberately hidden from the IRS. It might be someone you know: a high-school teacher painting houses on the weekend or a woodsman selling firewood from the back of a pickup truck—all for cash, of course.

If the underground economy is small in comparison to the gross national product, we do not have to worry about it affecting income distribution curves. Then it would not change the answer to the question, how rich is too rich?

How big is subterranean income? Nobody knows, of course, because it is *designed* to be hidden. However, some economists have investigated the question from an unusual angle. Friedrich Schneider and Markus Hofreither considered the amount of currency in circulation in 14 industrialized countries.[25] If there is one thing that someone who works in the underground economy wants to avoid, it is pieces of paper, such as receipts and cancelled checks, with names and amounts of money written on them.

So the more cash in circulation, all other factors being equal, the greater the size of the underground economy. The amount of currency *per capita* in 1986 in the United States was $846. Allowing for collections of Kennedy quarters at the back of drawers and unspent Susan B. Anthony coins, this is an enormous amount of cash per person. Most of us could not lay our hands on more than $100 in the next half-hour. Some people must possess enormous amounts of cash.

The economists, using currency amounts as a guide, found that the size of the underground economy varied greatly from one nation to the next. Their results are shown in Table 9.2.

Italy heads the list, with about 30% of their GNP below the table. The stories from Italy on how the authorities can be cheated are almost mythological in their scope, with a taxman turning the corner and coming across huge factories unaccounted for in his books.

The United States is at the bottom of the list, with only 5% of the national economy missing from the government's rolls. This may be due to the great and abiding honesty of the American people, as is carefully pointed out by politicians on the Fourth of July.

Or it may be that Americans are just more clever than Italians, being able to fool economists and everyone else.

Five percent may not seem that much. But 5% of a $4 trillion economy is $200 billion not reported to the IRS. If most of the money in the hidden economy goes to people in the lognormal income region (i.e., the lower 97% or so) the effect on our conclusions is likely to be small.

However, if a big chunk goes to the top income earners in the Pareto region, the income curves could be changed substantially. If the Pareto region contains about 3% of all taxpayers, and this group has about 20% of all *declared* income,[6] then 5% of the economy would correspond to about a 25% increase (5/20) in their income. Other estimates of the hidden economy are higher than that noted in the table, ranging from 7.5%[26] to 10% to 20%[27] of the economy. The latter range would correspond to between $400 billion and $800 billion unreported.

Table 9.2
Estimated Size of Domestic Underground Economy, Percent of Total Output, in 1978[25]

Country	Percent	Country	Percent
Austria	10	Italy	30
Belgium	21	Norway	11
Britain	7	Spain	23
Canada	11	Sweden	13
Denmark	9	Switzerland	7
France	7	United States	5
Ireland	8	West Germany	11

The amount of *tax* that would have been collected if these economic moles had performed their activities in the sunlight is much less than the amounts above, although still substantial. The IRS estimates that it lost $106 billion in revenue in 1986 on unreported cash transactions, from overstated deductions or unjustified tax credits.[28] This includes both of what we are calling the underground economy and tax cheating.

By way of comparison, the *total* amount of federal income taxes paid by everyone who earned $100,000 or more in 1987 (i.e., the entire Pareto region and then some) was about $119 billion.[6] The underground economy, whatever its precise size, is still a huge beast.

ARTS AND CRAFTS

The number of ways in which the IRS can be left holding the bag is vast. Estimators of tax losses must feel that they are searching for black frogs in a swamp, at midnight, in a driving rain.

An example from the art world was recorded a few years ago.[29] In studying 468 tax returns from 1982, the IRS found charitable contributions of art prints valued at $103 million, or an average of $220,000 per return. These were prints, not original works of art. Prints can be churned out by the thousands, if not millions. The IRS experts disagreed with every claim, and said that the gifts were worth a grand total of $702,000, or $1,500 per tax return. This represented a 99.3% reduction of the taxpayers' estimates of the prints' value.

According to the *Washington Post*, ''In a typical scheme, an investor will buy an art object for, say, $5,000 cash but an appraiser will value it at 12 times that price. The owner holds the object for a year to qualify it as a long-term capital asset, donates it to charity and takes a $60,000 deduction.''

In the year in which this scheme was revealed, the top marginal tax rate was 50%. If the art lover whose system was described in the news report fell into that tax bracket, he or she could save $30,000 in taxes (0.5 × 60,000) by laying out $5,000 for prints. This would be multiplying money six times in one year, an investment that most of us would like to have.

PERKS

To bilk the IRS as in the previous example, a conscious effort has to be made. Somebody has to buy a print, get a friendly appraiser to value it more than it is worth, then find a museum curator willing to look the other way. Each of these steps involves some risk in being detected.

Far easier is the role of executives in large corporations. They get the benefits of perquisites (the converse of greater deductions to charity) without the hassle of dealing with recalcitrant art appraisers or the IRS.

Even better, the IRS generally does not treat these executive prerogatives as taxable, so there are no worried sessions in the tax auditor's office.

Jan Pen, whose "grand parade" formed much of the first chapter of this book, said[30]:

> The company car is also used for private purposes. For top executives: the company plane. Generous expense accounts. Hospitality to business connexions, business friends, relatives and friends at company expense. The country house available for that purpose. All the firm's clerical and technical services are also available to the top executives. Neither managers of large firms nor their wives ever have to renew their passports or queue for tickets or for anything else. As someone moves higher up in the firm, these privileges increase, and if we forget to include them we find an income distribution that is less unequal than in reality. (Quoting R. M. Titmuss, *Income Distribution and Social Change*)

GETTING CAUGHT

For a long time, the penalties for getting caught for nonreporting were minor. You had to pay back what you owed, but not much more. According to former IRS Commissioner Jerome Kurtz,[28] the 1982 "substantial underreporting penalty" was only 10% of the understated tax, plus interest. If someone thought he or she had a better than one-in-ten chance of getting away with underreporting, it would be economically *wise* to cheat.

Even with this penalty, the IRS levied only 149 underpayment fines in the first year of their use. Either Americans are extremely upright and conscientious about paying taxes, or the IRS has little success in catching those who are not. As one IRS official put it, "We're still the best place in town to borrow from for many people."

HOW DO THE CURVES OF INCOME CHANGE?

Most of the benefits of reporting lower incomes go to the wealthy. In this section, we will estimate how this affects reported income distributions.

We'll start with tax shelters, described earlier. According to Meyer,[31] the average tax shelter owner earns $81,000 a year, putting him or her in the top 4% of the population. Stating it another way, 82% of tax shelter benefits go to people with incomes of over $100,000.[32]

The total extent of shelters will probably never be known precisely, but one estimate[33] was $49 billion in 1983. If we want to determine how this affects income distribution, we would have to know the income of each shelter user and the amount he or she has invested. So to do the calculations, we have to make some assumptions.

First, we will disregard the 18% of sheltered money that comes from people earning less than $100,000. This makes the amount invested in 1983 shelters by those above this income level $(1 - 0.18) \times \$49$ billion, or $40 billion. We still have to spread this amount among taxpayers in the above-$100,000 bracket, some of whom probably had nothing to do with shelters. Since we do not know who did or did not, we will assume proportional allocation.

The total adjusted gross income of those above $100,000 in 1987 was $464 billion.[6] If what we have said is valid, the true income, including shelters, was closer to $504 billion (= $464 + $40), or 8.6% more.

A recent IRS audit of about 50,000 taxpayers shows that those among the top 12% of taxpayers account for at least 40% of tax underpayments.[1] The top 1% of taxpayers *alone* accounts for 14% of underreporting. The survey says that 70% of audited returns showing more than $200,000 income—the top ½% of taxpayers—have unreported income.

What conclusions can we draw from this mass of numbers? If the top 12% account for 40% of underpayments, the bottom 88% must account for 60%. To translate these percentages into dollars, we note that the bottom 88% of taxpayers generated about $1.6 trillion in adjusted gross income in 1987.[6]

Recall that one estimate of the underground economy was 5% of total goods and services produced in this country.[25] If the size of the economy is about $4 trillion, there is a $200 billion economy undetected by the IRS. Not all of this is income, of course. If we assume that perhaps 70% of this amount is actually income, unreported earnings are about $140 billion.

Now we can compare the numbers we have calculated. For the bottom 88% of taxpayers—roughly corresponding to the lognormal region— unreported income is 60% of the total unreported income of approximately $140 trillion, as we noted above. So unreported income is about 5% of reported income for the bulk of taxpayers. This in turn corresponds closely to an IRS survey in 1983.[24] So the lognormal curve would change, but not by much.

Now consider the top 12%, those with 40% of underreporting. Using the calculations above, this corresponds to about $60 billion of income hidden from the IRS. The 1987 adjusted gross income of this group is about $1.1 trillion.[6] So the proportion of unreported to reported income for the top 12% (i.e., those earning more than about $50,000 in 1987) is about 5.5%. This in turn is about the same proportion, given all the uncertainties in data, as that of the lower 88%.

It is only when we get to the top 1% of taxpayers that we see a different trend. The IRS audit found that they account for 14% of total underreporting, or about $25 billion by our estimate. Their adjusted gross income was perhaps $260 billion in 1987.[6] So the proportion of unreported income is about 9.6% (25/260) for this group.

Suppose that all of the members of the top 1% shared proportionately in this underreporting. Then the results in terms of Figure 9.1 would be the broken line slightly above the "no-shelter" not far from dashed line.

We have assumed that underreporting is done *proportionately* within an income group. If someone with an income of $100,000 is assumed to leave out $10,000 (i.e., 10%) from his or her form 1040, we are assuming that someone with an income of $1 million will omit $100,000. While this simplifies the mathematics, it obviously will not hold in all cases. Nonetheless, the assumption fits with the credo: The more opportunity, the more action.

We have found that both the lognormal (the lower 97% or so) and Pareto top 3% or so) curves *do* change when we take account of unreported income. The nature of unreported income precludes a precise assessment of how the income curves will change. As far as we can tell, the kink between the two regions remains in about the same place.

SUMMARY

Tax evasion and avoidance can be described in terms of a spectrum. On one side, we have the time-hallowed tax exemptions and deductions, such as interest payments on mortgages. On the other side, we have people who have not reported their income in years, let alone paid any taxes on it. In between, we have a welter of tax shelters and tax-avoidance schemes, some shady and others mostly in the sunlight.

Trying to make mathematical sense from what is often a surreptitious activity is not simple. However, as far as we can tell, after taking into account sheltering and other forms of tax avoidance, our overall conclusions still stand. The Pareto region is still distinct from the lognormal income distribution, and there is *still* a kink between the two.

The story of tax evasion is more a tale of legends in the public mind than it is of cold statistical tables or graphs. The Leona Helmsley story in 1989 was just the latest in a long series of semimythological parables. Our approach here has been analytical, thus taking away some of the fun that people often have when talking about this subject.

The ambivalent feelings that many of us have about tax evasion was perhaps best expressed by Art Buchwald, the syndicated humorist. He wrote[34]: "Show me a rich man who doesn't pay any taxes to the government, and I'll show you an American hero."

10

A PERSONAL MEMOIR ON WEALTH

The rest of this book deals with the wealthy and their assets *en masse*. This is probably inevitable in a book devoted to studying mathematical concepts of income. Yet the wealthy are more than dots on a graph. They are real people. This statement is not made to curry favor from the rich, but simply to note a fact. Behind each of the terms in an economic equation are people—some good, some bad.

In 1944, at the height of World War II, an old man sat down with a notebook and started to write with a yellow pencil. Gnarled with age, he was in his eighty-seventh and last year. Somehow he sensed, as many aged people do, that the end of living was near. He and his beloved mother, who was the great-grandmother of one of our (SC) wives, were not wealthy. They were not in the du Pont or Mellon class. However, his mother, Belinda, did accumulate a modest fortune. Since the stories of Henry Ford, Edwin Land, Lee Iacocca, and other millionaires have been told and retold many times, like Hail Mary's over a string of beads, we thought it would be of interest, in a book devoted to studying wealth, to see how a small store of money was built up long ago.

The original notebook, written by Charles Randall, extended over many sheets in manuscript form. When typed, they yielded about ten pages of single-spaced legal-sized paper, too much to include here. To keep this excerpt to a reasonable length, we will concentrate on the wealth and income aspects, as opposed to the strictly personal yarns and stories. For simplicity, we will run otherwise separate passages together without the use of dots and ellipses. This will give what follows a more continuous look. We have also taken the liberty of correcting spelling and grammar[1]:

> Ireland must be heaven, for my Mother came from there. In 1827 in County Leitrim in the north of Ireland a fine lady was born and named Belinda

Notley, the twelfth child. Her mother died when she was born. About 300 miles across the Irish Channel on the Orkney Islands [in Scotland], in the same year [1827] a boy was born named James Randall. He was the youngest of four children and his mother died at his birth. His father's name was John Randall.

After [John Randall's] second wife died, he moved to St. Johns in Nova Scotia [Canada], where he engaged in ship building.

Belinda Notley and James Randall met [in Pawtucket, Rhode Island]. He was very quiet and timid but she took charge of him and in 1852 married him. She said that she had to train him how to take a girl around and to spend some money on her. She declared that she would buy every house they would ever live in and [that] included the house that they were married in. She was very ambitious.

Father [James Randall] was doing very well. He had started and developed a large furniture and piano factory and was making money, [and] was also the inventor of a machine to make seamless eyelets like they use in shoes today [1944]. The eyelet company expanded and combined with jewelry manufacturing and other articles. They formed a trust, but he objected, saying it wasn't honest to do so, and sold his stock and resigned the presidency, although he had a large salary, and quit.

Mother loved to travel and every year she would take Etta (my older sister) and me and one or two other children on a trip to New York. It was on one of these trips that she discovered something that started her speculative mind and her opportunity to make a lot of money. Her only difficulty was her husband. He could earn all that was necessary for the family and did not approve of making fortunes. He claimed that too much money ruined families and that the second generation should not have enough to keep them from work. It made them no account. A sufficient income secured for life, enough to educate the children and take care of them in their old age, was all that anyone should have. She, on the other hand, wanted a fortune and everything in the world for her children.

In [1861 the Civil War] broke out. Business was at a standstill. Mother noticed that whenever the South gained a victory the Government bonds would drop down [in value]. They were Government 6% interest income so when they dropped she would invest, and if they went lower, she would buy more.

There was a space over the upper drawer of her dresser and she would tack the bond up there and say nothing about it to anyone. I saw her do it but it made no impression on me. Twenty-one years later, after her death, Father remarked that she had never said anything about the bonds and didn't know how many of them there were. Mother and he respected her wishes to leave them there. We took them out and there was $17,000 worth of bonds with the coupons attached. I sold them for $1.15 a bond, a total of over $20,000.

On her trips to New York [Mother] discovered the —— [company]. They handled manufactured goods and imported goods. They established auction rooms and had samples of the various goods and auctioned them off. The bids were taken on lots of cases of this and gross lots of the other, and when you bid on that basis you bid for the whole lot, and it might be a cargo, or thousands of dozens, and the successful bidders would divide with other bidders when the allotment was too large.

Mother discovered these sales places and discovered what she was looking for, adventure into commerce. I was with her, and they passed cards of a new kind of button so cheap that she made a bid and they were knocked down to her. Then they made up the bill and she found that she had bought a carload of buttons. She was game and not knowing how to interest the other bidders, ordered the whole shipment to Providence [Rhode Island].

We had a large barn and we stored the whole shipment here, about filling it up. Mother took samples to Harwell and Richards [apparently a notions store] and told them they had to sell the buttons, they were a new design, etc. She induced them to put a man on the road to make a specialty of them.

In those days just after the [Civil] war goods of all kinds were scarce and anything new was quickly absorbed. Harwell and Richards didn't think it would pay to make a specialty of buttons, they didn't think the supply would last on good demand for them [i.e., if demand was good the carload of buttons would be all that was available]. She assured them she could get the supply. She then designed a dress that was covered with buttons.

They [the buttons] were about as large as a dime with a glass front and had colored lining, very pretty. On this dress was row after row down the front and back, across the front, down the sleeves, lots of buttons. She visited some dressmakers and interested them to make the design and introduce it. (I think that she gave away the buttons and guaranteed the sale of the dress; anyway, the dress was a hit, for at that time the styles were changing and everything new was immediately accepted.) Well, the new style took at once and it was buttons everywhere. She and Harwell and Richards made so much money on the deal that they encouraged her to buy anything that she wanted and they would handle it. So that set her off. Back to New York the next season and this time she bought a cargo from Africa of ostrich feathers—all kinds, sizes and colors—beautiful to look at. There were more of these than buttons. She also bought a large shipment from France of ribbons, from one-half inch to six inches wide, all colors and designs.

At that time the poke bonnet was the rage. Everyone alike and everyone wore them. They were rather plain, just two strings and a bow, but Mother planned what to do. She went around to the milliners. They were generally people that used one room of their houses to make bonnets.

She invited them to visit her at a certain date and she put the proposition to them. She employed a couple of smart young girls and began designing and she told the other milliners that she would furnish them on a credit, to be paid after their sales were made. She was to furnish models and stock and they were to meet every week to study new designs.

So I think she was the first to organize chain stores. It was a success. They trimmed the poke bonnets in narrow ribbon and ribbons six inches wide and they put feathers on them from small groups of tips to long plumes, and were they gay and did they sell.

She asked no profits from the girls that sold them, she was contented with the profits from the wholesale house in which she became a silent partner and selective buyer, and every time she went to New York she bought something.

At that time you couldn't buy a man's shirt. The home folks made them. They would make a body of cotton goods and the bosom of Irish linen. One of her purchases was a great shipment of bosoms, plaited and ruffled, and all kinds, and they were sold to retailers and tailors in the same way.

One shipment she bought was buckles, Mother-of-Pearl buckles they were, all sizes one inch to five inches, and lots of them shipped from the West Indies islands. Something had to be done about them, so she designed a dress of velvet and these buckles trimmed it.

She in some manner interested a debutante that was in the stylish set at Newport [the exclusive resort of the wealthy in Rhode Island]. She knew her very intimately and told her she wanted her to wear it, knowing that it would make a noise. She would not accept anything for it, telling the girl that she knew it would be copied, and then she could throw it away. The girl thought that it could not be copied because no one could buy buckles like them, but Mother knew they would flood the market. She wore it and the craze was on.

Mother's chain of dressmaker friends put them on the market, and did they sell and did we have lots of them. They adapted the buckles to the bonnets as well as dresses, and they never wore out. They were worn for years on dress after dress, year after year. I used to call them 'Mother's Buckles' whenever I saw them.

Mother was studying real estate with the idea of larger and more stable investments. She kept posted on affairs and especially realty and decided she wanted some of it, always inquiring about values in different parts of New York, which was growing fast, and studying the trend of movement of business and residences. We used to visit the zoo in Central Park and outside the parkway up town were hills and improved property covered with shacks on it. Mother remarked that some day all of that would be built up and valuable. Mother began an inquiry and found out the owners, they were generally land poor [owned potentially valuable land but had little cash].

She bought a yearly option for little money from some of the holders, but when she told Father about it he was mad, couldn't see any future in it and was afraid she would lose all we had on such property. After a while she regretfully sold her option at a good price, deciding to invest nearer home, but she always regretted it because it became worth millions. That district is now all built up with apartment houses and hotels.

But she wasn't discouraged. She kept her eyes and ears open for developments. She had her lawyer that she used to consult. Always I was with her and she would talk over her ambitions and plans with me.

She heard from a friend who was a councilman that they were going to straighten out North Main Street that had a big bend in it. He said that it would destroy some prize homes that were built on the bend but that the city would probably pay damages.

She studied the maps and discovered that the project would ruin the home of Dr. Crocker, the house she was married in. Right then she got interested in the plans. She called on Dr. Crocker and discussed with him what they were going to do. He was disgusted.

The plans would cut off all his front yard and about ten feet of the house. He wanted to get rid of it at once. He made a price, I think about $15,000; the lot was deep and wide, the house a three story mansion. She got an option, told him she could probably find a customer. She talked to the councilman, and he thought that the city would pay about that much [$15,000] damages, as it would ruin the property.

She went to the bank and contracted a loan if she should need it. Another house and grounds [on that street] were similar and she got an option on that too. It was a wider lot and deep. Then she waited and eventually found out what damages the city was about to pay. It was nearly enough to pay for the property.

She closed her options. In the meantime, Father objected very much, and said it would ruin her, so without his knowledge she bought one piece in his name and another in her own. He never knew it until the last paper was signed, then it was valuable.

The city paid the damages, but instead of tearing down the building or cutting it off, she had it raised about 12 feet, moved in back in line with the new line, built a brick store underneath, changed the upper part into apartments, and warehouse on the back in one place, did the same with the other place, and built a building adjoining this two stories high, having two stores underneath. All told, she came out of the deal with four stores, with apartments above them.

The city quickly changed the street and filled it in and Mother and Father were assured a good income all of their lives. In fact, Aunt Linnie and Lou still own these properties and that one deal has given them an independent income. They did not ever sell any of the property. Aunt Etta and I sold our interest to Linnie and Lou about thirty years ago.

When the big fire in Chicago occurred, Mother went to Chicago to visit her sister [in 1873]. She became interested and saw a chance to make a lot of money. She believed that the city would come back after the fire with a boom, but everyone was so shocked that they were very pessimistic.

There were a lot of people who had lost improvements on their property in the fire and were anxious to sell their lots. She took a number of options on business property and decided to wait and see how the city would react on rehabilitation. Father was very much opposed to the deal and foresaw heavy losses.

It worried him because she would have to borrow a lot of money and he thought she was taking a big chance, so in deference to his judgment when the reconstruction boom started she sold her options, and had her sister take over some of them. Well, the outcome was that her sister made a fortune on the deals. The city took on a tremendous boom and everything went skyhigh, and Mother was right and lost out in making a fortune.

She was a very generous person. She turned over all of her part of her parents' estates which she inherited to her brothers and sisters who needed it. She said that the reason she was always successful was that she cared for the poor and needy, and that the Lord attended to her income and safeguarded her.

It is a great shame that wisdom comes only with age and the young refuse to listen to it and look at it as a dottering [sic] harangue of the old. You should analyze your mistakes and take advantage of them so that they will not recur, but that takes a cautious brain. I have thrown my regrets into the corner for the cats to grow on, so it is all right.

What can we learn from this description of Civil War and post–Civil War wealth making in New England? Some of the points are clearly in black and white. Others are between the lines:

1. As in any narrative of events, the author can see only part of the picture. *The Seven Samurai* shows that the viewpoint of the observer colors what is perceived. If the ever-complaining Father or Dr. Crocker, whose house was to be destroyed, had told their story as well, we might come to different conclusions.

2. Mr. Randall was devoted to his mother. As a result, only her *positive* financial transactions are presented. Where they are not completely positive, as in the case of the Chicago land options, they were prevented from becoming so only through the interference of others—in this case, the father.

Teddy Roosevelt once said that if a man was right 51% of the time, he was doing well. Mrs. Randall, at least in this version of the story, scored close to 100%. We suspect that the complete story was not told.

3. The amounts of money changing hands are mentioned only briefly, so we cannot tell exactly how wealthy the family was. The government bonds that Mrs. Randall bought were worth between $17,000 and $20,000 around 1880, or over a century ago. To bring this into present-day dollars, we might multiply by around fifteen, making the bonds the equivalent of around $300,000 in modern funds. This family was clearly above the lognormal kink in wealth.

Income, as opposed to wealth, is not mentioned explicitly in the notes. We find this a little odd. Mr. Randall would have been about twenty-three in 1880, when some of this activity was taking place. He would have had *some* knowledge of the family's income by that age.

On the other hand, it is still regarded as *gauche* to mention income in family histories. This convention is still observed in the biographies of many wealthy people to this day. For example, when we read the doings of the Gettys or Hunts, we get the impression of great wealth, but their income-tax returns are not printed as appendices. We have to take the word of their biographer on how much they earn or have in the bank.

All of the action in the excerpt took place in the days before the federal income tax began in 1913. In those days, every penny of income or outgo did not have to be recorded. The omission of income data makes some sense historically.

We noted previously that great amounts of wealth are usually associated with high incomes, so it is fair to assume that the Randalls were also above the kink in terms of income. Mr. Randall is described as having a "large furniture and piano factory, and was making money."

4. The "donation" of the buckle-adorned dress to the debutante at Newport was an example of what today would be called a loss-leader. Mrs. Randall was not in the habit of giving out free dresses to Newport debs. These young ladies could afford to buy dozens on their own, or even buy and sell Mrs. Randall herself. She wanted to get her buckles sold by putting them in public view, pure and simple.

Some of those who have mythologized capitalism in recent years have described it as meeting people's needs. Undoubtedly it does. But in this case, the debutante did not know she needed a dress covered with buckles until she got it as a gift. The economists would call this a supply-driven transaction.

5. The story of all fortunes is, in part, the story of even *bigger* fortunes that could have been. Mrs. Randall's missed chances to buy slum land in New York and properties in fire-devastated Chicago are only two of the possibilities that are mentioned.

If Mr. Randall had spun out the story a little more, we can imagine his mother had a chance to become one of the towering figures of American wealth, perhaps lighting cigars with J. P. Morgan himself. Stretch this a bit further, and it could have been Mrs. Randall advising Morgan, in the celebrated anecdote, not to think about getting a yacht if he had to estimate how much the upkeep was, instead of Morgan telling that to a lesser mortal.

One of us (SC) remembers being driven, as a boy, through the streets of Shreveport, Louisiana, after the oil and gas boom that struck the city. On seeing a vagrant on the sidewalk, his father said that the man had gone through four fortunes. Presumably he lost them all through overreaching. Mrs. Randall might have made hills of money if her New York and Chicago deals had gone through. She might have lost it all through yet other transactions. Nobody will ever know.

6. Father Randall comes through as a bit of a heavy and a wet blanket, at least financially. Was he really like that? If he had not been around or had been of a different disposition, there would probably have been another Gloomy Gus nearby—the banker. The history of most speculators—and Mrs. Randall was undoubtedly one—is that they have far more ideas than money to put them into practice. If Mrs. Randall had been widowed at an early age, there almost certainly would have been others

to tell her to back off. Whether she would have listened to them any more than she paid attention to her husband is anybody's guess.

7. All this took place when women could not vote and were regarded legally as chattels of their husbands. The fact that Mrs. Randall could do all this when under such legal disabilities may occasion some surprise.

If Mrs. Randall did encounter prejudice in either word or deed, she either did not mention it to her son or he excised it from the manuscript. If the dates of the narrative were not given, we would have the impression of a thoroughly modern Millie, perhaps paying a bit more attention to her husband's wishes than is common today.

Regardless of the laws, regulations and customs of the day, some people find a way around them. According to the rules of the 1870s, women didn't exist financially. Yet there was Mrs. Randall, bigger than life.

8. Mrs. Randall apparently made a lot of money, or came close to it, in real estate. This still happens today. According to a 1978 *Fortune* study,[2] half the new multimillionaires made their money in land.

The implication given in the manuscript is that making money this way was fairly easy. Mrs. Randall noted that "outside the parkway up town [in New York] were hills and improved property covered with shacks on it . . . some day all this would be built up and valuable."

No details are given, so we cannot tell which part of present New York City this is. Mrs. Randall was certainly astute enough to find landowners who were land poor. Yet she would not have been granted an option to buy the land if she did not have a large amount of capital under her control. We will return to this point below.

9. It pays to be on the right side in a war. Mrs. Randall was shrewd enough to buy U.S. government bonds when their price was depressed following a Union military defeat. Others in Atlanta and Montgomery were probably equally observant, snapping up Confederate bonds when Johnny Reb fled the field.

The difference between Mrs. Randall and her Southern counterparts was not their financial cleverness, but which direction they looked toward the Mason-Dixon line. At the end of the war, Confederate bonds were no better than wallpaper. Union bonds made Mrs. Randall wealthy.

This lends credence to Lester Thurow's[3] theory of the random walk in creating wealth. In his theory, the random walk is a mathematical term describing what most of us would call "luck." For example, suppose at the beginning of the Civil War, we took a group of well-off people, both Northerners and Southerners, who would be in a position to buy government bonds from the warring sides. Then we flip a coin.

Heads means that people who buy Northern bonds make money, in some cases a lot. Tails means that people who purchase Confederate bonds, regardless of how astute they are, end up having a little extra paper for their fireplace. Such are the vagaries of the coin toss. Mrs. Randall's undoubted virtues do not play any part.

Some might say that the victory of the North was fore-ordained, and therefore any Southerner who bought Confederate bonds was, by definition, unwise. We can not refight the Civil War here. If that attitude was common, the South would never have seceded in the first place. Any Southerner who foresaw defeat and wanted to invest in Northern bonds could not have done so. It really does pay to be on the winning side.

10. In addition to living in about the right region, Mrs. Randall lived in about the right time. It was the "Gilded Era," as Mark Twain put it. Fortunes were made that have persisted to this day. As the chronicler put it, "goods of all kinds were scarce and anything new was quickly absorbed."

Not everyone made a bundle during this Era of Good Feeling about money. But from what we are told by economic historians, it probably was a lot easier in those decades than since.

11. Them as has, gets. This restatement of an ancient saw, still sharp enough to cut down forests, is necessary.

We see many examples of this in the manuscript. For example, consider the button incident, which apparently marked Mrs. Randall's entrance into the world of finance. She became interested in a "new kind of button" because it was "so cheap." She thought she was buying a small number, when she found out she had accidentally bought a carload. We are not told the cost of either the small amount of buttons or the carload. Most families of the time could have bought the small amount. Few could have afforded the carload.

Because Mrs. Randall had the money to purchase the carload, she could apply her imagination. There undoubtedly were many potential dressmakers of the day who had the vision to make button-covered dresses, but did not have the capital to buy the buttons in the first place.

About the same could be said about the bosoms of men's shirts and ostrich feathers from Africa. There is no indication in the manuscript of how much money was involved. Nonetheless, Mrs. Randall had enough capital to take a chance on her new fashions getting accepted. Few others could do this, due to lack of money.

How much wealth did the Randalls have with respect to other Americans? George Holmes[4] did research on the 1890 census figures. He found that the top 4,000 families, or about 0.031%, had a net worth of about $12 billion, or about 20% of the total net worth of the nation. Each of the top 4,000 families would then have a net worth of about $3 million. Mrs. Randall was not in this class.

In the top 1% of the nation in 1890, there were 127,000 families. They had an average net worth of about $123,000. This included factories, land, and other belongings.

We are not told how much Mr. Randall's factory was worth. But combining it with the $20,000 in bonds owned by Mrs. Randall might have put her family in the top 1%.

Related to the question of how much capital the Randalls possessed is that of financing and borrowing. Few if any of the wealthiest families acquired their wealth from saving and putting it in the bank. They almost always borrowed to finance business opportunities. The narrative does not describe how Mrs. Randall financed her purchases of buttons, buckles, or real estate. She did deal in real estate options to purchase. Getting these options would not have required much cash, but if she had exercised them she would have had to raise capital.

Any borrowing she did would have taken collateral. That would have come from her or her husband's business. Others saw the opportunities that Mrs. Randall seized, but did not have the cash or credit to follow up.

12. Them as knows, gets. This is a variation on the preceding comment. If Mrs. Randall had not known the councilman in Providence who told her about a street being straightened, she would not have been able to capitalize on this. She probably knew the councilman not because she subscribed to his political ideas or had licked envelopes in his last campaign, but because by then she and her husband were prosperous and upstanding citizens of the community. Councilmen—and indeed all politicians—have a habit of listening to these people and telling them interesting tidbits.

13. Is making money from changes in fashion as simple as described? The implication of the narrative is that all one has to do to make a fortune in this field is to devise some new design, get some prominent people to wear it, and then watch the money rolling in. While neither of us is an expert in fashion, we doubt that it is quite that simple.

The story about the poke bonnets illustrates our point. According to the story, all Mrs. Randall had to do was to get a number of hat-makers to make headcoverings in the new styles she had invented, with ostrich feathers and different types of ribbons. The story does say that Mrs. Randall did give the milliners financial credit, although it is not exactly clear what type of credit this was. It presumably was on the materials used for the new-style hats.

But in order to get this enterprise off the ground, Mrs. Randall needed some design ability. She also required the skill to convince hat-makers, whose livelihood up to that time depended on selling the prevailing style, to start working on new and untested designs.

Finally, she was unlikely to give the hat-makers credit for the time they spent conferring with her and in making the new-style bonnets. That is, suppose each hatmaker spent ten hours in meeting with Mrs. Randall and making new-style hats. Say that an average wage in those days might be 50¢ an hour. If nobody wanted to buy the new-style hats, each of the hat-makers would be out $5—a lot in those days—and Mrs. Randall would have lost nothing. Her only risk would have been confined to the special ribbons and feathers she supplied, as well as the time she invested in coming up with the new design.

We still don't know the exact strategy she used to convince tradition-bound hatmakers to take a chance, or the financing arrangements that were employed. If we did, new entrepreneurs in the fashion industry might be able to use her tactics.

14. Much of the above sounds, on second reading, as if we were denigrating Mrs. Randall's undoubted abilities. Even allowing for some exaggeration in the account of a devoted son, her foresight shines down through the years.

She took buttons that few others wanted, and apparently single-handedly created a demand for them. She did the same with buckles and ostrich feathers. Her chronicler claims that, in the process, she developed the concept of chain stores. This may be true, but we were unable to find her name in histories of inventions listed before Woolworth. She was clearly one of the many creators who made some money, but whose base was not large enough to carry the concept nationwide or worldwide.

Mrs. Randall obviously had a rare shrewdness and energy. There are two major questions which still pose themselves to us after this account. First, how much of these abilities are in others, but do not get used because their possessors are in the wrong place, living in the wrong era, or do not have access to capital? If Mrs. Randall had lived in a relatively static and poverty-stricken society like the European Middle Ages, she could not have accomplished what she did. Might Thomas Gray's musing in *Elegy Written in a Country Churchyard* that ''some mute inglorious Milton here may rest'' apply financially to your ancestors or ours?

Second, how much should society reward Mrs. Randall, or others like her, for her astuteness or risk-taking? Most of us would agree that, at least based on the manuscript, Mrs. Randall should have a higher income and net wealth than average. (We will leave aside the possibility that the narrative presents a false picture of Mrs. Randall's skills and history.) But should she receive an income twice as much as the average, ten times, a hundred times, or some other value? This brings us around again, like the painted horses on a merry-go-round, to our title: How Rich is Too Rich?

__ 11

A PROPOSAL FOR
AN ALTERNATIVE
DISTRIBUTION SYSTEM

We have made the case that the current wealth and income distribution is enormously skewed toward the highest few percent of the population. As we have noted before, 1986 figures suggest that the top 1% own 31% of total net worth; the lower 90% share 36%.[1] In this chapter, we will outline how wealth can be distributed so that eventually income moves closer to a lognormal distribution.

Our goal is to split assets, currently frozen in gargantuan fortunes, among many people in a yeasty infusion of capital. This would percolate through the economy in unpredictable but potentially beneficial ways. The changes would occur rather slowly—as the current wealth holders die—yet the effect over time could be profound.

Instead of leaving assets effectively locked beyond creative use by individual "beneficiaries," assets would be spread so that unfettered control is transferred, possibly quite early in life. This would give heirs the incentive to use these resources to make *their* own fortunes. The incentive system—the foundation of a vigorous entrepreneurial society—could be harnessed to encourage many with fertile minds and vigor to develop assets now managed by stolid banks and other financial institutions. This would release enormous energy throughout the economy.

Our plan would cut the Gordian knot between a rich man and his money on the day of his demise. Not a penny of the estate has to go to the IRS if one simple rule is followed—estate dispersion. No longer would the estate tax system generate an American royalty—those freed from the need ever to be economically productive. The ADS would generate for *all* the incentive that most of us have in the outcome of our own economic lives. No longer would a large part of our national wealth be beyond responsive use.

Wealth great enough to entitle one to membership in the elite comes from two sources—enormous earnings or inheritance. Prudent public policy should allow those who, through individual ingenuity, talent, or luck, gain a fortune to use and enjoy it for life. This will retain the financial encouragements that help fuel the economy.

However, these individuals have the power to transmit immense wealth to others after death—to progeny, a favorite charity, or a personal foundation. They can write the rules controlling this wealth, possibly many generations into the future. This breaks the chain of personal *effort* that is tightly bound, for most of us, to personal *reward*. Economic resources, controlled by rules set up by the dead, are denied to those who might well be more productive.

Estate tax laws are used in the United States to govern the transfer of wealth from one generation to the next. The *estate* is taxed. It makes no difference whether one person or one hundred inherit. The tax is the same.

Inheritance taxes differ fundamentally in both design and effect. They tax the *recipient*, not the estate. They can be used to cap individual lifetime inheritances. Implications for transfer of fortunes are quite different for the two systems. The inheritance tax is a much more flexible and effective tool for mitigating extreme distortions in wealth; and through wealth, income.

HOW THE ALTERNATIVE DISTRIBUTION SYSTEM (ADS) WORKS

The policy suggested here is called the Alternative Distribution System (ADS). Any policy attempting to shift wealth transmission patterns should take advantage of the *natural* inclinations of the wealth-holders. Money cannot easily be wrested away from those who have much. The history of taxation is littered with failed attempts. But people *can* be cajoled into distributing their legacies in ways beneficial to *both* their heirs and society.

The policy is simple. Taxes would be levied on inheritances, not estates. During a lifetime an individual could receive $1 million tax free, from inheritances and gifts from all sources. The second inherited million would be taxed at 25%; the third at 50%; the fourth at 75%, and the remainder at 100%. This tax would not be levied on earnings, only on inheritances.

The tax would be cumulative. Thus, the total inheritance one person could receive during his or her lifetime from all sources would be $2.5 million. This is made up of the first million (tax-free), plus $750,000 from the second million, $500,000 from the third million, and $250,000 from the fourth million. Included in these amounts are gifts from one person to another.

The aim is to limit the amount any person could hope to inherit—to add a cost to making a mistake with an inheritance. Jet setters, with sometimes unbounded wealth available from birth, have little incentive to use assets vigorously and creatively.

How the Amounts Were Chosen

The amounts chosen are semiarbitrary, in the sense that a total maximum from inheritance more (or less) than $2.5 million could be chosen. We use that amount to show that nobody receiving it could be called ''deprived'' in any sense. For example, if someone receiving that inheritance put it all in tax-free municipal bonds at 6%, he would receive $150,000 annually. Only about 960,000 tax returns in 1987 had a higher total. The inheritor would be in the top one in 110.

And that tax-free income would be the equivalent of about $200,000 in taxable income, at 1987 tax rates. The inheritor would have a higher income than all except about 500,000 returns in that year. He would be in the top one in 200.

Examine the relation between an individual and the amount of money available to him. As income goes up, expenditures rise, and overall satisfaction usually ascends. Eventually there is such an amount of income to be consumed that one is satiated. After this point, more income results in little or no increase in satisfaction. The key point here is that what the economists call the ''marginal utility of income'' is very low for the immensely wealthy.

Although it is difficult to motivate someone born to great wealth to be an economically productive citizen, for those with lower income there is considerable incentive. If money could be shifted to a large number of people, for whom each dollar is still meaningful, it would harness their energy and innovative ideas. This is better than passing it to a single person (or relatively few) who are near income satiation. Benefits would accrue to the economy as a whole.

Shifting Assets

The wealth-spreading effect of ADS would shift assets in at least two ways. First, after each designated heir is given his maximum allowable inheritance (and the tax paid), the remaining estate can be distributed tax-free if spread among enough people.

Second, the cumulative nature of the inheritance tax would limit all citizens to a maximum lifetime inheritance from all sources. The children of merger/marriages could not hope to inherit unlimited amounts from their many wealthy ancestors. But, for example, both sets of grandparents could give substantial annual gifts. This would convert the wealth behind the dam of inheritance into a stream of assets for the grandchild.

Current estate policies *encourage* retention of estates till the death of the holder. Average life expectancies are in the seventies, with many living much longer. Since most assets change hands as a result of someone's death, many are in late middle age (or even older) by the time they receive any money. By that time, youthful creative juices have vanished.

A MODEL SHOWS THE DIFFERENCE ADS WOULD MAKE

To illustrate the powerful difference between the current estate tax approach and an inheritance tax scheme—our alternative distribution system (ADS)—we will use a simple model.[2] We examine a wealth distribution—for wealth (not income) millionaires only—at the moment of transfer as the current generation inherits. Then, thirty years later, they pass the estate on to the *next* generation.

To keep the comparison focused on the difference between estate and inheritance taxation, we will assume that income tax codes, economic growth rates, interest rates, mortality tables, and other factors stay the same, and all estates pass simultaneously.

HOW MANY WEALTH MILLIONAIRES ARE THERE?

To develop our model, we have to know the number of wealthy people. As we noted earlier, wealth information is not collected annually, as income data is. The most authoritative numbers come from Federal Reserve Board surveys. In 1983, 1,310,000 families (about 2% of the total) had net worth of at least $1 million.[3] Inflation or other factors may have changed the number since then. As well, the specific individuals within this group do change over time. Yet the distribution itself has remained fairly stable.[4]

We can take the figure of 1.3 million families with net worth more than a million and apply the techniques of the economists Pareto and Van der Wijk to estimate the numbers at each financial level. For simplicity, we will not show the calculations here.

We then generate Table 11.1. It shows the relationship between the number of people with net worth over $1 million, the number of those between one and two million, and so on up the line. It also allows us to compute the average wealth of those in each of the categories.

So much for the theory. How well does the distribution we have calculated relate to reality? The data collected by the Federal Reserve brackets the top 1% (approximately 770,000 households) with a minimum net worth of $1.4 million and a maximum of $87 million.[5] The average per household in this lofty group is about $4 million. Our calculations

Table 11.1
A Wealth Distribution for the United States in the 1980s

Wealth Above (in millions)	People	Category (in millions)	People in Category	Average Wealth (in millions)
$1	1,310,000	1 to 2	982,500	1.33
2	327.000	2 to 5	275,000	2.86
5	52,400	5 to 10	39,300	6.7
10	13,100	10 to 100	12,970	18
100	131	100 to 500	126	167
500	5	above 500	5	1,000

say there will be 664,000 people with net worth above $1.4 million, with average fortunes of $2.9 million—an underestimate on both counts.

A secondary reality check, the *Forbes* magazine tallies, listed 51 billionaire households for 1988.[6] Our formulas estimate 5 families in this group, an insignificant difference if we are talking about the entire population of the United States. Even the Federal Reserve Board, with all of its resources, found the maximum fortune to be $87 million. They should consult *Forbes*.

Our numbers are thus in rough conformance with reality. If anything, our numbers are conservative. At worst, we underestimate those at the wealth apex.

ASSUMPTIONS OF THE MODEL

We made the following assumptions to generate a model focusing solely on the impact of estate *versus* inheritance taxation. We assume

1. each fortune is inherited by two heirs;
2. capital is not consumed. Since heirs cannot be expected to be hermits, *earnings* from capital are consumed at the following rates: 80% of the first $20,000 is consumed; as is 60% of the next $20,000, and so on in a continuous fashion;
3. the only wealth or income at issue is the inherited pile;
4. 100% of earned income (e.g., salaries) is consumed so that further accumulation comes entirely from the inherited fortune;
5. inheritance and consumption rules are the only ones that vary;
6. generations last thirty years;
7. all transfers occur simultaneously; and
8. no heir has inherited before.

Return on Investment

We also assume the after-tax rate of return on investments is 4.7%. This unusual number was chosen for two reasons. First, it is a fairly accurate reflection of the historical long-run rate of return. Second, it allows an investment that is quartered (i.e., divided between two heirs and subject to an estate tax of 50%) to return to the original undivided level in one generation of thirty years.

For example, suppose an inheritance of $1 million is divided between two heirs. The $500,000 each gets is cut in half by the tax of 50%, reducing each to $250,000. After 30 years and a growth rate of 4.7%, each of the two heirs now has $1 million. The cycle can now begin again, with division by two heirs.

THE TWO APPROACHES

The essence of the two approaches is when and to whom the estate is bestowed. In a nutshell, we have:

1. Estate: *Tax* the estate and *then* distribute the proceeds.
2. Inheritance (ADS): *Distribute* the proceeds and *then* tax the recipient.

The features of the two tax systems are outlined in Table 11.2. Under current U.S. death tax law, the tax is levied on the estate. After all assets and liabilities are tallied, $600,000 is deducted from the net value of the estate. The reduced amount is than taxed at rates varying from 37% to 55%. For simplicity, we are assuming a rate of 50%, as we noted above. This rate is reasonably accurate for estates in the rarefied financial group we are considering.

Under the present system *any* distribution of the remaining assets is theoretically possible. The donor can give it all to one person, dozens, or even thousands. In most cases, the number is very small. Every year, everyone is free to give—tax-free—$10,000 to anyone else. This is an invisible transfer of assets. It never enters any government computer.

Tax the Heir, Not the Estate

ADS works differently. The tax is on the heir, not the estate. The most an individual can inherit in a lifetime is $2.5 million. The first $1 million is inherited tax free. The second million is taxed at 25%, the third million at 50%, the fourth million at 75%, and all money above $4 million goes to the government. However, there is *no limit to the number* of individuals to whom the estate can be left. By limiting bequests to $1 million each

Table 11.2
A Comparison of the Features of Estate Taxation and Alternative Distribution System (ADS)

	ESTATE	ADS
1. Incidence (who pays tax)	estate	heir
2. Exemption	$600,000	$1 million
3. Tax-free annual gifts per individual	$10,000	
4. Cumulative lifetime inheritance limit	none	$4 million
5. Tax rates	50%	$1–$2 million 25% $2–$3 million 50% $3–$4 million 75% over $4 million 100%

to people who have not inherited before, it would be possible to distribute an immense estate entirely tax-free.

As with estate taxation, tax-free gifts can be given at any time. However, all gifts accumulate as part of the ADS inheritance limits. The lack of annual limits on gifts causes the dynamics of this sytem to differ drastically from those of estate taxation. There is no longer an obvious way to get around the inheritance limits by doling out the money annually to would-be heirs.

In many wealthy families, children stand to inherit not only from parents, but from grandparents. The discipline imposed by the lifetime limit on inheritances would give impetus to much greater annual giving, in which control of the asset would pass to the heir. Trusts controlled by the donor would fade away. Family power incentives would change. Given American ingenuity, ADS could stimulate very creative estate dismemberment.

A QUANTITATIVE EXAMPLE

Table 11.3 traces the effects of the two systems—estate and ADS—upon estates of varying size. We consider when the money is received, and when it is disbursed.

In the table, we assume that under the present system, two *primary* heirs split the whole estate. In the ADS, we assume both primary and *supplementary* heirs. The latter are given tax-free million-dollar dollops. This clearly changes the distribution of who gets what from large estates.

Table 11.3
The Impact of Death Taxation upon Wealth Distribution

The original estate				The inherited estate (under estate and ADS dispersal)			
Wealth (in millions)	People	Average Wealth (in millions)			Inher- itors	Average Wealth (in millions)	Average Wealth 30 Years Later (in millions
1 to 2	982,500	1.33	Estate	Primary	1,965,000	0.48	1.54
			ADS	Primary	1,965,000	0.67	2.16
2 to 5	275,000	2.86	Estate	Primary	550,200	0.86	2.84
			ADS	Primary	550,200	0.93	3.05
5 to 10	39,300	6.67	Estate	Primary	78,600	1.82	6.15
			ADS	Primary	78,600	2.34	7.97
10 to 100	12,970	18.2	Estate	Primary	25,940	4.70	16.4
			ADS	Primary	25,940	2.50	8.56
				Supple- mentary	46,600	1.00	3.30
100 to 500	126	166	Estate	Primary	253	41.7	154
			ADS	Primary	253	2.50	8.56
				Supple- mentary	9,700	1.00	3.30
over 500	5	1000	Estate	Primary	10	250	955
			ADS	Primary	10	2.50	8.56
				Supple- mentary	2,590	1.00	3.30

Results of the Calculations

The methodology is this: For estate taxation, 982,500 people have wealth between $1 and $2 million. (See the first line of Table 11.1). Their average wealth is $1.33 million. Given our assumptions, under either the estate system or ADS, there will be two primary heirs, hence the 1.96 million inheritors. This is shown in the topmost box in Table 11.3.

For estate taxation, the calculation subtracts the $600,000 exemption from the $1.33 million average wealth, leaving $730,000. This is taxed at 50%, resulting in a tax bill of $365,000. Subtracting the tax from the estate, $1,330,000 – $365,000, leaves an after-tax estate of $965,000 for two heirs. This is $482,500 for each.

Under ADS, each heir is taxed. We have assumed that we are dealing with inheritance virgins—absolutely nobody has ever inherited before.

Therefore under ADS the $1.33 million estate is divided in half and given to the two primary heirs. Since each heir has never inherited before, and the inheritance is less than $1 million, no tax is due.

Notice that the inherited estates are larger for ADS inheritors than estate-tax inheritors until the estate size exceeds $10 million. This is not a fundamental feature of the system. We could use alternative assumptions. Exemptions, tax-free annual gift amounts, lifetime inheritance limits, or tax rates could be changed. All of these could be adjusted to take account of inflation, much as personal exemptions do today.

The purpose here, however, is to emphasize the critical differences between estate and inheritance taxation, not to set a particular set of assumptions in concrete. While the impact of ADS would not be immediate, over generations the changes in the way wealth is distributed through inheritances could be profound. For each of the boxes in Table 11.3, we go through the same type of calculations. For brevity, they are not shown here.

There are at least two key conclusions we can draw from Table 11.3. First, the number of supplementary inheritors under ADS is large. There are almost 60,000 of them under the assumptions we have chosen. These are 60,000 people who each would get $1 million. Under the estate system and our assumptions for that system, they would get nothing. Out of those 60,000 individuals may come whole new businesses, industries that would not have started under the present system because of lack of capital.

Second, under the estate system, some receive enormous chunks of wealth. About 250 receive $42 million each; ten get $250 million. Under ADS, the maximum any one person gets is $2.5 million. This allows for the almost 60,000 supplementary inheritors, mentioned in the last paragraph.

REMOVING THE KINK

Stepping back now, we now view the entire parade of wealth, rather than the individuals marching in it. Figure 11.1 graphs in the now familiar Pareto way the original estates and each heir's estate 30 years later.

The horizontal axis is the by-now familiar cumulative probability scale. The cumulative percentages refer to the fraction of 1.3 million wealth millionaires described in the text, *not* the fraction of all Americans. For example, from Table 11.1, about 13,000 families have wealth above $10 million, according to our calculations. This is about 0.1% of the total of 1.3 million wealth millionaires. This then produces a point at around 99%, or slightly to the right of the 98.86% marker. Similar calculations can plot each of the other points. The graph exhibits about the same kink as previous wealth and income graphs. That is, even among the wealth millionaires *alone* there is the kink. The title of this graph includes the

Figure 11.1
Estate Taxation—at Inheritance and 30 Years Later

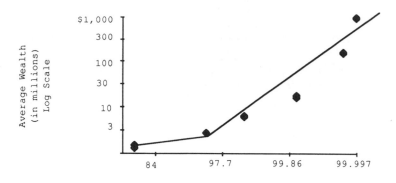

phrase, ''and 30 Years Later.'' The rate of return on investment of 4.7% was chosen to reproduce the wealth distribution subsequent to it being split at death. In other words, under the present estate taxation system the kink is perpetuated forever.

The ADS results of Figure 11.2 are quite different. The scale of this graph is exactly the same as the one immediately preceding. Yet note how different the curves are. The kink is vastly reduced in size. The curve does not sweep endlessly upward, as in the previous graph. The primary heirs, those given the largest share of any estate, are confined to a maximum of $10 million ($4 million after taxes). The secondary heirs, those who would probably receive nothing under the present system, all get $1 million, tax free. The extreme inequalities of the present system are reduced, but heirs still are quite comfortable by any conceivable standard. ADS can either modify or eliminate the kink in wealth distributions. It does not give everyone a shot at the same inheritance, but it allows the inheritances at the top to follow approximately the same distribution as those of the lower 99%. This is a way to decide How Rich is Too Rich, and then, over time, produce a solution.

Under ADS, more people are moderately well-off. No Brobdingnagian estates exist. The ADS curve simply does not climb to the astronomical heights of the estate curve (i. e., the present situation).

In summary, under the ADS system, about 60,000 more people inherit than under the estate system. And they do not inherit a pittance, either—it is $1 million. This money is large enough to develop a good-sized new

Figure 11.2
Alternative Distribution System—30 Years Later

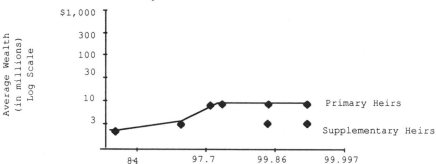

Cumulative percentage of people
(ordered from smallest to biggest wealth)
Probability Scale

business or other productive enterprises. It is more money than all except 1.3 million of us in the country possess.

IS IT IMPOSSIBLY COMPLICATED?

One possible objection to the ADS is that it would make bookkeeping
for the government more complicated. That is, it would have to keep tabs
on the inheritances of all taxpayers, and then hold them to the limits set
down in the ADS.

"Just too complicated," some might contend. "The government can't
possibly keep track of all the inheritances that people get, charging different tax rates according to what someone has inherited in the past.
Whatever the merits of the ADS, it is just too complex for the government to carry out."

This might have been true long ago, but not today. With the advent
of Social Security numbers tracking most legal financial transactions—
our publisher has ours on file for any royalty payments—the job is made
much more simple. Computers can track the inheritances of each person, over their entire lifetime.

The House of Representatives apparently thinks that an analogous
system is workable. In October, 1990, in the midst of the debates on reducing the federal budget deficit, the House introduced the "lifetime" capital
gains concept.[7] Briefly, it would allow a person to avoid tax on half of
capital gains of up to $200,000 earned in a lifetime. While we are not deal-
ing here with the issue of the appropriate rate of tax on capital gains

versus "regular" income, the House did imply that a lifetime concept for some income was feasible. That is, certain income, under the bill, would be considered apart from other income on a "lifetime" basis. This is precisely what we are advocating in the Alternative Distribution System.

A CLOSER VIEW

A number of points briefly made above are considered in more depth here.

Demographics dictate change. Since the days of Teddy Roosevelt, when the original estate/inheritance tax battle was fought in Congress, only slight tinkering has been done with elements of the original law. The tax rates have gone up and down, but the basic principles have remained the same.

We All Live Longer

In the meantime, dramatic shifts in the age of the population have occurred. Life expectancy in Teddy Roosevelt's time was of the order of fifty years. According to federal estimates, during the next twenty years the average life expectancy will climb from the present seventy-four to eighty-five.[8] In 1930, 0.2% of the people were over 85; by 1989, the figure had more than sextupled, to 1.3%. Three generations of a family were unusual at the beginning of the century. Today it is almost commonplace for *four* generations to be alive simultaneously.

Check your local newspaper's obituary column. In our local paper the day we checked, of those over 70 reporting offspring, 50% listed great-grandchildren.[9] In the early 1970s, only 25% of those in their late fifties had a surviving parent. By 1980, 40% did. So did 20% of those in their early sixties and 3% of those in their seventies.[10]

In 1989, more than 70% of all deaths are of people over 65; only 5% are children under 15. This is a dramatic reversal since the turn of the century, when 53% of all deaths were of children under 15.[11]

The trend is accelerated for the extremely wealthy. They have unlimited access to the very best health care from infancy and use it, further enhancing their prospects for long lives. The estate tax laws were fixed in stone when modern health care advances were undreamed of.

Do the Wealthy Spread the Wealth?

Second, will people who are clever enough to make incredible fortunes bend their creativity toward disbursing them? The rich have always made headlines, so anecdotal evidence is readily available. Some have publicly stated goals. J. Paul Getty's cardinal rule was to avoid taxes because the government wasted them. His second rule was to prevent his children and grandchildren from obtaining great wealth.[12] He was quite successful in achieving the first goal, but unsuccessful in the second. There were three Gettys in the 1989 *Forbes 400*.[13]

There have always been those who have made a determined effort to give away their fortunes. These attempts are favorite topics for media attention. A typical article of this type, entitled "Arnold Beckman's New Career: Donating His Fortune to Science," noted that in 1986 Mr. Beckman's $75 million in gifts (derived from his instrumentation fortune) placed him second only to the Ford Foundation.[14] Carnegie Libraries are still in existence all around the world for the same reason.

A third group, having made fortunes while quite young, simply quit working to enjoy their lucre. A newspaper headline reads, "Change of Heart: Arnold Kreiger Made $3 Million Last Year—Why Isn't He Happy? Banker's Trust Money Trader Tires of Frenzied Life. Quits at Peak of Success."[15]

Parents and Children

Third, wealthy parents worry about the impact of wealth on children. A *Fortune* cover story says, "Should You Leave It All to the Children? No, Says Self-Made Billionaire Warren Buffett—Among Other Wealthy Americans." A *New York Times* piece is called "The Perils of Raising Rich Kids: Easy Money Can Sap a Child's Ambition." *Inc.*, in a story titled "Share the Wealth, Spoil the Child," quotes a wealthy child as follows: "For a long time I was a kind of wealth junkie. Money had the same effect on me as a drug would to a drug addict. My self-worth seemed completely tied to my net worth."[16]

WHY IS IT NECESSARY TO HAVE THE INHERITANCE TAX CUMULATIVE?

A *cumulative* lifetime limit provides discipline to the system. Each portion of an inheritance wasted is irreplaceable. Coupled with the notion that assets must be given without strings, the lifetime limit has the potential to transform the heir's choices into the decision behind all economics— how to allocate scarce resources. The current estate system has *no* concept of scarce resources.

Further, the cumulative lifetime limit would eliminate the possibility of a new version of political action committees, where the wealthy form groups with the philosophy, "You give my child the limit and I'll do the same for yours."

The cardinal rule here is to limit the total accessions of wealth for a single individual to a less than egregious level (i.e., about $2.5 million). As we have noted above, this should be more than enough on which to scrape by.

HOW ARE INCENTIVES CHANGED WITH ADS?

The present system of estate taxation puts a premium on maintaining control of assets as long as possible, because of the power that accrues to those with wealth. The unspoken threat is, "If you don't do what I want you to do, I'll disinherit you." There is no reward for disbursing the money at regular intervals or early. At worst, strings are attached to the wealth. These strings persist long after the death of the original owner.

Inheritance taxation, or the ADS, will *encourage* rather than discourage the early dissemination of wealth, or what the economists call "de-cumulation." While the power motive would be decreased, we cannot claim that it would be completely eliminated. That would be asking too much of human nature.

Limiting inheritances could create competition among wealthholders to endow a child. The lifetime inheritance given at birth and the lavish gifts from relatives can be allowed to accumulate in the child's account. The power of compound interest would then work to build the child's eventual prize. Rather than devolving wealth on middle-aged or even elderly inheritors, the wealthy would often transfer the wealth to relatively young people.

The knowledge, from infancy, that this money will be released when the child becomes a young adult, and that there will be no more, would give a child incentive and motivation. That motivation has been demonstrated, for example, when college educations are unconditionally offered to ghetto elementary school children unlikely to have guaranteed access any other way.

A number of wealthy people in the last decade have made these offers to underprivileged school children. In a sense, the ADS does about the same for children of the wealthy.

Creating heirs without control of assets has produced generations of "poor little rich kids." That a significant portion of our national wealth is allocated to allow these few to live such lives is wasteful to the economy as a whole.

CONCLUSION

The Alternative Distribution System is both powerful and objective. It also provides a test to see how well the remedy is working: How far has the cumulative wealth line of the wealthy, as depicted on probability graph paper, moved toward the line of the majority?

By itself, ADS does not have a cap on *income*. If you earn it, you keep it, subject to current income taxes. Under ADS, fortunes you build for yourself are differentiated from perpetuated fortunes. The link of personal effort and personal reward is maintained and strengthened. Over time, ADS could dismantle the huge fortunes which pass to individuals in a Mendelian lottery.

The ends to which immense wealth can be applied are almost limitless in their variety, but for first fortunes there is a certain rationale. The perpetuated or inherited fortune has its recipients chosen haphazardly, with undeserving individuals picked in a genetic roll of the dice. You may have Bunker Hunt, Stewart Mott, or Sunny von Bulow controlling vast amounts of the nation's resources without any effective constraint or guidance. There is no recognized justification for such a choice of stewards for the wealth of a nation.

With ADS in place, no constituency could rightly object. The person who made the original fortune is only under a rule to spread the benefits around at his death. The potential heirs are limited by law in their inheritances, so they cannot blame their ancestor for lack of generosity.

ADS untangles the intertwined skein of money and genetics. It makes it simple for the dying rich person to leave his legatees with enough and yet provide for the dispersal of wealth without a great deal of anguish. After a generous jackpot is settled on individual heirs, the government would be the prime beneficiary if the wealthholder failed to spread the estate sufficiently. Society as a whole would benefit with smaller, yet still significant, resources available to more people.

_ 12

A NEW START ON INCOME DISTRIBUTION

In Chapter 11, we showed how the Alternative Distribution System could make our wealth distribution, and ultimately our income spread, more rational. This final chapter explores what others have proposed, and outlines our conclusions.

A FLOOD OF MILLIONAIRES

The 1980s brought some unusual economic phenomena. Some of the negative aspects have been an enormous public debt and the most severe recession since the Great Depression of the 1930s. Positive events include a strong growth in employment; much lower inflation than the 1970s; and a long sustained period of economic growth, from 1982 to the end of the decade.

Almost unremarked in the debates over economic policy has been the tremendous growth in the number of millionaires. Note that these are _income_, not wealth, millionaires. The latter group is much larger.

Figure 12.1 shows how their numbers have increased from 1951 to 1987.[1]

The vertical axis is in thousands. The lower curve shows the rise from 1951 to 1987, in _current_ dollars. The upper curve takes account of the almost four-fold inflation during these years (i.e., it is based on inflation-adjusted or _constant_ dollars). The last two open dots for the right-hand side, for 1986 and 1987, are superimposed on the black dots for those years. For both cases, we see a huge increase of millionaires in recent years.

In 1951, the entire nation recorded only 171 millionaires. We noted in Chapter 7 that in the 1920s, the number of millionaires was of that order. There had been little growth in their number over a generation.

Figure 12.1
A Deluge of Millionaires

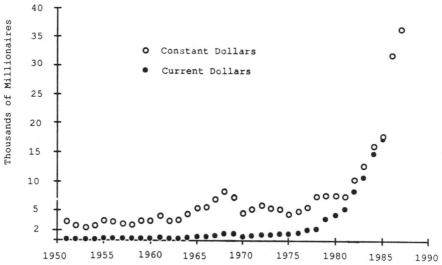

During the Eisenhower years, the number went up considerably, although the scale of Figure 12.1 is too compressed to show it. By 1961, the first Kennedy year, there were 398 millionaires, over twice that of a decade previously.

There were minor dips in the figures in the 1960s, yet the seemingly inexorable rise continued. By 1969, after eight years of Democratic rule, there were 1200 millionaires, three times that of the beginning of the decade. It's only around those years that the dots are really distinguishable from the horizontal line indicating zero.

For the next few years, however, their ranks fell on hard times. The stock market dipped, and so did their numbers. The next year, 1970, saw only 642 millionaires, about half that of the previous year. It took until 1976 before the previous peak of 1969 was surpassed. If anything, this hiatus showed that the number of millionaires can drop substantially without utter economic ruin being visited on the nation.

From 1976 onward, the number proceeded only one way—up. The corps of millionaires increased at a rate unprecedented in modern history. From 1976 to 1979, they almost tripled; from 1979 to 1983, they exactly tripled; from 1983 to 1986, they *more* than tripled. The number recorded in 1987, 36,299, marked an increase of 21,100% over the level of 1951.[2]

Now some of this is due to inflation. An income of $237,000 in 1951 was about equivalent to $1 million in 1986,[1] using the Consumer Price Index for scaling. So to make a fair comparison to 1951, we should count up everyone in the former year who made more than $237,000, and compare the group to the millionaires in the latter years. We can follow the same procedure for the intervening years.

Obviously, there were a lot more people earning $237,000 or above in 1951 than a million. This is reflected in the top curve of Figure 12.1. But inflation does not explain *all* the rise in millionaires.

The inflation-adjusted number was about 3,200 in 1951. It remained about constant in the 1950s, in spite of two recessions. It climbed slowly in the 1960s, reaching a peak of 8,400 in 1968. From there it dropped dramatically, falling to about 4,600 in 1975. That was about the same level as in 1962. In twenty-four years, the number had increased by less than 50%.

After 1975, it was another story. The number of millionaires, adjusted for inflation, rose steadily. By 1981, it was 7,500, still below the peak of 8,400 in 1968. That is, the number had not increased in 13 years. But three more years brought a doubling, to 16,000. Two more years, bringing us up to 1986, brought another doubling, up to 31,900. The inflation-adjusted number of millionaires had risen, from 1951 to 1986, by about 880%. Most of that increase had taken place since 1981.

None of this tells us how many millionaires there *ought* to be. We will reserve this for later in the chapter.

Our main points in this section are three-fold. First, the number of millionaires has increased enormously over the years, most especially in the 1980s. Second, even if we take inflation into account, the number of millionaires has *still* risen.

Third, when the number dropped, or remained constant, the country still went on. The number of inflation-adjusted millionaires remained about the same from 1951 to 1963, years of great economic growth. No increase in their number seemed to be necessary.

WHO EARNS WHAT IN THE TOP RANKS

So far, we have been treating all millionaires as if they are equal. They are not.

The average income of all millionaires, taken together, has changed very little over the years. For most of the 1951–1986 period, the average income of a millionaire was $2 million, give or take a few percent. This meant that for everyone who barely got into this top income bracket, there was someone else who earned $3 million.

But these generalities do not tell us the number who earned more than $2 million, $5 million, or $10 million. The IRS does not supply these figures, so we have to estimate them.

The data on which the calculations are based are the preliminary IRS returns for 1987.[2] For the top income earners, there are four brackets: $100,000 to $200,000, $200,000 to $500,000, $500,000 to $1 million, and above $1 million. The Pareto equation ($N = AY^{-a}$) was used to interpolate between and extrapolate beyond those numbers. In this equation, N is the number of taxpayers who earn beyond an income level Y, A is a constant, and a is the Pareto constant.

This equation relates the number of people who earn more than a given level of income to that level mathematically. It applies only to the highest income earners, not the average Joe or Jane. For the three ranges, $100,000 to $200,000; $200,000 to $500,000; and $500,000 to $1 million, the values of the logarithm of A were 10.155; 9.687, and 9.495, respectively. The values of a were 1.920, 1.713, and 1.645, respectively. Dollar values were in units of 1,000.

The problem of estimation becomes more difficult above $1 million. This is because in order to estimate the two parameters in the Pareto equation, A and a, both the upper and lower range of income must be known. The IRS states only that the top income bracket is over $1 million, not what the highest income in that group is.

To get around that problem, we note that the *average* income for those at or above $1 million in 1987 was $2.4 million. This means that half the total income in this bracket of $87.2 billion derives from those with incomes of less than $2.4 million. By mathematically integrating the Pareto equation noted above and using these facts, we find that a is 1.792 and log A is 9.935 for those above $1 million. These values of a and A are higher than the corresponding ones for the $500,000 to $1 million bracket. Results are shown in Table 12.1.

Table 12.1
Estimated Number of Top Income Earners in 1987

Income Level	Estimated Number of Tax Returns above that Level
$100,000	2,060,000
200,000	545,000
300,000	270,000
400,000	170,000
600,000	84,000
800,000	52,000
$1 million	36,000
2 million	10,500
3 million	5,100
4.5 million	2,500
6 million	1,500
8 million	870
10 million	590
15 million	280
20 million	170
25 million	110
30 million	82
50 million	33
80 million	14
100 million	9
150 million	5
200 million	3
360 million	1

While estimating the *highest* income earner is speculative, according to our calculations there probably was someone between $300 and $400 million in 1987.

Michael Milken, the junk-bond financier, made about $550 million in 1987. This value was derived not from a gossip columnist or other unreliable source, but from a court case in which he figured. Because the amount is based on court records and not speculation, it is as accurate as income information ever gets.

The total given was for Milken's salary and bonuses. If he was like other wealthy men, he may have been able to take large deductions and exemptions. So it is possible that his adjusted gross income—the basis on which we are comparing all incomes—may have been substantially less than $550 million. Is it too much to expect that it was in the range of $300 to $400 million?

It is possible, though not likely, that someone bested Milken in the income derby that year. If nobody did, we have made a reasonable estimate—given all the uncertainties—of Milken's income in 1987 without knowing anything about him other than what we read in business journals. We thus have some confidence that the parameters we used in the Pareto equation yield something not far from the truth.

As a footnote to this, in 1990 Milken was sentenced by a federal court to ten years for violations of securities and tax laws. He had pleaded guilty to the charges, and was expected to serve a total of approximately three and one-half years.

Tallying the Number of Millionaires

Table 12.1 starts off at the $100,000 mark, about where the Pareto region begins. The IRS says that, in 1987, there were about two million taxpayers at or above the $100,000 level; about 113,000 at or above $500,000; and about 36,300 at or above $1 million. These points are fixed, and the Pareto equation allows us to interpolate between them.

In the interests of brevity, we will skip over all those below $1 million in income, and start right in with the millionaires. Their ranks start thinning out immediately after that commanding level is reached. By the $2 million stratum, only 10,500 (or less than a third of the total number) are left.

By $3 million, only about half those who survived to the $2 million level remain. About 5,000 earn more than $3 million, or about 0.005% of all tax returns.

The ranks diminish ever more rapidly from this point on. Only about 1,500 make it to the $6 million level. By the $10 million plateau, only about 590 survive. This is about 1.6%, or one in sixty of all millionaires, or about 0.00075% of all tax returns.

By the $30 million level, we could fit all the recipients into one fairly large room. Only about 80 are still around. About seven-eighths of those who made it to the $10 million landing have fallen by the wayside.

From this point up, any numbers we calculate become more and more speculative. We estimate that there were about a classroom full—about 33—who made more than $50 million. A minivan could hold all those (nine) who made more than $100 million. The front seat of a car could accommodate the trio who cleared the $200 million level. We guess possibly one between $300 and $400 million, as noted above.

This, then, is a shortened rerun of the parade we described back in Chapter 1. There are two main differences between the parade and our discussion here.

First, the parade was concerned with *all* income, not just the top earners. Here we have concentrated on those who made more than $100,000 in 1987.

Second, the parade generally avoided numbers, being descriptive in nature. Here, as well as in the accompanying table and graph, we have been much more specific.

The table and graph tell us what *did* happen, but do not say what *should* take place in the ranks of the high earners. The next section outlines some ideas.

WHAT SHOULD BE DONE—SOME OTHER IDEAS

In previous chapters, we discussed what should or could be done about income and wealth disparities. We evaluated the various nostrums that had been proposed by economists, philosophers, seers, and prophets over the centuries. Our conclusion? Almost all the remedies suggested were so vague as to be unworkable. In spite of this, some have continued to work on the question of what constitutes a "fair" income distribution.

Heilbroner and Thurow

Robert Heilbroner, the distinguished economist and philosopher, and Lester Thurow, the Dean of the Sloan School of Management at MIT, and an equally noted economist, have come up with an ingenious standard for setting income distribution.[3,4] Their reasoning is seductive, and goes as follows in our paraphrase:

> There is a widespread discrimination in society, in spite of the plethora of laws we have passed since World War II. It is obvious that it will never go away completely, no matter how many fingers Washington has in our pies. Until the happy day when income unfairness disappears, why not take as a standard a group which has relatively little discrimination levelled against it?

The group which probably suffers the least discrimination is white men who have worked full time during the year. Of course, since these white men have minorities such as Jews, Italians, Poles, and the like in their ranks, there is still some prejudice directed at them in certain parts of the country.

But surveys have shown that a few of these minorities, such as Jews, actually earn more on average than the majority WASPs. And by definition we are excluding those who suffer tremendously from income disparities, such as women, the unemployed, blacks and Hispanics, the disabled, part-time workers, and so on. If all those excluded had the same income distribution as full-time white males, then we would have an equitable income distribution. If the gap between our 'standard' and the rest widens, then we are moving in the direction of more unfairness.

Reasonable enough. There are, however, a number of problems with this formulation from our viewpoint. Two are major, and the others minor.

First, this supposedly "fair" income distribution is in terms of eliminating or reducing racial, gender, and other types of discrimination. While we are in favor of getting rid of these vestiges of the past, doing it would not tell us how rich is too rich.

Consider gender discrimination. There are many women in the ranks of the highest income earners. Frequently their income is derived by inheritances, as in the case of the daughter of H. L. Hunt, Caroline Hunt Schoelkopf. The Heilbroner-Thurow formulation does not tell us whether this woman's enormous income and wealth is appropriate or too high.

Second, the white male income that Heilbroner and Thurow discuss applies to the *whole* population. We are primarily concerned here about the *rich*. For example, the Census Bureau figures on which they rely[5] has only one category for those earning $50,000 to $75,000 annually. The highest category is for those earning above $75,000.

The income tax returns which we have used in our graphs and tables have the identical $50,000 to $75,000 bracket, and then five more: $75,000 to $100,000; $100,000 to $200,000; $200,000 to $500,000; $500,000 to $1 million; and above $1 million.

The kink between the lognormal and Pareto regions was around $110,000 in 1987. We were able to detect the kink because there were some data points above it. If the income information had stopped shortly above $50,000, we would never have been able to say how rich the rich should be.

This then is the biggest drawback to the Heilbroner-Thurow theory. It may work for the general population, but does not tell us much, one way or the other, about the rich. It runs out of financial gas before it gets to the interesting part.

There are other data problems. The Census Bureau listed about 49 million white men as working full time during 1982. Of these, only 36.2

million worked between 50 and 52 weeks. The rest worked less. (We are assuming that "working" includes vacation time.) This army of almost 13 million full-time workers who work somewhat part time distorts the figures.

We run into more difficulties when we ascend into the upper reaches of income, the areas about which we are most concerned. The Census Bureau deals with individuals; the IRS deals with tax returns. These returns may be joint, that is, including more than one income. For example, the Census Bureau listed about 1.7 million white men earning between $50,000 and $75,000 in 1982. But the IRS had about 2.8 million tax returns in that category, not listed by race, for that year.[6] A difference of a few tens of thousands is reasonable, given the varying definitions. Yet we have here a difference of a million.

Above $75,000 annually, the Census Bureau listed 789,000 white males working full-time, and 876,000 whites of both sexes, including full- and part-time workers. The IRS had 1.3 million returns above that income, a difference of about half a million.

The major reason for these discrepancies is—as we've mentioned above—a substantial part of the income of the wealthy does not come from salaries. The Census Bureau lists the income of its respondents as *earnings*, almost all from salaries. But of the total income of those who made more than $200,000 in 1982, only 42% derived from salaries.[7]

So the Heilbroner-Thurow proposal *can't* tell us how rich the rich should be. It expires through lack of data before it gets to the crucial point. Philosophically, it makes some sense; operationally, it still needs work.

Pechman

Joseph Pechman, of the Brookings Institution in Washington, probably wrote more about income distribution than anyone else in the United States for decades. His thoughts influenced many of the writers we have quoted. Pechman was president of the American Economics Association (AEA), the largest group of economists in the nation, when he died in August 1989. His last paper was presented at a later meeting of the AEA.[8]

In it, he noted that from 1952 to 1981, the top 1% of taxpayers had a share of total reported income of between 8% and 10%. This took place under Democratic and Republican administrations, during surges of "soak the rich" feeling and contrary "let them have all they want—they deserve it" sentiments. Since 1981, Pechman noted, things have been different. The share of the national wealth of the top 1% of the population went from 8.1% to 14.7%. Obviously the unspoken social compact that reigned from 1952 to 1981 has disappeared.

What would Pechman do to restore that compact? He would raise the marginal tax rate on incomes above $250,000 to 48% for a start. It was

50% or more from 1942 to 1986, so there is historical precedence for this. The 1986 Tax Reform Act lowered it to 28%.

Pechman noted that a lot of interest and dividend income, much of it received by the wealthy, is not reported to the IRS. Pechman would institute withholding on these sources of income, in the same way that taxes on salaries are withheld. This step, in principle, would boost the reported income of the wealthy, and at the same time increase the total taxes they pay.

In the early 1980s, Congress did pass a law withholding taxes from savings from banks and other financial institutions. But because of pressure from these banks, the law was repealed before it went into effect. One of us can remember getting an urgent appeal in the mail from his credit institution, urging him to write his Congressman advocating repeal. Apparently many people heeded these messages.

In 1989, President Bush proposed that capital gains be taxed at a lower rate than ordinary income. He had some historical precedence for this, just as Pechman had for higher marginal tax rates on the wealthy. As Pechman noted, "For the first time since 1921, realized capital gains were made taxable as ordinary income [in 1986]."[8]

Pechman opposed any change in the capital gains law, disagreeing with President Bush: "This [regarding capital gains as ordinary income for tax purposes] is the keystone of comprehensive tax reform. It reduces the incentive to convert ordinary income into capital gains, and removes one of the major elements of tax-shelter arrangements."

Pechman advocated an allowance for inflation on capital gains, however. If the average rate of inflation were 4%, say, and a stock went up 4% a year, there would be little or no tax on the gain made from selling the stock under his scheme.

The economist made other suggestions, not described here. Many of them are worthy, in our opinion. But Pechman does not outline a theoretical framework for advocating a specific tax rate on ordinary income or capital gains. Why a 48% marginal tax rate on the wealthiest, and not 46% or 50%? The proposed increase over the present marginal rate of 28% he proposes is 20%, a round number. Should tax increases—or decreases, for that matter—be chosen on the basis that they are in multiples of ten? Without some theoretical underpinning, we do not know where Pechman got his figures.

Jesse Jackson

A political campaign brings out those few who are willing to talk about the wealthy and how affluent they could or should be. In the 1988 presidential race, Jesse Jackson, as a candidate for the Democratic nomination, had the temerity to do so.

He advocated a marginal tax rate of 38.5% on people earning more than $200,000, saying that this had been the rate in 1987. The 1988 rate on these people had declined to 28% because of the income tax reform act. Jackson claimed that this increase would raise an extra $20 billion.

Some questions come to mind. First, what would the tax increase do to income distribution? The extra tax would clearly reduce the size of the kink between the two income distributions that we have found. But would it be a measurable difference?

Second, why the rate of 38.5%? Is there reason other than the fact that it had been in effect the previous year?

The 38.5% rate had been signed and approved by President Reagan, hardly one of the Reverend Jackson's heroes. In other words, if Jackson had wanted to radically rearrange income distribution—and he has been accused of that by many critics—why not a marginal rate of 50%? That would have soaked the rich even more. And *that* rate had been in effect for much of the Reagan administration on the highest income bracket.

The gist of these questions suggests that, while Jackson was clearly concerned about maldistribution of income, his proposal had no theoretical basis. Saying that the 38.5% margin rate he proposed was based on the previous year's value would have been fine if last year's rate in turn had had some economic underpinnings. But nobody, either allies of Mr. Jackson or his opponents, claimed that.

In defense of the Reverend Jackson, in politics (or at least the American variety) there is often little to be gained for giving a rationale for policies. Just state a goal, even if it comes out of the air, and that is that. Demand to cut the poverty rate in half, or punish the rich, and that should be enough for the electorate. The overwhelming majority of politicians do precisely that. Yet if there is one point to be made in this book, it is that general prescriptions of that type are not sufficient to produce real change.

Still, the fact that Reverend Jackson brought the question up at all at a Democratic platform hearing was an accomplishment. Candidates are all too often given to slogans like "fair jobs at fair wages" which, upon reflection, mean close to nothing from an income distribution standpoint. Jackson took the first step by saying, "I want a marginal tax rate of X% on those who earn more than Y dollars annually." The second step, much more difficult politically, would require, "I have suggested these income and estate tax rates because I want the nation to have one income distribution, not two."

What became of the Jackson proposal? It was defeated, along with a variety of other suggestions. The Democrats, avoiding their usual platform battles, were content to hear out Reverend Jackson's thoughts, and then vote them down quietly. To our knowledge, not one of the participants, either pro or anti-Jackson, raised the question of the *basis* for tax rates, either existing or proposed. Such is the state of economic inquiry at a Presidential platform hearing.

Saskatchewan

Very few governments in North America—federal, state, provincial, or local—have ever considered how rich the rich should be, although most of them have tried to levy more taxes on the affluent than the poverty stricken. The Saskatchewan provincial government in Canada did float a trial balloon in the mid-1970s.

Ruled at the time by the New Democratic Party, roughly similar in outlook to the British Labor Party, the provincial government suggested a maximum income for all its residents. As far as we know, this was the first time this had been done on a quantitative basis on the continent by a major government body. By "quantitative," we mean statements that are more precise than, "the rich are getting too rich."

Saskatchewan said that nobody should make four or five times the average wage in that province. How would this translate to present-day dollars? Doing the calculations is complicated by the economic transfer factors to go from a Canadian prairie province in the 1970s to the United States today, the inflation since that time, and the varying exchange rate of Canadian to U.S. dollars. However, the Saskatchewan maximum in modern times is not too far below the $110,000 kink we have identified. This may be a coincidence, or the Saskatchewan government may have put their finger on an economic law before anyone else did.

The difference between the Saskatchewan proposal and ours is two-fold. First, when questioned about the basis for their factor of four or five times the average wage, their theoreticians merely said that "it felt right." No real reason was supplied for the numbers they chose. Twice the annual average wage was obviously too small for a maximum income. One thousand times would be regarded by most people—though not all—as too big. The question was, and still is, if you suggest a concept like a maximum income, how do you choose the level?

Second, Saskatchewan suggested an absolute cut-off, beyond which *all* income would be taxed away. We think this would contribute to economic inefficiency in the long run, although filling up government coffers in the short run. In our proposal, there is no upper limit to income.

What happened to the idea from the Great Plains? In Canada at the time, provincial income taxes were tied to the federal tax level, much as county taxes in some U.S. states are tied to the state tax level. That is, the provinces (with one exception) allowed the federal government to collect all income taxes, and were given a fixed share of federal taxes collected in that province.

We go into the abstruse details of the Canadian tax system to explain why, even if the maximum income-level proposal in Saskatchewan had been hailed as the greatest event since the locusts left in the Great Depression, it would not have gotten far. Saskatchewan taxes were tied to federal levels. There was thus very little they could do to implement the scheme, unless they persuaded the federal government to go along. The federal government had no interest in levelling income at the time.

Politically, the results were mixed. The provincial government that came up with the idea was eventually defeated. The conservative government that followed was elected in part on promises to throw out the woolly minds on the government benches.

Nonetheless, that long-ago government deserves some credit for at least thinking out loud about income equality and inequality. Tax rates and schedules are set by almost all other governments as if they had no relationship to income fairness.

Heilbroner, Thurow, Pechman, and others have elements of what we have proposed here. Some have an abstract platform for wealth and income redistribution, but founder on the shoals for lack of data. Others may produce many numbers, but those tax levels do not have a logical foundation.

THE CEOS AND THE WORKERS

Another way of considering what is a fair or just distribution of income is to see what chief executive officers (CEOs) of corporations are making. The ratio of their incomes to those of ordinary workers may tell us something about the income hierarchy.

Eckhouse[9] writes that the average compensation for a CEO among the largest U.S. industrial companies was $2.2 million in 1988. By way of comparison, the fifth-ranking executive in the same company earned about a fifth of that—$463,000. In the previous five years, the CEOs' total compensation jumped from forty-one times that of a skilled production worker to fifty-five times greater.

Doug Stanton, a consultant in international compensation, says, "The value of bonuses and stock options [to upper management] is so high in the United States compared to anywhere else around the world that it just blows away the ratio." He found that if stock options are included, U.S. CEO pay multiples are higher than in any other country except Brazil.

Some have paid a lot of attention to these numbers. Graef Crystal, a professor at the Haas School of Business at the University of California at Berkeley, says, "This is the stuff of which revolutions are made." If anything, the ratios are getting larger. The average compensation for a CEO rose 14.3% in 1988. The increase for the fifth-ranking executive in the same company was 9.6%.

Peter Drucker Speaks

The same theme was echoed by Peter Drucker, perhaps the best-known writer on business organization. In an article entitled "Reform Executive

Pay—Or Congress Will,''[10] he decried the enormous compensation being given to top executives.

Drucker described the old finding of the financier J. P. Morgan around the turn of the century:

> The only thing that businesses who were clients of J. P. Morgan & Co. and did poorly had in common was that each company's top executive was paid more than 130% of the compensation of the people in the next echelon and these, in turn, were paid more than 130% of the compensation of the people in the echelon just below them, and so on down the line. Very high salaries, Morgan concluded—and he was hardly contemptuous of big money or an anti-capitalist—disrupt the team. They make even high ranking people in the company see their colleagues as adversaries rather than as colleagues.

Drucker proposed a CEO-skilled-worker multiple of no higher than twenty. At the time he wrote, he estimated that this might top CEO compensation at perhaps $850,000, affecting no more than about 500 executives in the entire nation. If the multiple were set at fifteen, Drucker says that about 1,000 executives would have their compensation reduced. In his opinion, such a cap would be "eminently acceptable."

Drucker, as is the case with almost all his writings, makes considerable sense. Yet only in his example derived from J. P. Morgan's empirical research is there a theoretical basis. Morgan apparently found that a ratio of more than 130% in compensation from one level of management to the next doomed a company. This *does* tell us how to organize pay structure in a corporation if we want it to survive, but *does not* say how rich is too rich.

Drucker says that a multiple of fifteen or twenty between CEO and skilled worker would be reasonable. It would clearly be lower than the ratio of fifty-five in recent years, and around forty at the time that Drucker was writing. But why fifteen or twenty? Drucker sheds no light on this.

Drucker's suggestion would, at first glance, appear to have a major effect on many of the top income earners. He does imply that compensation of some top executives might be cut in half without much loss to the economy. But the proportion of top income earners affected would not be great. In 1984, the year he wrote, perhaps 22,000 income-tax returns were above $850,000. He says that his ratio of twenty would reduce the salaries of about 500 executives, or one in forty-four at that high level.

Drucker's "ratio of 15" implies a cap on CEO compensation of about $640,000. In 1984, about 34,000 people filed income-tax returns at or above that level. Drucker says that about 1,000 executives would have their compensation drop under his rule-of-fifteen system. This would be about one in 34 at that level.

We have pointed out elsewhere the reason behind these tiny proportions. Much of the income in the highest reaches is based on investments and inherited wealth. We have tried to deal with this in our Alternative Distribution System. Drucker, while undoubtedly well-meaning, would tilt the scale even further toward *unearned* income by putting a cap on *earned* income. We find this a peculiar result of his suggestions.

The ratio of the compensation of CEOs to workers provides a rough measure of income equality or inequality. Yet because so much of high incomes is traceable to unearned income, setting an arbitrary ratio of CEO compensation to that of skilled workers does not affect the top income brackets significantly.

THE JAPANESE MODEL

No longer do Japanese-produced articles fall apart in our hands. No longer do the Japanese feel it necessary to rename a town "Usa," so goods produced there could be labelled "Made in USA." Now the trend is to genuflect before all things Japanese. Best sellers on the Japanese way of doing things crowd the bookshelves. In a *Washington Post* survey in January 1990, more Americans ranked Japan as the world's greatest economic power than they did the United States.

Do the Japanese have something to teach us about income distribution? Perhaps. Before evaluating their way of spreading income and wealth, we should recall two facts. First, income distribution is partly cultural in nature. That is, Japan may have adopted a certain income distribution through historical forces, not because of a conscious decision.

Second, the income distribution of another nation may be different from that of the United States, but there is no way to prove that one is "better" than another. Some countries, such as Japan, do have close to a one-segment income distribution, in contrast to the two segments of the United States. In our opinion, it is more logical. A statement of this type is as close as we can come to comparing the income distribution of one country to that of another.

In spite of these two *caveats*, there is great interest in Japan and the way they handle money. That country, since World War II, has been the world's greatest economic success story. They must be doing *something* right.

Let us return to the ratio of CEO to skilled worker compensation that we evaluated in the last section. In Japan, the ratio has *narrowed*, not increased, over the years.[9]

In 1927, the president of a large Japanese company received about 101 times the cash compensation of the most recently hired male college graduate. The multiple dropped to twelve in 1963, nine in 1973 and just seven and one-half in 1980, according to the Federation of Japanese

Managers Association. The numbers are not directly comparable to the U.S. figures we quoted above. The American data refer to skilled industrial workers, and the Japanese to new male college graduates.

In spite of this, the contrast is stark. The Japanese ratio has fallen from one-hundred to seven and one-half, in the direction of greater equality. The U.S. ratio in five recent years has risen from forty-one to fifty-five, in the direction of greater *in*equality.

Do Taxes Make a Difference?

What about taxes? It may be that the Japanese have a lower CEO to new college-graduate ratio, but perhaps the CEOs and other executives escape unscathed at tax time. If this were true, the low ratio in Japan would not matter as much.

Not true. Joseph Pechman, who we quoted above, wrote a book entitled *World Tax Reform: A Progress Report*, in which he debunked this view.[11] He found that in 1984, the combined national, state, and local taxes in the United States for the highest income bracket was 55%. By 1988, they had declined to 33%. These numbers are not in complete agreement with others we have listed in this book, because we have not been considering state and local taxes. Pechman did.

In Japan, the situation was radically different. In 1984, the highest marginal tax rate was 88%. By 1988, it had dropped, but only to 76%. While high, these rates are comparable to those which prevailed in the United States for over two decades, from the early 1940s to the mid-1960s. These decades marked the greatest economic advance in American history.

Michael Kinsley of the *New Republic*, writing in early 1990,[12] comes to the same conclusions, although using somewhat different numbers. He finds that the average American top rate of income tax is more than a third less than Japan's. In addition, Japan has a higher inheritance tax. Kinsley concludes that overall, the Japanese system "taxes capital, and the affluent in general, more heavily than the U.S."

Much of Japan's relative egalitarianism is based on the past. Lehner[13] writes:

> Their society historically has considered conspicuous consumption distasteful. The Buddhist and Confucian ethic encouraged even the old samurai nobility to live poorly and purely. Merchants, at the bottom of the social ladder in feudal Japan, were expected to hide their wealth. (Some wore kimonos with cotton outers and silk linings.) In the economic rebuilding after World War II, an industrialist's fondness for sardines and rice, the poor man's diet, won him widespread respect.

This does not mean that wealthy Japanese are only slightly above the level of the poor. A recent television show filmed Japanese students as they crowded into French restaurants to order $100 courses and vintage wine.[13] But the burst of superwealth, as exemplified by the different Pareto income distribution above the lognormal region, simply did not happen in Japan.

Whenever an economic story is told, it is often difficult to distinguish between cause and effect. Did the Japanese economic miracle come about mostly because it was a relatively classless society, or was the lack of great income disparities only a minor factor? Conversely, did the *absence* of great fortunes on the American scale hold back the Japanese? Would they have accomplished even more—we admit that this is not easy to visualize—if their incomes had had the Pareto-region kink of the U.S.?

The evidence is clear. The Japanese shook the world economically in large part because they avoided the tremendous sinks of wealth in Western countries. As they developed financially, the money was spread around more evenly than in their competitors' countries. Because more people shared in it, the ideas of the multitudes could go forward. This, we suggest, is the hidden benefit of Japan's relatively equitable income distribution.

WHAT SHOULD THE INCOME DISTRIBUTION LOOK LIKE?

In much of this book we have advocated a one-segment income distribution, in which the Pareto region would become an extension of the lognormal or Gibrat region. We have carefully drawn this line below the steeply rising portion. See, for example, the right-hand side of Figure 3.1.

Some readers may feel more comfortable seeing our conclusions in black and white, as opposed to stripes on an unusual type of graph paper. Our proposed income distribution is shown in tabular form in Table 12.2.

We said previously that the kink between the two distributions was around $110,000 in 1987, so the actual and proposed incomes at that level are the same. But the two paths soon start diverging.

By the $200,000 level, the proposed income is $170,000, for a total "tax" of 15%. Instead of someone with an income of $200,000 being in the top 540,000 tax returns in 1987, he or she would be in the top 750,000.

A Story About Mount Everest

If we were to use the height of Mount Everest (about 29,000 feet) as corresponding to the total number of taxpayers, someone with an actual income of $200,000 would be 146 feet from the top. After his income is reduced to the proposed level, he would have dropped down, to about 203 feet from the summit.

Table 12.2
Actual and Proposed Pareto-Region Income Levels in 1987

Actual Income Level	Proposed Income Level
$120,000	$115,000
200,000	170,000
300,000	224,000
400,000	273,000
600,000	359,000
800,000	434,000
$1 million	503,000
2 million	790,000
3 million	$1.0 million
4.5 million	1.3 million
6 million	1.6 million
8 million	2.0 million
10 million	2.3 million
15 million	3.0 million
20 million	3.6 million
25 million	4.2 million
30 million	4.7 million
50 million	6.5 million
80 million	8.9 million
100 million	10.0 million
150 million	13 million
200 million	16 million
360 million	24 million

The divergence between the actual and proposed income rises with earnings. By the $600,000 level, the proposed income is $359,000, for a total "tax" of about 40%. This is still lower than the marginal tax rate of 50% that prevailed until 1987. In that year, someone with an income of $600,000 would be in the top 84,000 in the nation. Someone earning $359,000 would still be in the top 200,000. Back at Mount Everest, the $600,000 level lies about twenty-three feet from the peak. Sliding back to the $359,000 level would put one about thirty-two feet lower.

At the $1 Million Level

At the $1 million level, the proposed income would be about half that. The total "tax" would be close to 50%. That was the marginal rate from 1981 to 1986, most of the Reagan years. During that time, with the exception of the 1982 recession, the nation experienced great economic growth. An income of $1 million in 1987 would put an individual in the top 36,000; an income of half that would put her in the top 110,000. Returning to Mount Everest, the millionaire would be within ten feet of the top. The half-millionaire would be about twenty feet—about a car length—lower.

The "tax" goes up sharply with income. Consulting our original graphs shows that the Pareto line pulls away more and more from the extension of the lognormal or Gibrat distribution as income rises.

At the $6 million level, we propose an income of about $1.6 million. This corresponds to a total "tax" of about 73%, close to the marginal rate of 70% that was the law from the mid-1960s to 1981, about fifteen years.

At the rarefied $6 million income level, only about 1,500 people are between this amount and the top. This would put the hardy climber about six inches—less than a handspan—from the top of Mount Everest. At the proposed income of $1.6 million, there would have been about 16,000 people in front in 1987. This corresponds to about five feet—the height of a rather short person—from the top of the mountain.

At the $20 million level, the proposed income would be $3.6 million, for a total "tax" of 82%. This would still be less than the maximum marginal rate during World War II and for years afterward.

How are the climbers doing? At $20 million per year, someone would be within 0.7 inches—a finger's width—from the top. About 170 people would be ahead. Knocked back to $3.6 million, he or she would be 1.2 feet from the top, about the length of two handspans. There would have been only 3,500 people ahead in 1987.

At the $100 million level, the proposed total "tax" would be about 90%, which we agree is steep. But those in that income class would still have $10 million annually, more than all except 590 people in 1987.

At the Very Top

In terms of the Himalayan giant, someone at the $100 million level would have nine people in front, or be within a millimeter of the crest. Someone with $10 million would, as we said above, have 590 citizens ahead. This is the equivalent of 2.4 inches from the top, or about the length of a finger. The peak would clearly be visible.

The beauty of our proposed system is two-fold. First, there is *no cap* on income, as has been proposed by Drucker and other philosophers and economists. This is in accordance with the American attitude of "get all you can while the going's good." Second, there is a *logical framework* for the proposed income as a fraction of actual income. We do not pull tax rates out of the air. All of the rates are based on how American incomes are *actually* distributed.

HOW MANY MILLIONAIRES SHOULD THERE BE?

The income level starting at seven figures has a peculiar fascination. Nobody knows or cares about what a "hundred-thousandaire" is, even those people—in the top 3% of the population—who have that income.

Yet everyone knows, or think they know, what a millionaire is. A logical question, in the light of the proposed income distribution of Table 12.2, is: How many millionaires should there be?

The question can be answered using Tables 12.1 and 12.2. At the middle of Table 12.2, a *proposed* income (right-hand column) of $1 million corresponds to an *actual* income (left-hand column) of $3 million. Returning to Table 12.1, an actual income of $3 million was exceeded by about 5,100 individuals in 1987.

This is a large drop from the 36,000 who earned more than $1 million in 1987. But how does the value of 5,100 millionaires compare with the historical record?

Referring to the bottom curve of Figure 12.1, there were only six years from 1951 to 1987 when there were more than 5,100 millionaires. Those years were the last in the group—1982 to 1987. The *average* over the thirty-seven years was 4,100 millionaires.

Adjusting for Inflation

The upper curve of Figure 12.1 shows the inflation-adjusted number of millionaires. About half the years had more than 5,100 millionaires, about half below. Recall that in 1951, you needed only an income of about $237,000 to qualify as the equivalent of a 1986 millionaire.

The average for the thirty-seven years (1951 to 1987) was 7,430 inflation-adjusted millionaires. If the years 1986 and 1987 are removed from the calculations, the average drops to 5,910 millionaires. This is not far from the value of 5,100 we suggested.

The nation got along in most of the post-World War II era with fewer than 5,100 millionaires, even when inflation is taken into account. Under the proposed income distribution, we would go back to the conditions that prevailed during much of that time. If that is not a definition of conservatism, we do not know what is.

HOW RICH IS TOO RICH?

There *is* an answer to the question, how rich is too rich? The solution is not found by envy, or fine words, or vague generalizations. We have replied to the question posed as the title of this book by mathematical analysis. Fortunately, much of this analysis could be presented in a simplified form, to reach many readers.

Incomes up to about $110,000 (in 1987 dollars) do not really qualify for the word "rich". Above that point, superwealth or superincomes appear. We call this region the Pareto segment, after the Italian economist who first discovered it.

No Caps on Income or Personally Earned Wealth

We do not propose a specific cap on income or the wealth an individual accumulates during his lifetime. In that sense, one might claim that nobody is *ever* too rich.

But we do propose a two-pronged approach to bring the "superwealth" segment in line with the more natural lognormal segment below it. First, we propose progressive levies on annual incomes above $110,000. Second, an inheritance tax system we call the Alternative Distribution System (ADS) would replace our current death taxes. The two would work together so that the kink represented by the explosive riches of the top few percent in both distributions would bend to the lognormal distribution. That distribution describes the economic fate of almost all of us. We even provide the test to gauge our progress toward these goals.

Make no mistake about it—the question of income and wealth distribution will be around as long as income itself is. Fernando Collor de Melho, elected President of Brazil in December 1989, said as much before taking office[14]: "In Brazil, 70 percent of the wealth is in the hands of 1 percent of the population. . . . This is our great challenge—the distribution of income."

In the United States, our problems are not as severe as they are in Brazil. Yet in terms of income and wealth distribution, we are heading *toward* the Brazilian example, not away from it. We hope this book will help avert this trend.

REFERENCES

CHAPTER 1

1. Alexis de Tocqueville, *Democracy in America*, J. P. Mayer and A. P. Kerr, editors [New York: Doubleday, 1969], Chapter 17.

2. The genesis of this argument was presented in Herbert Inhaber, "How Rich Should the Rich Be?," *New Leader*, 67 (7) 9-12 (April 16, 1984).

3. Sidney Carroll, "Taxing Wealth: An Accessions Tax Proposal for the U.S.," *Journal of Post-Keynesian Economics*, 12 (1) 49-69 (1989).

4. William S. Gilbert and Arthur S. Sullivan, *The Authentic Gilbert and Sullivan Songbook*, James Spero, editor [New York: Dover, 1978], "The Gondoliers," Act II.

5. Robert Samuelson, "The Coming Car Crunch," *Newsweek*, Oct. 16, 1989, p. 62.

6. Jan Pen, *Income Distribution: Facts, Theories, Policies* [New York: Praeger, 1971], p. 48.

7. Susan Hostetter and Jeffrey Bates, "Individual Income Tax Returns, Preliminary Data, 1987," *Statistics of Income Bulletin*, 8 19 Table 1 (April, 1989). About 20 million tax returns were nontaxable.

CHAPTER 2

1. Lord Acton, *Historical Essays and Studies*, J. N. Figgis and R. V. Laurence, editors [Salem, N.H.: Ayer Co., reprint of 1907 edition].

2. Confucius, *Analects*, Book 14, in George Seldes, *The Great Quotations* [Secaucus, New Jersey: Citadel Press, 1983], p. 173.

3. Plato, *The Republic*, Book 4, James Adam, editor [Cambridge, England: Cambridge University Press].

4. Cicero, *De Officiis*, Book 1 [Cambridge, Mass.: Harvard University Press, 1930].

5. Lucretius, *De Rerum Natura*, Cyril Bailey, editor, 1798 edition [Oxford, England: Oxford University Press].

6. 1 Samuel 2:7.

7. Proverbs 30:8.

8. Leviticus 25:8-13.

9. *The Abingdon Bible Commentary*, F. C. Eiselin, Edwin Lewis and D. G. Downey, editors [New York: Abingdon-Cokesbury Press, 1929], pp. 78, 295.

10. Mark 10:23.

11. Luke 12:16 ff.

12. Mark 10:17 ff.

13. Mark 15:43.

14. Luke 8:3.

15. *Pastoral Letter on Catholic Social Teaching and the U.S. Economy* [Washington, D.C.: National Conference of Catholic Bishops, Nov. 11, 1984], first draft.

16. St. Chrysostom, *Homilies*, part 388, Jean Dumortier, translator (in French) [Paris: Cerf, 1981].

17. St. Jerome, in Seldes, *Great Quotations*, p. 375.

18. St. Ambrose, *Letters*, quoted by Mortimer Adler, Ideas of Freedom, in Seldes, *Great Quotations*, p. 253.

19. St. Augustine, *On the Christian Conflict*, quoted in Seldes, *Great Quotations*, p. 71.

20. Internal Revenue Service, *Income Tax Compliance Research: Estimates for 1973–1981* [Washington, D.C.: U.S. Government Printing Office, 1983], p. 3.

21. Abd-el-Raham, Caliph of Cordoba, in Seldes, *Great Quotations*, p. 35.

22. Dante Alighieri, *The Convivio*, C. E. Norton, translator [Albuquerque, N.M.: Found Classic Reprints, 1985].

23. John Wycliffe, "To the Duke of Lancaster," 1381, in Seldes, *Great Quotations*, p. 759.

24. Desiderius Erasmus, *In Praise of Folly*, H. H. Hudson, translator [Princeton, N.J.: Princeton University Press, 1941].

25. Martin Luther, *Werke*, vol. 18 [Amsterdam, Holland: De Gruyter, 1982], p. 327.

26. Noah Webster, in Seldes, *Great Quotations*, p. 731.

27. Francis Bacon, "On Riches," in *Essays*, M. Kiernan, editor [Cambridge, Mass.: Harvard University Press, 1985].

28. Miguel de Cervantes, *Don Quixote* [Cutchogue, N.Y.: Buccaneer Books, 1981].

29. Thomas More, *Utopia*, Edward Surtz, editor [New Haven, Conn.: Yale University Press, 1965].

30. Samuel Johnson, in *Boswell's Life of Johnson*, April 14, 1778.

31. Thomas Jefferson, Letter to John Adams, in Seldes, *Great Quotations*, p. 370.

32. Thomas Carlyle, *The French Revolution* [Darby, Penn.: Arden Library, 1986 reprint of 1900 edition].

33. Adam Smith, *An Inquiry into the Nature and Cause of the Wealth of Nations*, Edwin Cannan, editor [New York: Modern Library of Random House, 1937], p. 670.

34. James Madison, *The Federalist*, Number 10, in Seldes, *Great Quotations*, p. 458.

35. Andrew Jackson, Veto, Bank Renewal Bill, July 10, 1832. (A considerable portion of this message was written by Roger B. Taney.) In Seldes, *Great Quotations*, p. 355.

36. Peter Cooper, quoted by A. J. Cummings, U.S. Attorney General, in a letter to Samuel Gompers, read at the A.F.L. convention, Philadelphia, December, 1892. In Seldes, *Great Quotations*, p. 180.

37. Lee Soltow, "Wealth Inequality in the United States in 1798 and 1860," *Review of Economic Statistics*, 444 (Table 3) (August, 1984).

38. Matthew Arnold, in Seldes, *Great Quotations*, p. 69.

39. George Baer, in a letter to W. F. Clark, Wilkes-Barre, Pa., during the great anthracite coal strike in 1902. In Seldes, *Great Quotations*, p. 75.

40. J. P. Morgan, *Autobiography*, p. 437, in Seldes, *Great Quotations*, p. 506.

41. Benjamin Franklin, *Poor Richard*, 1734, in Seldes, *Great Quotations*, p. 259.

42. Joseph Patterson, *Confessions of a Drone*, and *A Little Brother of the Rich*, 1908.

43. M. K. Gandhi, quoted by Edgar Snow, *Journey to the Beginning* [New York: Random House, 1958].

44. George Orwell, *Animal Farm* [New York: North American Library, 1983].

45. George Bernard Shaw, *An Intelligent Woman's Guide to Socialism and Capitalism* [New Brunswick, N.J.: Transaction Books, 1984].

CHAPTER 3

1. Susan Hostetter and Jeffrey Bates, "Individual Tax Returns, Preliminary Data, 1987", *Statistics of Income Bulletin*, 8 19 (April, 1989).

2. For an elegant yet understandable discussion, see Jan Pen, *Income Distribution: Facts, Theories, Policies* [New York: Praeger, 1971], p. 235.

3. For a more detailed discussion, see Vincent Tarascio, *Pareto's Methodological Approach to Economics* [Chapel Hill, N.C.: University of North Carolina Press, 1968].

4. Jim Henderson, "How Rich is Rich," *USA Today*, October 12-14, 1984, p. 1.

5. F. Thomas Juster, editor, *The Distribution of Economic Well-Being* [Cambridge, Mass.: Ballinger, 1977].

6. Mortimer B. Zuckerman, "Dreams, Myths and Reality," *U.S. News & World Report*, July 25, 1988, p. 68.

7. Elliott W. Montroll and Michael F. Schlesinger, "On the Wonderful World of Random Walks," in J. L. Lebowitz and E. W. Montroll, editors, *Non-Equilibrium Phenomena II: From Stochastics to Hydrodynamics* [Amsterdam, Holland: North-Holland, 1984], pp. 1-121.

CHAPTER 4

1. Robert B. Avery and Arthur B. Kennickell, "Measurement of Household Saving Obtained from First-Differencing Wealth Estimates," presented at Twenty-First General Conference of the International Association for Research in Income and Wealth, Lahnstein, Germany, August 20-26, 1989, p. 11.

2. Robert B. Avery, Gregory E. Elliehausen, and Arthur B. Kennickell, "Measuring Wealth with Survey Data: An Evaluation of the 1983 Survey of Consumer Finances," *Review of Income and Wealth*, 358 (December, 1988).

3. *Ibid.*, p. 356.

4. *Forbes 400*, 232 (October 23, 1989).

5. *Forbes 400*, 248 (October 24, 1988).

6. *Household Wealth and Asset Ownership 1984: Data from the Survey of Income and Wealth Participation*, Current Population Reports, Household Economic Studies, Series P-70, No. 7, Bureau of the Census, Tables 3 and 4, pp. 16, 18-19.

7. Jim Luther, "Richest People in U.S. Control 28% of Wealth," *Buffalo News*, August 23, 1990, p. A-9.

8. Alan Murray, "Senate Panel Democrats Opposed Gains Tax Cut but Voted for Giant Loopholes in Estate Levies," *Wall Street Journal*, October 13, 1989, p. A16.

9. Quoted in Chris Pond, "Wealth and the Two Nations," in Frank Field, editor, *The Wealth Report II* [Boston: Routledge and Kegan Paul, 1983], p. 21.

10. Ronald Chester, *Inheritance, Wealth and Society* [Bloomington, Ind.: Indiana University Press, 1982], p. 79.

11. A. B. Atkinson, *The Economics of Inequality* [Oxford: Clarendon Press, 1975], pp. 181-183.

12. Pond, "Wealth and Two Nations," p. 18.

13. Susan Hostetter and Jeffrey Bates, "Individual Income Tax Returns, Preliminary Data, 1987," *Statistics of Income Bulletin, 8* 19 (April, 1989).

14. Donald R. Katz, "Of Capital, Taxes and Death," *Esquire*, 55 (March, 1987).

15. *1990 World Almanac* [New York: Pharo Books, 1989], pp. 84-85, 96.

16. Marvin Schwartz, "Trends in Personal Wealth, 1976-1981," *Statistics of Income Bulletin*, 4 (Summer, 1983).

17. Robert McIntyre, "Tax the *Forbes 400!*" *New Republic*, 15 (August 31, 1987).

18. *Wall Street Journal*, June 8, 1988, p. 1.

19. "Top and Bottom of the Art Market," *Economist*, 83 (October 28, 1989).

20. "Sotheby's, Christie's Report Auction Sales Rose in 1989," *Wall Street Journal*, December 21, 1989.

21. *Forbes 400*, 124 (October 1, 1984).

22. Lester Thurow, *Generating Inequality—Mechanisms of Distribution in the U.S. Economy* [New York: Basic Books, 1975], p. 154.

23. Chester, *Inheritance, Wealth*, p. 81.

24. 1962 data was converted to that for 1989 by using a ratio of the Consumer Price Indexes for the two years. See Thomas Osman, "The Role of Intergenerational Wealth Transfers in the Distribution of Wealth Over the Life Cycle: A Preliminary Analysis," in F. T. Juster, *The Distribution of Economic Well-Being* [Cambridge, Mass.: Ballinger, 1977], p. 403.

25. Atkinson, *Economics of Inequality*, p. 188.

26. Quoted in Pond, "Wealth and Two Nations," p. 27.

27. John Brittain, *Inheritance and the Inequality of Material Wealth* [Washington, D.C.: Brookings Institution, 1978], p. 8.

28. Thurow, *Generating Inequality*, p. 154.

29. *Ibid.*, pp. 134-140.

30. *Ibid.*, p. 141.

31. P. L. Menchik and M. David, "Income Distributions: Lifetime, Savings and Bequests," *American Economic Review*, 672 (September, 1983).

32. Lee Soltow, "Wealth Inequality in the United States in 1798 and 1860," *Review of Economics and Statistics*, 448 (Table 3) (August, 1984).

CHAPTER 5

1. Robert B. Avery, Gregory E. Elliehausen, Glenn B. Canner and Thomas Gustafson, "Survey of Consumer Finances, 1983," *Federal Reserve Bulletin*, 689 (September, 1984).

2. Jan Tinbergen, *Income Distribution: Analysis and Policies* [New York: American Elsevier, 1975], p. 147.

3. "The Rich Get Richer," *Parade Magazine*, 21 (October 22, 1989).

4. Gardner Ackley, *Macroeconomic Theory* [New York: Macmillan, 1961], p. 6.

5. Susan Hostetter and Jeffrey Bates, "Individual Income Tax Returns, Preliminary Data, 1987," *Statistics of Income Bulletin*, 8 19 (April, 1989).

6. "Whatever Happened to Thrift?," *Economist*, 77 (October 14, 1989).

7. Gene Koretz, "Why Asian Countries Blossomed While Latin America Wilted," *Business Week*, 16 (August 28, 1989).

8. George Gilder, *Wealth and Poverty* [New York: Basic Books, 1981], p. 56.

9. Stanley Lebergott, *The American Economy* [Princeton, N.J.: Princeton University Press, 1975], p. 245.

CHAPTER 6

1. Jan Pen, *Income Distribution: Facts, Theories, Policies* [New York: Praeger, 1971], p. 193.

2. F. A. Cowell, *Measuring Inequality* [Oxford: Philip Allen, 1977], p. 2.

3. Gian Singh Sahota, "Theories of Personal Income Distribution: A Survey," *Journal of Economic Literature*, 16 1 (March, 1978).

4. *Oak Ridger*, Oak Ridge, Tennessee, July 2, 1984.

5. John Rawls, *A Theory of Justice* [Cambridge, Mass.: Harvard University Press, 1971].

6. John Rawls, "Rawls' 'A Theory of Justice': Reply to Alexander and Musgrave," *Quarterly Journal of Economics*, 633 (November 1974).

7. George Bernard Shaw, *Major Barbara* [London: Penguin, 1950], Act IV.

8. *Knoxville News-Sentinel*, Knoxville, Tenn., Jan. 10, 1985, p. 1.

9. I. Kant, *Foundations of the Metaphysics of Morals* (1786) [New York: Bobbs-Merrill Co., 1969].

10. In film *Every Day's a Holiday*.

11. George Gilder, *Wealth and Poverty* [New York: Basic Books, 1981], p. 11.

12. H. T. Davis, *Political Statistics* [Bloomington, Ind.: Indiana University Press, 1954]; H. T. Davis, *The Analysis of Economic Time Series* [Bloomington, Ind.: Indiana University Press, 1941].

13. Cowell, *Measuring Inequality*, p. 175.

14. Gilder, *Wealth and Poverty*, p. 304.

15. *Ibid.*, p. 205.

16. H. Daly, "How to Stabilize the Economy," *Ecologist*, 90 (March, 1973).

17. Mortimer Zuckerman, "Dreams, Myths and Reality," *U.S. News & World Report*, 68 (July 15, 1988).

18. Gilder, *Wealth and Poverty*, p. 124.

19. Alfred North Whitehead, *Adventure of Ideas* [New York: Macmillan, 1933], Part III, Chapter 16.

20. Robert B. Avery, Gregory E. Elliehausen, Glenn B. Canner and Thomas Gustafson, "Survey of Consumer Finances, 1983," *Federal Reserve Bulletin*, 689 (September, 1984).

21. Jan Tinbergen, *Redelijke inkomsverdeling* (in Dutch), 1953.

22. "The Rich Get Richer," *Parade Magazine*, 21 (October 22, 1989).

CHAPTER 7

1. Joseph P. Thorndike, Jr., *The Very Rich: A History of Wealth* [New York: Crown, 1976], p. 13.

2. Ferdinand Lundberg, *America's 60 Families* [New York: Citadel Press, 1946], p. 26.

3. James D. Smith and Stephen D. Franklin, "The Concentration of Personal Wealth, 1922—1969," *American Economic Review* (May, 1974).

4. Thorndike, *Very Rich*, p. 330.

5. Jan Pen, *Income Distribution* [Harmondsworth, England: Penguin, 1971], p. 289.

6. Fernand Braudel, *Civilization and Capitalism, 15th–18th Century*, volume II: The Wheels of Commerce, Sian Reynolds, translator [New York: Harper & Row, 1982], p. 467.

7. *Delle Lettere di Messer Claudio Tolomei* [Venice: 1547].

8. Braudel, *Civilization*, p. 382.

9. C.A.B.F. de Baert-Duholand, *Tableau de la Grande-Bretagne*, An. VIII, IV, p. 7.

10. C. R. Boxer, *The Dutch Sea-Borne Empire, 1600–1800* [1965], p. 11.

11. H. L. Gray, "Incomes from Land in England in 1436," *English Historical Review*, 49 607 (1934).

12. Lee Soltow, "Long-Run Changes in British Income Inequality," in A. B. Atkinson, editor, *Wealth, Income and Inequality* [Oxford: Oxford University Press, 1980], Chapter 5.

13. J. C. Williamson and P. H. Lindert, "Long-Term Trends in American Wealth Inequality," in J. D. Smith, editor, *Modeling the Distribution and Intergenerational Transmission of Wealth*,. National Bureau of Economic Research, Studies in Income and Wealth, vol. 46 [Chicago: University of Chicago Press, 1980], p. 9.

14. Lee Soltow, "Wealth Inequality in the United States in 1798 and 1860," *Review of Economics and Statistics*, 448 (August, 1984).

15. L. Saunders, "The 'Rich List' of 1845," *Forbes 400*, 44 (October 1, 1984).

16. Alexis de Toqueville, *Democracy in America*, J. P. Mayer and A. P. Kerr, editors [New York: Doubleday, 1969], p. 161.

17. Thorndike, *Very Rich*, p. 332.

18. W. Sidney Ratner, *New Light on the History of the Great Fortunes*, 1953, quoted in S. Lebergott, *Wealth and Want* [Princeton, N.J.: Princeton University Press, 1975], p. 169.

19. *Congressional Record*, August 1913. Quoted in Lebergott, *Wealth and Want*.

20. "America's 30 Richest (of 1918) Own $3.68 Billion," *Forbes*, 49 (Fall, 1983).

21. "Seven-Figure Incomes," *Wall Street Journal*, June 21, 1983.

22. Frederick Lewis Allen, *Only Yesterday* [New York: Harper Brothers, 1931], p. 136.

23. Lundberg, *America's Families*, p. 28.

24. Lebergott, *Wealth and Want*, p. 170.

25. Lundberg, *America's Families*, p. 23.

26. Susan Hostetter and Jeffrey Bates, "Individual Income Tax Returns, Preliminary Data, 1987," *Statistics of Income Bulletin, 8* 19 (April, 1989).

27. "The Forbes Four Hundred," *Forbes*, 99 (Sept. 12, 1982).

28. E. Ray Canterbury and E. Joe Nosari, "*The Forbes Four Hundred*: The Determinants of Super-Wealth," *Southern Economic Journal*, 1077 (April 1985).

29. Lester Thurow, *The Zero-sum Society* (New York: Penguin Books, 1981), p. 172.

30. Joe Queenan, "The Many Paths to Riches," *Forbes 400*, 148 (October 23, 1989).

CHAPTER 8

1. Gian Singh Sahota, "Theories of Personal Income Distribution: A Survey," *Journal of Economic Literature, 16* 1 (March, 1978).

2. "What Value Education? Counting the Ways," *New York Times*, Oct. 3, 1987, p. 28.

3. Susan Hostetter and Jeffrey Bates, "Individual Income Tax Returns, Preliminary Data, 1987," *Statistics of Income Bulletin, 8* 19 (April, 1989).

4. Mark Blaug, "The Empirical Status of Human Capital Theory: A Slightly Jaundiced View," *Journal of Economic Literature, 14* (3) 827 (September, 1976).

5. Jacob Mincer, "Progress in Human Capital Analyses of the Distribution of Earnings," in A. B. Atkinson, editor, *The Personal Distribution of Incomes* [London: Allen and Unwin, 1976], p. 136.

6. Harold F. Lydall, "Theories of the Distribution of Earnings," in A. B. Atkinson, *Personal Distribution*, p. 15.

7. J. Ryan, "IQ: The Illusion of Objectivity," in K. Richardson and D. Spears, editors, *Race and Intelligence* [Baltimore: Pelican Books, 1972], p. 36.

8. J. Stamp, *The Science of Social Adjustment* [London: Macmillan, 1937].

9. H. T. Davis, *The Theory of Econometrics* [Bloomington, Ind.: Principia Press, 1941].

10. B. Mandelbrot, "Stable Paretian Random Function and the Multiplicative Variations in Income," *Econometrica, 29* (4) 517 (1961).

11. B. Mandelbrot, "Paretian Distributions and Income Maximization," *Quarterly Journal of Economics* (February, 1962).

12. Francis Galton, *Natural Inheritance* [London: Macmillan, 1889].

13. K. Pearson and F. Lee, *Biometrika 2* 357 (1903).

14. Christopher Jencks et al., *Inequality: A Reassessment of the Effect of Family and Schooling in America* [New York: Basic Books, 1972].

15. David B. Champernowne, "A Model of Income Distribution," *Economics Journal, 63* (250) 318 (June, 1953).

CHAPTER 9

1. James S. Henry, "Tax Tips from Leona," *Washington Post*, August 13, 1989, p. B1.

2. Hearings before the Joint Economic Committee on the 1969 Economic Report of the President, 91st Congress, first session, January 17, 1969, p. 6.

3. Philip Stern, *The Rape of the Taxpayer* [New York: Vintage Books, 1973], p. 67.

4. *Individual Statistics of Income* [Washington, D.C.: U.S. Department of Treasury, 1982].

5. Richard Meyer, *Running for Shelter* [Washington, D.C.: Public Citizen, 1985], p. 8.

6. Susan Hostetter and Jeffrey Bates, "Individual Income Tax Returns, Preliminary Data, 1987," *Statistics of Income Bulletin, 8* 19 (April, 1989).

7. Meyer, *Running*, p. 3.

8. "595 Paid No Tax Despite Income above $200,000," *Knoxville News-Sentinel*, October 22, 1989.

9. Jeffrey H. Birnbaum, "Senate's Tax Panel Measure is Jammed with Billions of Dollars in Giveaways," *Wall Street Journal*, October 5, 1989.

10. *Public Papers and Addresses of Franklin D. Roosevelt*, Vol. 4, 1935 [New York: Random House, 1938], p. 313.

11. Meyer, *Running*, p. 7.

12. Charles K. Ebinger, "Eclipse of Solar Power Leaves a Burning Need," *Wall Street Journal*, October 29, 1984.

13. Matthew Cooper, "Tilting at Windmills—with Energy," *People and Taxes, 13* (2) 8 (February, 1985).

14. James Abdnor, "Tax Law Effect on Agriculture," *Congressional Record*, June 29, 1984.

15. Martha Hamilton and Ward Sinclair, "Tax Law Effect on Agriculture under Scrutiny," *Washington Post*, May 28, 1984.

16. Robert McIntyre, "Tax the *Forbes 400!*" *New Republic*, August 31, 1987, p. 15.

17. "Tax Reform can Help Real Estate," *People and Taxes, 13* (2) 6 (February, 1985).

18. Albert B. Crenshaw, "Tax Break Expiring: Loophole Benefits Bequests from the Rich," *Washington Post*, October 1, 1989, p. H11.

19. Shelby White, "Easing the Tax Bite for Your Heirs," *New York Times*, January 1, 1984.

20. "Tax Report," *Wall Street Journal*, April 4, 1984.

21. Jane Perlez, "Congress is Moving to Limit Tax Breaks on Luxury Vehicles for Business," *New York Times*, March 3, 1983, p. A25.

22. Jim Luther, "Efficient Tax System Can be Simple or Fair," *Oak Ridger*, Oak Ridge, Tenn., September 12, 1984, p. 12.

23. "Our Tax System," *USA Today*, March 13, 1984.

24. Daniel Goleman, "The Tax Cheats: Selfish to the Bottom Line," *New York Times*, April 11, 1988, p. 1.

25. *Economist*, September 19-25, 1987.

26. "$222 Billion is Seen Hidden from U.S. Tax," *Washington Post*, December 25, 1983.

27. Robert D. Hershey, Jr., "Underground Economy is Not Rising to the Bait," *New York Times*, January 24, 1988.

28. Alan Murray, "IRS is Losing Battle Against Tax Evaders Despite Its New Gear," *Wall Street Journal*, April 10, 1984.

29. "IRS Claims Vast Overevaluation of Art Prints," *Washington Post*, August 5, 1983.

30. Jan Pen, *Income Distribution: Facts, Theories, Policies* [New York: Praeger, 1971], p. 28.

31. Meyer, *Running*, p. 43.
32. *Ibid.*, p. 1.
33. *Ibid.*, p. 20.
34. Art Buchwald, "Luck and Loopholes," *Washington Post*, March 13, 1984.

CHAPTER 10

1. *Recollections of Charles J. Randall*, unpublished hand-written manuscript, in the possession of Sidney and Betty Carroll, Knoxville, Tenn.: Written 1944.
2. George Gilder, *Wealth and Poverty* [New York: Basic Books, 1981], p. 260.
3. Lester Thurow, *Generating Inequality* [New York: Basic Books, 1975].
4. George K. Holmes, *Political Science Quarterly*, 8 (4) 589 (1893).

CHAPTER 11

1. R. Avery and A. B. Kennickell, "Measurement of Household Saving Obtained from First-Differencing Wealth Estimates," presented at International Association for Research in Income and Wealth, Lahnstein, Germany, August, 1989; revised February 1990.
2. Sidney Carroll, "Taxing Wealth: An Accessions Tax Proposal for the U.S.", *Journal of Post-Keynesian Economics*, 12 (1) 49 (1989).
3. R. B. Avery and G. Elliehausen, "Financial Characteristics of High-Income Families," *Federal Reserve Bulletin*, 163 (March, 1986).
4. Avery and Kennickell, p. 11.
5. Avery and Kennickell, Table 3.
6. *Forbes*, 347 (October 24, 1988).
7. "Comparing the Budget Bills," *Buffalo News*, October 21, 1990, p. A-12.
8. Patti Thorn, "Rise of Old Folks to Have Social Impact," *Knoxville News-Sentinel*, December 8, 1989.
9. Obituaries, *Knoxville News-Sentinel*, January 20, 1990.
10. "Ill Parent: The Woman's Burden Grows," *New York Times*, November 13, 1989.
11. L. Kutner, "Parent and Child," *New York Times*, December 21, 1989, p. Y29.
12. Jane O'Reilly, "Isn't It Funny What Money Can Do: Review of Robert Lenzner: *The Great Getty*," *New York Times Book Review*, March 30, 1986, p. 4.
13. *Forbes 400*, 344 (October 23, 1989).
14. Julie Flynn, "Arnold Beckman's New Career," *Business Week*, March 24, 1986.
15. C. W. Stevens, "Change of Heart," *Wall Street Journal*, March 24, 1988, p. 16.
16. Ellen Wojahn, "Share the Wealth, Spoil the Child," *Inc.*, 66 (August, 1989).

CHAPTER 12

1. Janet McCubbin and Fritz Scheuren, "Individual Income Tax Shares and Average Tax Rates, Tax Years 1951-1986," *Statistics of Income Bulletin*, 8 (4) 39 (April, 1989).
2. Susan Hostetter and Jeffrey Bates, "Individual Income Tax Returns, Preliminary Data, 1987," *Statistics of Income Bulletin*, 8 19 (April, 1989).

3. Robert Heilbroner and Lester Thurow, *Economics Explained* [Englewood Cliffs, N.J.: Prentice-Hall, 1980].

4. Lester Thurow, *The Zero-Sum Society* [New York: Basic Books, 1980].

5. *Current Population Reports*, Series P-60, No. 142, Bureau of the Census, p. 197.

6. *1986 World Almanac* [New York: Pharo Books, 1985], p. 46.

7. *Statistical Abstract of the United States* [Washington, D.C.: U.S. Government Printing Office, 1984], p. 331.

8. Hobart Rowen, "Joseph Pechman's Simple Solution for Fairer Taxes," *Washington Post*, December 31, 1989, p. H1.

9. John Eckhouse, "Salary Gap Wider in U.S. Than Others," *Knoxville News-Sentinel*, June 19, 1989.

10. Peter Drucker, "Reform Executive Pay or Congress Will," *Wall Street Journal*, April 24, 1984.

11. Quoted in "The Outlook: Lower U.S. Tax Rates Go International," *Wall Street Journal*, April 4, 1988.

12. Michael Kinsley, "Two American Myths About Japan," *Washington Post*, January 11, 1990, p. A23.

13. Urban C. Lehner, "Disparities in Wealth Affront Japan's Vision of Itself as Classless," *Wall Street Journal*, June 20, 1989.

14. Eugene Robinson, "Brazilian to Tackle Inflation," *Washington Post*, December 23, 1989, p.A16.

BIBLIOGRAPHY

Ackley, Gardner. *Macroeconomic Theory*. New York: Macmillan, 1961.

Allison, Paul. "Measures of Inequality," *American Sociological Review*, 865 (December, 1978).

Andrews, William D., "The Accession Tax Proposal," *Tax Law Review*, 22 589 (1967).

Atkinson, A. B. "The Distribution of Wealth in Britain in the 1960s—The Estate Duty Method Re-Examined," *Studies in Income and Wealth*, 39 277 (1975).

——. *The Economics of Inequality*. Oxford: Clarendon Press, 1975.

——. *Wealth, Income and Inequality*. Oxford: Oxford University Press, 1980.

Atkinson, A. B., A. K. Maynard and C. G. Trinder. *Parents and Children: Income in Two Generations*. London: Heinemann Educational, 1983.

Avery, Robert B., Gregory E. Elliehausen, Glenn B. Canner and Thomas Gustafson. "Survey of Consumer Finances, 1983," *Federal Reserve Bulletin*, 689 (September, 1984).

Avery, Robert B., Gregory E. Elliehausen, Glenn B. Canner and Thomas Gustafson. "Survey of Consumer Finances, 1983: A Second Look," *Federal Reserve Bulletin*, 857 (December, 1984).

Avery, Robert B. and Gregory E. Elliehausen. "Financial Characteristics of High-Income Families," *Federal Reserve Bulletin*, 163 (March, 1986).

Avery, Robert B., Gregory E. Elliehausen and Arthur B. Kennickell. "Measuring Wealth with Survey Data: An Evaluation of the 1983 Survey of Consumer Finances," *Review of Income and Wealth*, 358 (December, 1988).

Brittain, John. *Inheritance and the Inequality of Material Wealth*. Washington, D.C.: Brookings Institution, 1978.

Bureau of the Census. *Household Wealth and Asset Ownership 1984: Data from the Survey of Income and Wealth Participation*, Current Population Reports, Household Economic Studies, Series P-70, No. 7. Washington, D.C.: U.S. Government Printing Office.

Cain, L. P. "Incomes in the 20th Century U.S.: Discussion," *Journal of Economic History*, 43 241 (March, 1983).

Campbell, Colin D., editor. *Income Distribution*. Washington, D.C.: American Institute for Public Policy Research, 1977.

Canterbury, E. Ray. "A Vita Theory of the Personal Income Distribution," *Southern Economics Journal* 12 (July, 1979).

Canterbury, E. Ray, and E. Joe Nosari. "The *Forbes 400*: The Determinants of Super-Wealth," *Southern Economic Journal*, 1073 (April, 1985).

Carroll, Sidney. "Taxing Wealth: An Accessions Tax Proposal for the U.S.," *Journal of Post-Keynesian Economics*, 12 (1) 49–69 (1989).

Chester, Ronald. *Inheritance, Wealth and Society*. Bloomington, Ind.: Indiana University Press, 1982.

Cowell, F. A. *Measuring Inequality*. Oxford: Philip Allen, 1977.

Cowell, F. A. and F. Mehta. "The Estimation and Interpolation of Inequality Measures," *Review of Economic Studies*, 49 273 (April, 1982).

Dagnum, C. "The Generalization and Distribution of Income, the Lorenz Curve and the Gini Ratio," *Economic Applications*, 33 326 (1980).

Dagnum, C. "Inequality Measures Between Income Distributions with Applications," *Econometrica*, 48 1791 (November, 1980).

Dalton, H., *Some Aspects of the Inequality of Income in Modern Communities*. London: Routledge and Kegan Paul, 1920.

Field, Frank, editor. *The Wealth Report II*. Boston: Routledge and Kegan Paul, 1983.

Forbes 400, 1982–1990 (usually appears in the fall).

Gilder, George. *Wealth and Poverty*. New York: Basic Books, 1981.

Griliches, Zvi, Wilhelm Krelle, Hans-Jürgen Krupp, Oldrick Kyn, editors. *Income Distribution and Economic Inequality*. New York: Wiley Halstead, 1978.

Heilbroner, R., and L. Thurow. *Economics Explained*. Englewood Cliffs, N.J.: Prentice-Hall, 1980.

Inhaber, Herbert. "How Rich Should the Rich Be?," *New Leader*, 67 (7) 9–12 (April 16, 1984).

Internal Revenue Service. *Income Tax Compliance Research: Estimates for 1973–1981*. Washington, D.C.: U.S. Government Printing Office, 1983.

Jencks, Christopher, *et al. Inequality: A Reassessment of the Effect of Family and Schooling in America*. New York: Basic Books, 1972.

Juster, F. Thomas, editor. *The Distribution of Economic Well-Being*. Cambridge, Mass.: Ballinger, 1977.

Kakwani, N. *Income Inequality and Poverty*. New York: Oxford University Press, 1980.

Kuznets, Simon. *Share of Upper Income Groups in Income and Savings*. Chicago: National Bureau of Economic Research, 1953.

Lampman, Robert J. *The Share of Top Wealth Holders in National Wealth*. Princeton, N.J.: Princeton University Press, 1962.

Lebergott, Stanley. *The American Economy*. Princeton, N.J.: Princeton University Press, 1975.

Levy, Frank. *Dollars and Dreams: The Changing American Income Distribution*. New York: Russell Sage–Basic Books, 1987.

Lundberg, Ferdinand. *America's 60 Families*. New York: Citadel Press, 1946.

———. *The Rich and the Super-Rich*. New York: Lyle Stuart, 1968.

Lydall, Harold. *A Theory of Income Distribution*. Oxford: Clarendon Press, 1979.

Mandelbrot, B. "Stable Paretian Random Function and the Multiplicative Variations in Income," *Econometrica*, 29 (4) 517 (1961).

Menchik, P. L., and M. David. "Income Distribution: Lifetime, Savings and Bequests," *American Economic Review*, 672 (September, 1983).

Meyer, Richard. *Running for Shelter*. Washington, D.C.: Public Citizen, 1985.

Miller, Herman P. *Income Distribution in the United States*. Washington, D.C. U.S.
Government Printing Office, 1966.

———. *Rich Man, Poor Man*. New York: Thomas Y. Crowell Co., 1971.

National Conference of Catholic Bishops. *Pastoral Letter on Catholic Social Teaching
and the U.S. Economy*. Washington, D.C.: 1984.

Osman, Thomas. "The Role of Intergenerational Wealth Transfers in the Distribution of Wealth Over the Life Cycle: A Preliminary Analysis," in Juster,
Distribution, p. 403.

Packard, Vance. *The Ultra Rich: How Much is Too Much?*. Boston: Little Brown, 1988.

Pechman, Joseph. "Taxes Abroad: Pressures for Tax Reform," *Current*, 295 30
(September, 1987), Reprinted from "Tax Reform Prospects in Europe and
Canada," *Brookings Review*, 11 (Winter, 1987).

Pen, Jan. *Income Distribution: Facts, Theories, Policies*. New York: Praeger, 1971.

Pestieu, P., and U. M. Possen. "A Model of Income Distribution," *European
Economic Review*, 17 279 (March 1982).

Polanyi, George, and John B. Wood. *How Much Inequality*. London: Institute of
Economic Affairs, 1974.

Ranadive, K. R. *Income Distribution: The Unsolved Puzzle*. Bombay: Oxford University Press, 1978.

Reich, Robert B. "As the World Turns: U.S. Inequality Keeps on Rising," *New
Republic*, 200 23 (May 1, 1989).

Rostow, W. W. *Why the poor get richer and the rich slow down: Essays in the Marshallian
long period* . Austin, Tex.: University of Texas Press, 1980.

Sahota, Gian Singh. "Theories of Personal Income Distribution: A Survey," *Journal
of Economic Literature*, 1 (March, 1978).

Schwartz, Marvin. "Trends in Personal Wealth, 1976–1981," *Statistics of Income
Bulletin*, 4 (Summer, 1983).

Smith, James D., and Stephen D. Franklin. "The Concentration of Personal
Wealth, 1922–1969," *American Economic Review* (May, 1974).

Smith, J. D., editor. *Modeling the Distribution and Intergenerational Transmission of
Wealth*. Chicago: University of Chicago Press, 1980.

Soltow, Lee. "Long-Run Changes in British Income Inequality," in Atkinson,
Wealth, Income, Chapter 5.

———. "Wealth Inequality in the United States in 1798 and 1860," *Review of Economic
Statistics*, 444 (August, 1984).

Tarascio, Vincent. *Pareto's Methodological Approach to Economics*. Chapel Hill, N.C.:
University of North Carolina Press, 1968.

Taubman, Paul. *Income Distribution and Redistribution*. London: Addison-Wesley,
1978.

Thorndike, Joseph J., Jr. *The Very Rich: A History of Wealth*. New York: Crown, 1976.

Thurow, Lester. *Generating Inequality—Mechanisms of Distribution in the U.S.
Economy*. New York: Basic Books, 1975.

——. *The Zero-Sum Society*. New York: Basic Books, 1980.

——. "A Surge in Inequality," *Scientific American*, 256 (5) 30 (May, 1987).

Tinbergen, Jan. *Income Distribution: Analysis and Policies*. New York: American Elsevier, 1975.

——. "Two Approaches to Quantify the Concept of Equitable Income Distribution," *Kyklos*, 33 3 (1980).

Williamson, J. D., and P. H. Lindert. "Long-Term Trends in American Wealth Inequality," in Smith, *Modeling the Distribution*, p. 9.

INDEX

ABOUT THE AUTHORS

HERBERT INHABER is a physicist and a principal at an environmental consulting firm in western New York. Formerly Coordinator of the Office of Risk Analysis at Oak Ridge National Laboratory, he has held various senior consulting positions. He has published over 100 papers on physics, risk analysis, sociology of science, economics, and other fields in such journals as *Science, Nature,* and *Risk Analysis.* His previously published volumes include *Environmental Indices* (1976), *Physics of the Environment* (1978), *Energy Risk Assessment* (1982), and *What in the World?* (1985) (on foreign affairs).

SIDNEY CARROLL is Professor of Economics at the University of Tennessee in Knoxville, specializing in industrial organization and microeconomic theory. His concern with issues in wealth and income distribution stems from graduate studies in public finance under Richard Musgrave at Harvard and from Bernard Sliger, now president of Florida State University. His work has been published in *Challenge, The Journal of Post-Keynesian Economics, Southern Economic Journal, Public Choice, The Quarterly Journal of Economics, Law and Human Behavior,* and *Research in Law and Economics,* among others.